DRAGON'S SPINE

BEIT BRIDGE TO CAPE TOWN

SA'S ULTIMATE MTB TRAIL

58 ROUTES & MAPS

David Bristow & Steve Thomas

First published in 2012 by Struik Travel & Heritage
(an imprint of Random House Struik (Pty) Ltd)
Company Reg. No. 1966/003153/07
Wembley Square, First Floor, Solan Road, Gardens,
Cape Town 8001, South Africa
PO Box 1144, Cape Town 8000, South Africa

Publisher: Claudia Dos Santos
Managing editor: Roelien Theron
Editorial assistant: Alana Bolligelo
Editor: Mariëlle Renssen
Designer: Catherine Coetzer
Cartographers: Steve Thomas and Ricky Thomas
Proofreader: Lesley Hay-Whitton

Reproduction by Hirt & Carter Cape (Pty) Ltd

FSC
www.fsc.org
MIX
Paper from
responsible sources
FSC® C105735

Printed and bound in South Africa by Interpak Books, Pietermaritzburg

ISBN 978 1 43170 030 1 (Print)
ISBN 978 1 92054 529 1 (ePub)
ISBN 978 1 92054 530 7 (PDF)

10 9 8 7 6 5 4 3 2 1

The route maps in this guidebook are supplemented by GPS tracks, which are available as free downloads from **www.dragontrax.co.za**

Get monthly updates and news by subscribing to our newsletter at **www.randomstruik.co.za**

CONTENTS

ABOUT THIS GUIDE

The Spine of the Dragon trail and this guide to riding it are not an exact science: the riding was designed to be fun, and the route was designed to be flexible. The book provides just about everything you need to do the trail: route descriptions and distances, trail gradings, maps, contact information and even our own home-baked philosophies about life and riding. In between all this you'll find bits of history, geography, philosophy and other nonsense that came into our heads as we were riding.

We have divided the trail – and the book – into **nine discrete sections**, each one of which could be ridden as a shorter mountain bike touring holiday. Each section is further broken down into stages, amounting to a total of 58 day stages, each equivalent to a day's riding. Some people will want to try to ride the whole thing in one huge bite, or to knock off entire sections one after the other over time. Others might want to spend only a couple of days on the trail, in which case they'll have a multitude of options to choose from.

Each stage is described in detail. It is introduced by a **brief summary of what you can expect** along the route and is followed by an **overview of the experience**, offering insights into the day's journey. It might not be exactly as you experience it, but then that is the beauty of it: it will be unique to each person as he or she goes, or else why bother?

The overview is followed by a **full description of the day's route**. Mostly the routes are straightforward – following pretty much the same way most people would go if they had to connect the dots from one end of the country to the other. However, in some cases things became far from straightforward, such as when we had to get over or around mountain ranges, or swollen rivers, or when the distance between places to stay was too great to be done by the average cyclist in one day. Where possible we have given alternative routes on the maps as well as in the narrative, but not always; this is because we cannot anticipate exactly what you want to do, and we'd like to give you some leeway to make your own adventure. Like when the weather bowls you a googly and you have to make plan B.

To remove some of your stress, we have included recommendations about **where to stay** at the end of each day's ride as well as the contact details for the various establishments. We have asked each place we used, with the exception of community facilities or small local establishments, to give Spine riders a special rate, so do ask for it.

The **maps** you'll find in this guide are pretty good approximations of the route as you ride it, but of course they are not detail-perfect. A person with a really good sense of direction would almost certainly be able to complete the trail using just the route descriptions and the maps. After all, we did not have any route map to follow when we made up the trail.

The maps show many things, most importantly, the start and end points, together with their GPS co-ordinates, and the kind of track you are on at every stage, from tarred or dirt roads to dirt tracks, jeep tracks, footpaths and railway lines (there is a useful key to the maps on page 6). They also show the most pertinent towns, mountains, rivers and points of interest along each route to help you interpret the landscape.

Only where relevant, alternative routes suggested in the book are indicated on the maps. When choosing which route to take, you should consider the experience, fitness and abilities of the members of your group. Some people will be able to ride further than us, others less.

For people with a less well-developed sense of direction, we have posted all the **GPS tracks** on our **Dragon Trax website** (www.dragontrax.co.za). However, you would have to be a veritable Henry the Navigator to use only the GPS tracks without cross-consulting this guide, which fills in the detail along an otherwise featureless map on a small electronic device. Together, though, they make fine bicycling music.

BRISTOW-THOMAS GRADING SYSTEM

Since the international mountain biking grading system of green, red and black routes (taken from skiing) hardly applies to bicycle – or mountain bike – touring routes, we developed our own. We call it the Bristow–Thomas system, and it looks like this:

- **Short, easy/moderate** – typically 30–50km (sometimes less), no very hard climbs or technical sections
- **Short, hard** – similar distance but with physically hard and/or technical sections
- **Medium, easy/moderate** – typically 50–70km, no severe sections
- **Medium, hard** – similar distance but with hard ascents and/or technical sections
- **Long, easy/moderate** – more than 70km, no sustained or severe ascents or technical sections
- **Long, hard** – similar distance but with strenuous riding and/or technical sections

All routes in this guidebook have been ranked using this system.

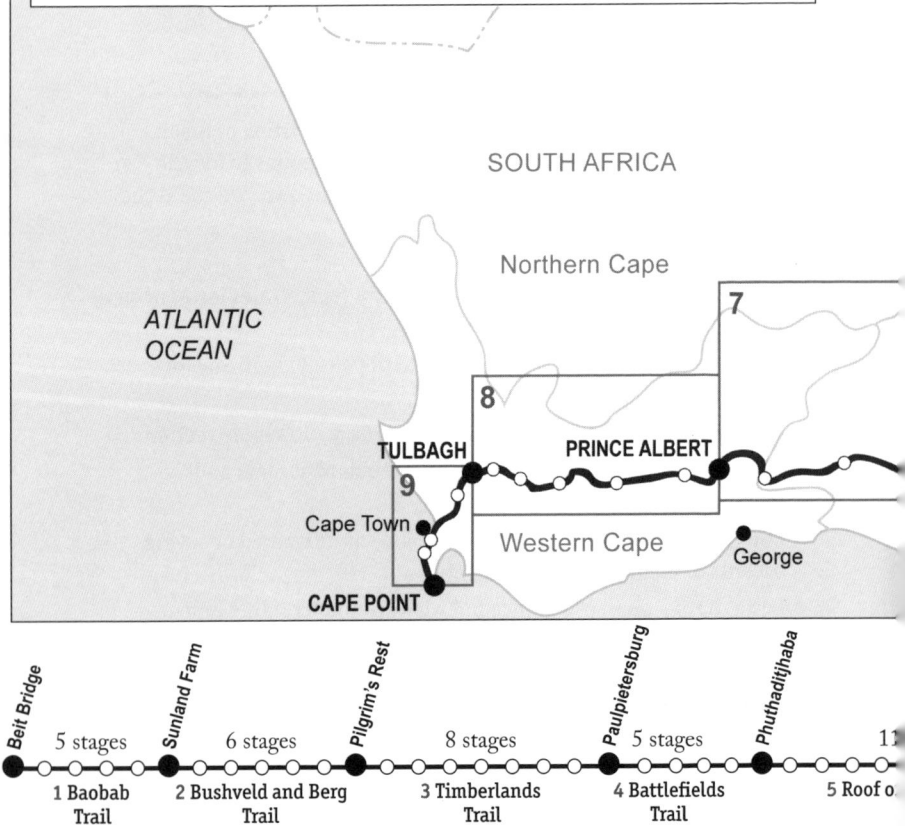

KEY TO STAGE MAPS

National road		Border post	
Main road		River	
Secondary road		Tributary, stream	
Railway track		Dam, lake, vlei, pan	
Tarred road (mtb route)			
Untarred road (mtb route)		National park, nature reserve	
Single track (mtb route)		Town, village, settlement	
Jeep track, sandy track (mtb route)		Point of interest	
Alternative mtb route		Railway station	
START Start (mtb route)		Farm	
ALT. START Alternative start (mtb route)		Accommodation	
N1 Route number national road		Plantation	
R525 Route number main road		Radio tower	
D104 Route number minor road			
International boundary			

SOUTH AFRICA

Northern Cape

ATLANTIC OCEAN

7

8

TULBAGH

PRINCE ALBERT

9

Cape Town

Western Cape

George

CAPE POINT

Beit Bridge

Sunland Farm

Pilgrim's Rest

Paulpietersburg

Phuthaditjhaba

5 stages   6 stages   8 stages   5 stages   1

1 Baobab Trail   2 Bushveld and Berg Trail   3 Timberlands Trail   4 Battlefields Trail   5 Roof o

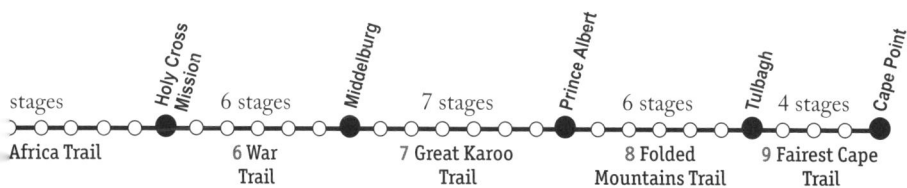

OVERVIEW: SPINE OF THE DRAGON TRAIL

1 BAOBAB TRAIL (5 stages)

Summer or winter, this section (which takes you through the far north) is as hot as hot gets in South Africa, which is why you should ride this trail in the milder seasons. If you are planning on doing the entire Spine of the Dragon route in one go, you should time riding the Baobab section in spring or autumn, provided that you take into account when that will get you through Lesotho and the Cape Folded Mountains, where the cold and rain are formidable factors. The biggest attraction of the area is how rural and African it is, so make a point of stopping often and engaging the locals.

Stage 1:	Beit Bridge to R525 T-junction	89km
Stage 2:	R525 T-junction to Gundani	55km
Stage 3:	Gundani to Thohoyandou	60km
Stage 4:	Thohoyandou to Middle Letaba dam	57km
Stage 5:	Middle Letaba dam to Sunland farm (Modjadjiskloof)	60km

2 BUSHVELD AND BERG TRAIL (6 stages)

Enter one of the least-visited regions of South Africa, with places you might have heard of but are unlikely ever to have gone to, such as Chuenespoort, Burgersfort, Steelpoort and Ohrigstad. The crux of this trail is the Wolkberg, a vast mountain wilderness that lies across our path and has to be got over, around or otherwise through. Even less expected is how rampant mining activity is in parts, transforming this former apartheid-era dumping ground into a vibrant rural socio-economic powerhouse.

Stage 1:	Sunland farm (Modjadjiskloof) to Kurisa Moya Nature Lodge	53.7km
Stage 2:	Kurisa Moya Nature Lodge to Haenertsburg	30km
Stage 3:	Haenertsburg to Chuenespoort	79km
Stage 4:	Chuenespoort to Burgersfort	157km
Stage 5:	Burgersfort to Ohrigstad	45km
Stage 6:	Ohrigstad to Pilgrim's Rest	68km

3 TIMBERLANDS TRAIL (8 stages)

Once, long ago, the eastern escarpment area was a fertile region of montane grasslands where birds and antelope played. Then came gold mines and timber plantations, and first the antelope and then the birds started to disappear. Yet, the cool climate and extensive timber plantations lend the area a feeling of being somewhere else, maybe in some mountainous part of Europe. Did we mention mountains? And some lovely villages, and hundreds of natural lakes? Enjoy.

Stage 1:	Pilgrim's Rest to Long Tom Pass	51.4km
Stage 2:	Long Tom Pass to Alkmaar/N4	56km
Stage 3:	Alkmaar/N4 to Kaapschehoop	30.5km
Stage 4:	Kaapschehoop to Badplaas	75.5km
Stage 5:	Badplaas to Chrissiesmeer	58km
Stage 6:	Chrissiesmeer to Amsterdam	72km
Stage 7:	Amsterdam to Piet Retief/Mkhondo	64km
Stage 8:	Piet Retief/Mkhondo to Natal Spa (Paulpietersburg)	84.5km

4 BATTLEFIELDS TRAIL (5 stages)

Talk about an area that drips with history. Around just about every corner is a historic battlefield, where Zulus, Boers and Brits set about lambasting one another in a series of wars that lasted pretty much the entire 19th century. And, looking at the sometimes rolling, sometimes rugged, intensely green land carved by looping rivers and dotted with fat cattle, you can understand what they were fighting over. The riding here is also pretty awesome, and it does infuse the trail with a sense of drama – especially if you have some notion of the dramas that forged the human landscape.

Stage 1:	Natal Spa (Paulpietersburg) to Blood River	105km
Stage 2:	Blood River to Rorke's Drift Lodge	68km
Stage 3:	Rorke's Drift Lodge to Elandslaagte	93km
Stage 4:	Elandslaagte to Swinburne	93km
	Alternative route: Elandslaagte to Harrismith	114km
Stage 5:	Swinburne to Oliviershoek Pass to Phuthaditjhaba	48km + 46km
	Alternative route: Harrismith to Kestell to Ha Napo/Ha Mphakha	53km + 55km

⛭ 5 ROOF OF AFRICA TRAIL (11 stages)

Lesotho is serious adventure territory, and definitely not for novices, anyone with a fear of heights or depths, or anyone who cannot fix a mountain bike with just a multi-tool and wire. Much of the route is off-road and off the map; it will tax the most proficient mountain biker. Be prepared for lots of walking, bike-hiking, clambering, and getting down and dirty. We strongly recommend you employ the services of a local guide, or do the section with Detour Trails. Either way, you should have backup and some sort of a plan B.

Stage 1:	Phuthaditjhaba or Kestell to Ha Napo/ Ha Mphakha	35km
Stage 2:	Ha Napo/Ha Mphakha to Oxbow Lodge	26km
Stage 3:	Oxbow Lodge to Motete	36km
Stage 4:	Motete to Ha Lejone	40km
Stage 5:	Ha Lejone to Katse	56km
Stage 6:	Katse to Thaba-Tseka	69km
Stage 7:	Thaba-Tseka to Mantsonyane	59km
Stage 8:	Mantsonyane to Semonkong	75km
Stage 9:	Semonkong to Ketane	57km
Stage 10:	Ketane to Ha Qiqita/Bethel	42km
Stage 11:	Ha Qiqita/Bethel to Holy Cross Mission	49km

⛭ 6 WAR TRAIL (6 stages)

In the realm of stories in two parts, this is the trail of two parts: the first part is tacked onto the end of Lesotho and consists of fairly high, hilly terrain, while the second half morphs into the Great Karoo, where the rides are long and often rather flat. But there is no shortage of mountains for riding, the trail having to negotiate the tail end of the Drakensberg, the Stormberg, Witteberg and Bamboesberg, and ending in sight of the Sneeuberg.

Stage 1:	Holy Cross Mission to Reedsdell farm	75km
Stage 2:	Reedsdell farm to Barkly East	38km
Stage 3:	Barkly East to Dordrecht	99km
Stage 4:	Dordrecht to Molteno	118km
Stage 5:	Molteno to Hofmeyr	84km
Stage 6:	Hofmeyr to Middelburg	92km

7 **GREAT KAROO TRAIL** (7 stages)

We all have a mental image of a Karoo that is a vast, flat, semi-arid expanse with scattered flat-topped koppies and windmills. But ride it on a bicycle and you soon discover that, while it is indeed vast, it is seldom flat. In fact, in places it's extremely mountainous and in others unexpectedly fertile. Each successive layer of land here represents a period during which sediments were laid down when this part of the earth was much wetter. Prototype plants and trees grew profusely in the wetlands, and the earth's first land animals, primitive amphibians, evolved through a zoological phantasmagoria of primitive mammal-like reptiles. The remains of some of these creatures exist right there where they died, in stream-bed sediments.

Stage 1:	Middelburg to Nieu Bethesda	75km
Stage 2:	Nieu Bethesda to Graaff-Reinet	108km
Stage 3:	Graaff-Reinet to Jansenville	114km
Stage 4:	Jansenville to Steytlerville	63km
Stage 5:	Steytlerville to Willowmore	112km
Stage 6:	Willowmore to Klaarstroom	97km
Stage 7:	Klaarstroom to Prince Albert	77km

8 **FOLDED MOUNTAINS TRAIL** (6 stages)

When the super landmass Gondwana started splitting up and the parts began drifting off, the southern edge of what became Africa crumpled like a carpet end that has been pushed back. These rumples are the Cape Folded Mountains, the most extensive mountainous region in Southern Africa. The Spine trail enters them via the spectacular Swartberg Pass and traverses some of the most legendary places of the many linear ranges. Much of this section lies within the Cape Floral Kingdom World Heritage Site, which celebrates the world's most extraordinary vegetation type, the fynbos biome.

Stage 1:	Prince Albert to Gamkaskloof	60km
Stage 2:	Gamkaskloof to Rouxpos	58km
Stage 3:	Rouxpos to Anysberg Nature Reserve	64km
Stage 4:	Anysberg Nature Reserve to Touws River	76km
Stage 5:	Touws River to Forgotten Highway Manor	70km
Stage 6:	Forgotten Highway Manor to Tulbagh	53km

9 FAIREST CAPE TRAIL (4 stages)

Mirror, mirror on the wall, which is the fairest Cape of all? The Cape, of course, Sir Francis! Super mariner Francis Drake reckoned as much only from his vantage on the poop deck of his *Golden Hind*. We on our bikes have the luxury of seeing this 'fairest cape in all the circumference of the earth' from a landward aspect. The trail starts off in the bucolic Tulbagh valley where vines abound and ragged mountain peaks are etched against the sky. From there it traverses gentle farmlands before reaching the Atlantic coast that is then followed for the last two and a half days of riding. May the winds fill your sails and the beauty – not least when you first see Table Mountain rise like a lithographic galleon on a sea of wheat – fill your heart.

Stage 1:	Tulbagh to Riebeek Kasteel	54km
Stage 2:	Riebeek Kasteel to Bloubergstrand	30km
Stage 3:	Bloubergstrand to Cape Town	22km
Stage 4:	Cape Town (City Centre) to Cape Point	73km

©Steve Thomas

The Dragon questers gather their wits before crossing the stone bridge into Pilgrim's Rest.

INTRODUCTION

Riding on the backs of giants

When Eardstapper (David Bristow) and the Daytripper (Steve Thomas) first met, they discovered a mutual fondness for the philosophical ramblings of Henry David Thoreau on the fine art of walking (only ever for pleasure, never for exercise or conquest), Little Feat and mountain biking – not the 'get there first' kind; more the ambling, smell-the-fynbos kind. So when the Eardstapper got a thought about riding across the country's pointy bits, his second thought was to tell the Daytripper. 'When do we leave?' was the response.

The spirit of Mr Thoreau was very much the guiding spirit of the Spine of the Dragon ride. What he wrote in his essay 'Walking', in 1863, can be directly equated to our love of riding today:

> *The best part of the land is not private property: the landscape is not owned, and the [rider] enjoys comparative freedom. But possibly the day will come when it will be partitioned off into so-called pleasure-grounds, in which a few will take a narrow and exclusive pleasure only – when fences shall be multiplied, and man-traps and other engines invented to confine men to the public road, and [riding] over the surface of God's earth shall be construed to mean trespassing on some gentleman's grounds. To enjoy a thing exclusively is commonly to exclude yourself from the true enjoyment of it. Let us improve our opportunities, then, before the evil day comes.*

We first agreed on a number of shared objectives:
- to find and map a mountain bike touring trail across South Africa, accessible to all,
- to make each stage do-able for the average off-road rider, with a roof, bed and bath available at the end of each day's riding,
- to keep the trail to an absolute minimum of tar and maximum of gravel and single track,
- to invite all mountain bikers to participate in improving this, 'the people's trail', by refining stages and posting the GPS tracks on our Dragon Trax website,
- to always ride in the spirit of Thoreau, with a song and a smile, no matter the weather or the obstacles.

The meeting of paths and minds

Our mantras became: 'even the uphills are down' and 'wherever you are, there you are'. This idea seems to have been a matter of what the intrepid Steve calls

If you cannot get reliable directions, just follow the cows home – a strategy that worked for us on some occasions.

synchro-destiny – the crossing of paths of various people working (sometimes unwittingly) towards a common end. Apart from the venerable Mr Thoreau, a more recent notable of this story is David Waddilove, who invented the mother of all mountain biking trails: the Freedom Challenge.

Crisscrossing his path is the likes of Kevin Davie, who pioneered the Spine Route along the Mpumalanga and KwaZulu-Natal Drakensberg escarpments, and a year later did his solo Ganna ride from Beit Bridge to Cape Point. Roughly the same time, Jaco Strydom had dreams of a circular route from Cape Town to Beit Bridge and back, which would link with the Freedom Challenge. After three attempts – dogged all the way by a succession of unfortunate health and injury issues – he finally made it (his route goes around the Drakensberg through KwaZulu-Natal and then through Swaziland) as we were going to press.

Our epiphany was to create a mountain biking **touring** route, rather than a hell-for-rubber Freedom Challenge-style ride. Not racing-snake types ourselves, the trail had to be something any off-road rider could do, or dream of doing, either in one big push or over time in sections and stages. The result is our Spine of the Dragon mountain biking trail – approximately 4000km from end to end (but ever changing as it gets improved), and broken up into nine sections, each with several stages. It attempts to provide the least amount of tar possible, and is suitably long and tough without being a Special Forces training course.

There are plenty of competitive mountain biking events where you can test yourself and impress your friends – this is not one of them. The Spine trail is about keeping it slow and steady, smelling the flowers, chatting to the locals and taking an interest in the physical and cultural landscape along the way. We purposely tried to connect the interesting dots: South Africa's biggest tree, many of KwaZulu-Natal's battlefield sites, the off-the-beaten-track trifecta of Swartberg Pass, Die Hel and Die Leer (some might wish we hadn't).

Since Lesotho seems to be number one on every mountain biker's bucket list, we decided to help David Waddilove in his mission to forge the ultimate route right across that country – the Trans Lesotho. This section is not for the soft of flesh or frail of heart; it will test you to the limit. There are many shorter or easier options within or around Lesotho; it will be up to other mountain bike riders to track and make available these in the future (see the box 'Dragon Trax: 'Wiki'ing' the Spine of the Dragon trail' below).

'The people's trail'

Our route should, we agreed, form the backbone of a mountain biking trail system that would eventually spread across the whole country, so we created the website **www.spineofthedragon.co.za** on which to post everything about the trail as we rode it. The name was a combination of things: Kevin Davie's first Spine Ride route; the idea of our trail as the skeleton of a larger trail system to be fleshed out over time; and, of course, the Drakensberg, forming the main part of our Great Escarpment mountain chain.

Our next mission, we agreed, was to open our route to the 'Wiki' review process. Creating a second website, **www.dragontrax.co.za**, we uploaded all our own GPS tracks from the Spine of the Dragon ride, then opened it to the

DRAGON TRAX
'WIKI'ING' THE SPINE OF THE DRAGON TRAIL

The Spine of the Dragon trail is our own creation, figured out on the road as we went, so we're aware it could be improved in many places by decreasing the tar and other less appealing aspects – and increasing the fun factor. In some places it could do with a complete rerouting.

The main reason we started the Dragon Trax website, from where GPS tracks for each section can be downloaded for free, is this: if you've found a better route that has access rights and is doable by the average mountain biker, we invite you to submit your track to the website.

Our webmaster, in consultation with us, will evaluate your track. If it meets our criteria, it will become the default route, or an optional track. Your name will also be attached to this new route.

Secondly, Dragon Trax facilitates the important function of peer review; in this way the best available information becomes accessible to all, while bad routing is eventually eliminated.

Thirdly, over time and with your participation we'd like to develop a network of trails off the main Spine, so that the Spine of the Dragon trail eventually becomes an entire body of mountain bike trails across and around the country. So ... ride the trail, enjoy the trail, and, where you can, improve and extend the trail.

mountain biking community to expand. There were, for example, a number of times when we got hopelessly lost, or had to abandon a section due to really foul weather, or realised there was a better option than the one we took. This is the essence of our concept for a 'people's trail' – for, by and of the people who ride it.

For the most part, we were making up the route as we went along. Google Earth and Garmin RoadTrip were not always very helpful when it came to fine detail in parts of Limpopo province and Lesotho, so there local knowledge became key. Although your best tool for navigating any route is a set of topographical maps (1:250 000 and 1:50 000) obtainable from the Government Printing Works, even these could not always help to untangle the maze that constitutes deep rural Limpopo. The Spine of the Dragon route is perfectly rideable, though, just as we tracked and described it; but given seasonal and weather variations, and riding ability, there are many places we've posed alternatives to either shorten or lengthen a day. Every mountain biker in this country who tracks his or her rides with a GPS device can help expand the Spine of the Dragon network by submitting his or her tracks to our webmaster. Ultimately Dragon Trax will become the repository of all mountain biking trails across South Africa.

Land access issues

Our old friend Mao Tzedung used to say: every journey of 4000km starts with the first pedal stroke. It struck us at some stage that, while the USA has any number of fine road and off-road cycle trails, South Africa is a whole lot wilder with realms of untapped mountain biking territory (albeit much closed off by national parks and private land). It seemed like a good plan to unlock some of it. That meant asserting access rights to what are, or should be, rights of way (old wagon roads, mountain passes, public roads that landowners have illegally closed off). The trick is to do it in a way that, while asserting our legal rights, coerces rather than alienates landowners: be friendly, respectful and attentive to the other party and his or her point of view.

It's a tricky road for sure – particularly when dealing with farmers wielding shotguns, the national parks system or timber companies who control so much of the mountain areas. When confronting an organisation, however, you should get advice from local or national mountain biking organisations. Your number one contact is AMA Rider (www.amarider.co.za), run by mountain biking and trail organiser supremo, Meurant Botha, in the Boland. AMA Rider is his growing endeavour to create an umbrella mountain biking organisation that deals with issues such as trail building, youth development (the Spur mountain biking league), land access and (even trickier) landowner indemnity. The other fountain of knowledge in land access is David Waddilove of the Freedom Challenge (www.freedomchallenge.org.za).

The Forgotten Highway Manor had forgotten about us (tring-tring, no one home), so we pushed into the cold front to find an inn in Ceres.

Whatever you do, don't be arrogant, confrontational or aggressive – or trespass when you know to do so will jeopardise future access. Okay, there are times when people just won't listen to reason; sometimes mass rogue access can overcome a stubborn landowner (we're talking about riding along existing tracks on public land where some jerk of a land manager has decided mountain bikers are the devil's disciples).

Giving back

Another stimulus in creating this ride was to do some good and leave a legacy. We are aware that our great fortune of living in this amazing country has, in some ways, come at a cost to others. There are those who are invariably worse off than we are. Giving back is an integral part of our vision, and the cause we've chosen is Operation Smile. Here all the resources are directed towards improving the lives of children in poor, mostly rural areas, whose lives have been traumatised by facial deformities. Read more about it on our site **www. spineofthedragon.co.za/index.php/ride-for-smiles**.

We raised a lot of money directly from our ride. In addition, our Dragon Trax website asks simply for a donation, however small, each time you download a free track. It's the right thing to do.

Tame your own dragon

On our websites we've created a Dragon Master order consisting of everyone who has ridden the entire Spine of the Dragon trail. To qualify, you need to have ridden the entire distance of around 4000km from Beit Bridge to Cape Town, Cape Point or Agulhas on a track, or any version of it, that constitutes the Spine of the Dragon trail. (This is a self-regulating system; we mountain bikers are decent, honest people.)

At the time of going to press there were four Dragon Masters (the two Dragon trail pioneers, Ganna-rider Kevin Davie and Beit2Cape Jaco Strydom), and a further three had just set off on the trail. We look forward to the time when it's a well-populated community conducting regular board meetings out on the trail, then trading stories while imbibing recovery drinks afterwards.

What we learned

We rode nearly 4000km across some of the most pointy bits of the country, and these are the lessons we now hold to be inalienable truths:

- There are more uphills than downhills.
- The prevailing wind is an easterly–westerly.
- All winds are headwinds.
- All potholes are on the left, except when they're on the left **and** right.
- All people are friendly when you are – except for some who are born with thorns in their asses.

Our backup Amarok and amaDriver also liked to have some fun when they got the chance, as they did here in full view of the Kompasberg near Nieu Bethesda.

- There are more unemployed people than employed; most sit (or lie) under trees and drink beer. They seem happy.
- It's a big country, end to end.
- It's great fun to ride a mountain bike.

Credit where it's due

People and organisations that need to be mentioned start with Volkswagen SA, the first supporter to come on board; they offered us a 4x4 double-cab as our backup vehicle, and we fell rather wantonly in love with the Amarok. The only problems we had with it were inflicted by ourselves; it proved to be a tough but racy workhorse (that bi-turbo engine is a pocket rocket). Check out www.vwcommercial.co.za/models/amarok.

Driving the Amarok were our three voluntary backup drivers: bike mechanic Philippe Samouilhan took us from Beit Bridge to Phuthaditjhaba; Steve's brother Denis Thomas took over from there to Nieu Bethesda; and Ray Wat, owner of Thaba Tours in Himeville, handled the final leg to Cape Town.

Next is the Liberty Trust, which gave a generous donation to cover some of our costs, without which we couldn't have taken off the time or have afforded the expenses of a two-month trip.

Then there is Operation Smile South Africa (www.southafrica. operationsmile.org), an amazing nonprofit, volunteer medical services organisation that helps to make the world a better place. It deserves to be acknowledged and rewarded for the selfless work it does.

On the cycling side, Stirling Kotze of Revolution Cycles in Cape Town (www.revolutioncycles.co.za) very generously helped us out with free services, parts and cycling gear, all of which we used and greatly appreciated. Specialized South Africa (www.specialized-sa.co.za) gave us a 29" Rockhopper test bike to ride, and provided a brand-new one to be auctioned off in aid of Operation Smile.

Thanks to Bruce Wright (bruce@mnemonic.co.za) of Mnemonic, who developed our Spine of the Dragon and Dragon Trax websites, and Josephine Bestic (napoleonsprincess@gmail.com) of Honeyguide Social Media, who did the daily administration on the web and who runs our Facebook page.

The Spine of the Dragon cycle shirts and the Goth-style T-shirts we produced and rode in were the inspiration and work of talented artist and long-standing friend James Berrangé.

Finally, to all the people along the trail who helped us, especially those who provided us – often for free – with soft beds and warm meals, a big thank you. You will find their contact details in a list at the back of the book.

Stay cool and ride easy,
David and Steve

PREPARING FOR THE TRAIL

Initial planning

How you prepare will depend on how far you plan to ride – a single section or the whole enchilada. Also, all sections are not the same: 10 days in Lesotho versus five days in the Karoo are different echidnas (like an enchilada, but more spiky). The real crux is whether or not you will have backup to carry stuff.

The trail is planned so that each night you are sure to find a bed, meal and bath of some kind (in some places it might be a basin of hot water). That means you need to carry very little on your bike – but in many cases you do need to book your accommodation in advance to ensure there is a bed at the inn.

Make sure your bike is in tiptop condition, because the riding can get hectic in places. In most cases you'll be far from any bike shop or a hardware store (that's the point of mountain biking, to get off the beaten track). And always carry a spare derailleur hanger (drop-out). If you're not a proficient can-do and bike-repair person, consider avoiding the more out-of-the-way places like Lesotho and rural northern Limpopo.

If you are aiming to go to Lesotho, check that your passport is in order – and remember to pack it. You'll need it to get in and out of the Mountain Kingdom.

Check weather conditions for when you will be riding and plan accordingly. Anywhere with mountains is going to be tougher in all respects than the flat Karoo. The best times to ride are March to May and September to November.

Other than that, all you need to carry is a big smile, a can-do frame of mind, and a bit of spare cash for the spaza shops along the way, tips for help proffered, or the occasional emergency Basotho pony hire.

Clothing

Since you carry very little – that means usually only one change of riding gear – you have to wash it every day. Most places will have some washing facilities (five-star means the place has a washing machine and tumble drier!).

You need to tailor your gear to the place and the season: mountains mean rain, in general, and unpredictability, so you need warm and wet (waterproof) layers. Winter in the Western Cape means rain – serious rain – so be prepared.

Don't forget to pack your toiletries and a basic medical kit.

A good check list is:
- helmet
- riding shoes
- overshoes, waterproof (optional)

- spare cleats
- buff, and/or beanie
- gloves x 2 – light, fingerless; warm, fingers
- gloves, waterproof (optional)
- socks x 2
- riding shorts x 2
- riding longs (stretch)
- undershirt x 2 (polyprop only)
- riding shirt x 2
- arm warmers (also for sun)
- riding jersey, lightweight, polyprop
- sleeveless windbreaker
- rain jacket
- wind bib (optional)
- waterproof riding suit from First Ascent or Cape Storm (optional)

A set of casual clothes can include:
- underwear
- socks for cold
- trainers/sandals
- T-shirt x 2
- shorts
- tracksuit-type longs
- warm top

Bike maintenance and repair

On our entire ride we needed to fix only three punctures, replace two broken derailleur hangers, fix one bent brake disk and repair one free-wheel hub. Of course, that's on top of the planned replacement of tyres (once), drive trains (chain rings, chain, cassette cluster) and gear cables (around halfway).

However, on certain rides we've had to make running repairs, like breaking the derailleur clean off and converting the bike to a single-speed (choose a gear and shorten the chain to bypass the derailleur); or having a hydraulic brake cable sheer off (nothing to be done); or a pedal crank fall off (cable ties and a stick).

While you have to hope for the best, you do need at least one person in your party who is a 'fixer'. And you should carry all the basic repair stuff (see page 22 for a list). But by far the most important task is daily to clean your bike, check it over, and lube the chain. It's like feeding and watering your horse at the end of a day's ride – you have to do it if you want your mount to survive.

If you're not bike-repair whizzes, including a bike-repair manual in your kit is worth the weight. Make sure you know how to fix small and large punctures

AmaDriver Philippe tended our bikes for the first 2000-odd kilometres of the ride, and they did not give one groan, moan or squeak.

(the most common repairs), as well as side-wall tears (snake bites). We strongly recommend you use tubeless tyres, which are easy to repair if you have the experience – not so if you don't. With tubeless, you won't even notice at least 90% of punctures, while another 9% are easy fixes with slime and tyre plugs. But you have to carry a gas cartridge inflator to get the pressure kick when you reinflate (trying to pump up tubeless tyres with a hand pump can be a life-altering experience, in a bad way).

A final recommendation is to make both your brake rotors (disks) the same, so you need carry only one spare. We standardised all our brake and gear parts and it proved to be a very good idea when we needed to carry out on-trail repairs.

Probably the worst-case scenario is a damaged freewheel hub: if you don't have all the right tools and don't know what to do inside the thing, you're pretty much finished. Best is to use the old phone-a-friend bail-out technique: have the number of a really good bike-fixer on your speed dial, so you can call when you have to and let him or her talk you through the repair.

Gear to carry
Short ride
- cable ties
- spare gear cables
- spare tyre
- spare tubes – can be used when you can't fix a tubeless puncture

- tube or tubeless puncture repair kit (know how to use it)
- tyre gaitors
- tyre lever x 2
- gas-bomb tyre inflator
- lots of spare bombs
- derailleur hanger (each bike has a unique one)
- chain breaker and spare snap link
- combination toolset
- small-nose pliers
- backpack hydration pack
- extra water bottle
- GPS unit
- cellphone
- laptop
- camera
- batteries (or rechargeables)
- leads for recharging GPS unit/cellphone/laptop/camera
- adaptor plug
- spare tyre slime (prefill tyres with extra slime)
- spare tubeless valve
- head torch
- long-bristle cleaning brush

Long ride

- all the short-ride gear listed above
- spare brake pads
- spare brake rotor (disk) and key (if a star key)
- extra derailleur hanger
- handlebar/crossbar panniers
- shock pump
- spoke tension tool
- chain cleaner
- plenty of chain lube
- first-aid kit

Tyres and wheels

By now the tube/tubeless debate should be over, with tubeless the preferred option for all mountain bikers. If you have the old tube rims, you can save money by doing a Stan's tubeless conversion (any bike shop can), or you'll have to buy tubeless rims. There are websites that show you how to make a home conversion; worth a try if cash is a factor.

Once fitted properly (and there is a bit of technique here to get the beading to sit in its track), they should give no trouble. Punctures are sorted out by the slime which is forced out under pressure and seals most thorn-like intrusions. Bigger holes are fixed, just like a car tyre, with a tubeless plug kit.

Tubeless tyres run on lower pressure than tubed, so mostly snake-bite cuts are a thing of the past. Side-wall slits can happen, but are rare. If they do, you'll need to use a gaitor. You need to learn how to use it because there's no tube to keep it in place. Carry a tube just in case.

Running on lower pressure means better traction in mud, dust and sand, and overall it's a much more comfortable ride. If you cannot repair a tubeless tyre, insert a tube – but make sure you remove all thorns from the inside or the exercise is futile. You'll need to remove the tubeless valve too, or the Stan's conversion rim band with valve.

Now for the 26"/29" debate: we firmly believe it's a means for bike manufacturers to increase sales when the development curve tapers off. Scientifically speaking, on uphills and flats a 29" bike should roll better over obstacles. On the other hand, the higher centre of gravity works against you on technical downhill sections. Try them both, then you decide.

Trail sustenance

Whether for calorie replacement or emergency rations, you should always carry some kind of trail nosh. Energy bars, chocolate bars, jelly babies, Super Cs (the gel ones are best) – they're all good. If you're riding long and hard, you should try to take in calories soon after finishing the day's riding. We don't buy into the whole recovery drink fad; rather, we believe in Coke, beer (the Dr Castle programme), buns, pies or anything packed with calories. The point is, you need to replace lost carbohydrates as soon as you can (within an hour of ceasing exercise) in order for your tired muscles to recuperate.

Raisins are very good carbohydrate-rich foods, and nuts supply added protein. Your trail food should be something you like – else why bother? You'll be using up to 4000 calories a day, even more on the most extreme sections, so you'll need to refuel during the day. This applies even more on multi-day rides.

In rural areas, you'll find spaza shops with cold drinks and some snacks – sweets, salty crisps and those orange puff-worms, sometimes even dried mopane worms. Otherwise towns are generally spaced far apart; sometimes you won't find any commercial enterprise between the start and end of a day, so you should stock up the day before riding a stage. Always carry cash just in case.

Using GPS

You can ride the Spine of the Dragon trail without using Global Positioning System (GPS) technology by following the maps and route descriptions in this guide. When we rode it, we had no GPS tracks to follow, as we were laying them down as we went. However, we highly recommend using a GPS device as it simply makes navigation so much easier. You can buy the Garmin RoadTrip software and read the tracks off that like a map, but then you'd have to carry a laptop. Learning how to use Garmin, and the associated software, is beyond the scope of this book.

You don't need a computer to use a GPS, although you do need one to download tracks from Dragon Trax or any other website. Once you have the tracks loaded onto your device, all you need do is follow the line and arrow as it goes. Using your GPS in conjunction with software like RoadTrip or Oz Explorer, as well as Google Earth, is amazing fun once you get going, and increases navigational accuracy exponentially.

Of course, using a map or two, a compass and common sense is really the purest way to go – but recommended only for expert navigators with an excellent sense of direction.

Personal safety

We never had a single incident that threatened our personal safety, other than a theft from our backup vehicle in Mbombela (Nelspruit) when our Amarok was cleaned out.

The biggest danger is the sun: that includes dehydration and possible heat exhaustion. Use sunscreen liberally and drink plenty. South Africa's municipal tap water is safe, but in rural areas you can't always be sure. Foreigners can also succumb to local *goggas* to which locals are immune. While we are not advocates of buying bottled water, sometimes it is the safest option.

You do need to carry a basic medical kit which, as well as the plasters, bandages and antiseptics, should include antihistamine medication (tablets and/ or cream) for any bites or allergies. Merthiolate spray is the very best thing for healing cuts, blisters or open sores (it hurts like blazes when first applied).

Always carry a whistle and keep it in an easily accessible spot. It has saved more than one rider from wild animals and/or robbers, and in one known case was vital for locating a fallen, injured rider, and getting that person out of a difficult situation in the dark.

The most important thing to carry is common sense. Take necessary precautions (we often chose to walk a difficult technical section rather than risk riding it), don't leave valuables lying around and always ensure your bicycle cannot be lifted. Keep important stuff – cash, credit cards, passports/ID documents, camera, GPS device, cellphone – close to hand at all times.

You'll find many people along the trail are incredibly friendly and willing to help. However, you will often be riding through areas where they are dirt poor: be sure not to give anyone the temptation to steal from you.

RECOMMENDED
5 days

Baobab Trail

Beit Bridge to Sunland farm (Modjadjiskloof)
•321km

STAGE 1
BEIT BRIDGE TO R525 T-JUNCTION   89km

GRADE: Long, moderate
OVERNIGHT: Popallin Ranch; Forever Resorts Tshipise

IN A NUTSHELL

This is baobab country – hot, low-lying bushveld where massive old trees dot the rocky hills and sandy washes along the great, green, greasy Limpopo River. The first half of the stage is more strenuous than you might imagine, with some stiff hill climbs, while the second half is a long, flat haul. For a first day out on the trail, it's a good tester of things to come.

Snapshot of the experience

Daytripper Steve swung a leg over his Morewood Zula and I, Eardstapper, followed suit on my Specialised 29" Rockhopper. Our backup man, amaDriver Philippe, was captaining the amazing Amarok. We headed east into the wind. Riding into the wind would become the score for almost the entire trip.

The decrepit military road, outside the Beit Bridge army base, was built by the old-regime defence force to prevent 'terrs' from crossing the Limpopo into South Africa. Nowadays the SANDF infantry (men, and women *nogal*, in camo gear) patrol the razor wire for cigarette smugglers from Zimbabwe. Judging by the multitude of holes in the fences, and the din of the shredding machine nearby, we are not winning this battle any more than did the previous regime.

The Limpopo was in spate, averaging around 200m or more across, with the country alongside green as tyre slime and the grey-green river all set about by luminous-trunked fever trees. We stopped and talked to soldiers, walkers and tomato farmers, both black and white, all seemingly happily busy and prosperous. Apparently the tomato business is flourishing there under the giant baobabs in the far north.

Birds were atwitter, monkeys and baboons fat and shiny, and the insects – Limpopo has some serious goggas – were abundant in the extreme. When you look at maps, the experience is a sterile one of lines and topo details: there is no texture, no substance, no soul. There are no sounds, or smells, or lactic acid build-up in your legs, no sweat on your brow and wind in your face, no birds calling, insects chittering and autumn-dry leaves tinkling like chimes.

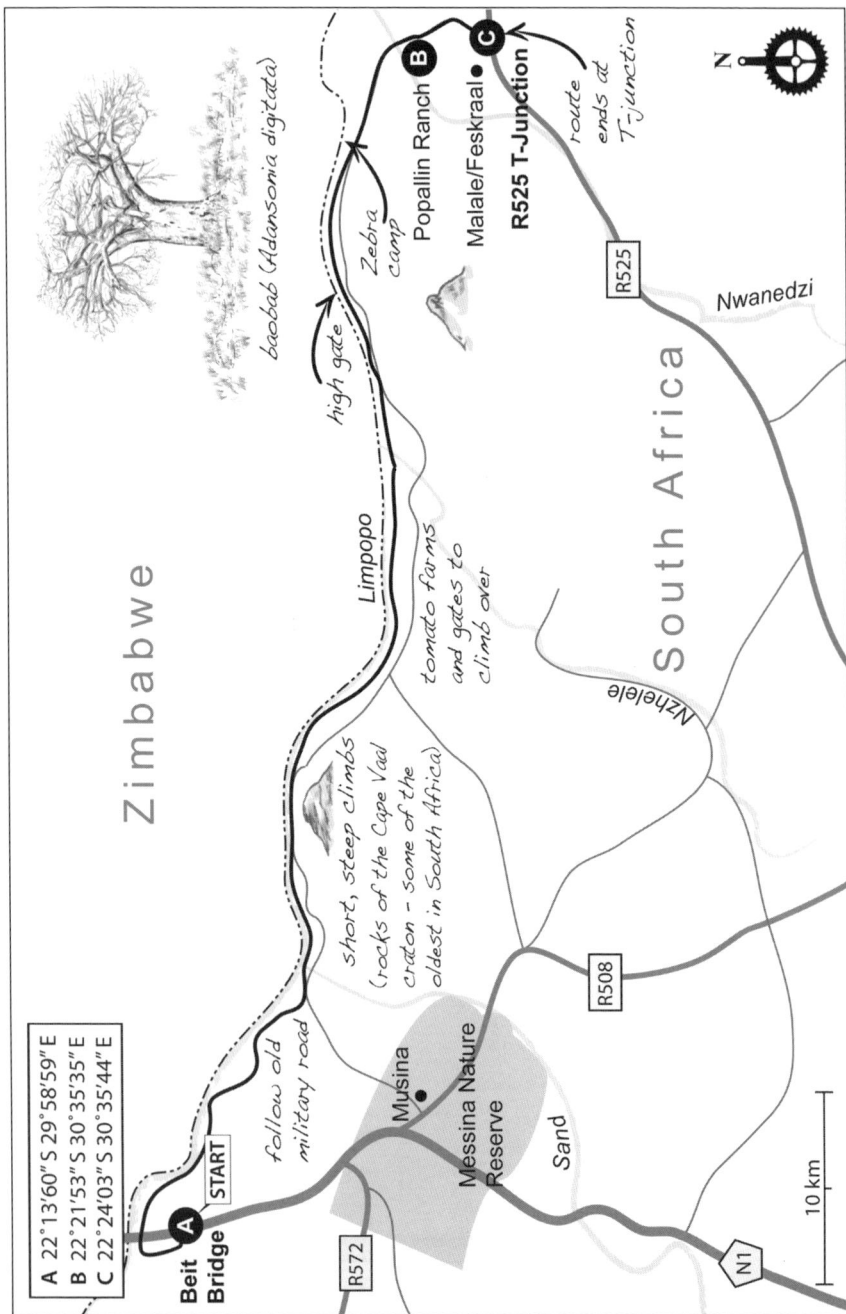

A 22°13'60"S 29°58'59"E
B 22°21'53"S 30°35'35"E
C 22°24'03"S 30°35'44"E

Beit Bridge

START

A

Zimbabwe

baobab (Adansonia digitata)

Popallin Ranch

B

C

Malale/Feskraal

R525 T-Junction

route ends at T-junction

Zebra camp

high gate

Limpopo

R525

Nwanedzi

South Africa

Nzhelele

tomato farms and gates to climb over

short, steep climbs (rocks of the Cape Vaal craton – some of the oldest in South Africa)

follow old military road

Musina

Messina Nature Reserve

Sand

R508

R572

N1

10 km

N

The route

The hardest part, as is so often the case with trails, is locating the starting point. Travelling north on the N1, just before the Beit Bridge border post, turn left at the stop street, immediately right at a T-junction, then right again to find your way under the twin road-rail bridges. This is the old military road that travels east along the Limpopo River all the way to the Kruger National Park. It is tarred, kind of. Given that virtually no vehicles use it, it's a very off-road riding experience ... no easy ride, up-down all day, and several hills requiring the old zigzag climbing technique to breach.

Follow the military road, over dongas, gates and game fences, no matter what. There are several places, where the road breasts ridges, in which legs and lungs are tested to the extreme, if for only short distances. The road crosses a few intermittent watercourses, such as the Sand at around 12km and the Nzhelele about 20km further. After unexpectedly rugged landscape, the road flattens out and first small, then larger farms appear. Here you start to clamber over fences and lift your bike over gates, some double height. In places it might require some scrambling around to make sure that you're on the right track.

The military road has right of way. However, where you do cross farmlands (tomatoes, mainly), be engaging and polite because you are kind of intruding. After another 20km you start to cross small subsistence farms; from about 35 to 40km they become more commercial. At the 69km mark, at a high gate, hop over the fence on your right and get onto the district gravel road – very corrugated and lined with thorn trees. It's another flat 20-odd kilometres to the tarred R525 (the Pafuri Road). At around 70km, before you reach the Pafuri Road, you cross the Nwanedzi River (actually a seasonal stream), where the main development of Popallin Ranch and a golf course can be seen.

Popallin Ranch is in the weekend game-lodge style, with a self-catering camp (Zebra) 10km before you reach the river (or 20 km from the end of the day's route at the lodge). It's the only option in the area, unless you have transport and can bus back to Forever Resorts Tshipise.

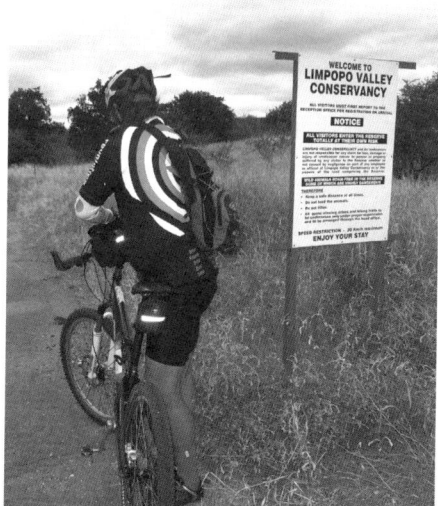

Steve stops to check the fine print before climbing another gate.

STAGE 2
R525 T-JUNCTION TO GUNDANI 55km

GRADE: Medium, easy; one tough climb
OVERNIGHT: Gundani Mutsiwa Campsite (community campsite, arrange ahead through BirdLife South Africa)

IN A NUTSHELL

It's tracks and cattle paths most of the way from Popallin Ranch to the Sagole Big Tree, passing several villages and buying litres of cold Cokes at spaza shops along the way (April was *hot*, one reason not to ride here in midsummer). The giant Sagole baobab is officially acknowledged as the largest indigenous tree in South Africa, measured as the circumference of the trunk 1m above the ground times the height times the circumference of the crown. The tree is 10.47 x 22 x 38.2m. It's quite magical, spiritual possibly, to lie in its ancient shade and dream dreams of dragons' spines and hominid tracks.

A rider needs carbs and protein – Coke and dried mopane worms at Klein Tshipise.

Snapshot of the experience

We had a sense of riding deep into *terra incognita* – no two maps had the same information, and local names and road signs bore no relationship to anything on any map. The *lekker* thing is to stop under the shade of a big tree and shoot the breeze with the local community. We declined kind offers of dried mopane worms (though no doubt a great protein boost) – the people here regard them as a snack food.

The ride from near Klein Tshipise to the Soutpansberg was on gravel roads, and invigorating in its harsh African beauty – first through maize lands dotted with outrageous-looking baobabs, then through thorn and mopane bush to the base of the mountains. Not sights you see every day, unless you are a local

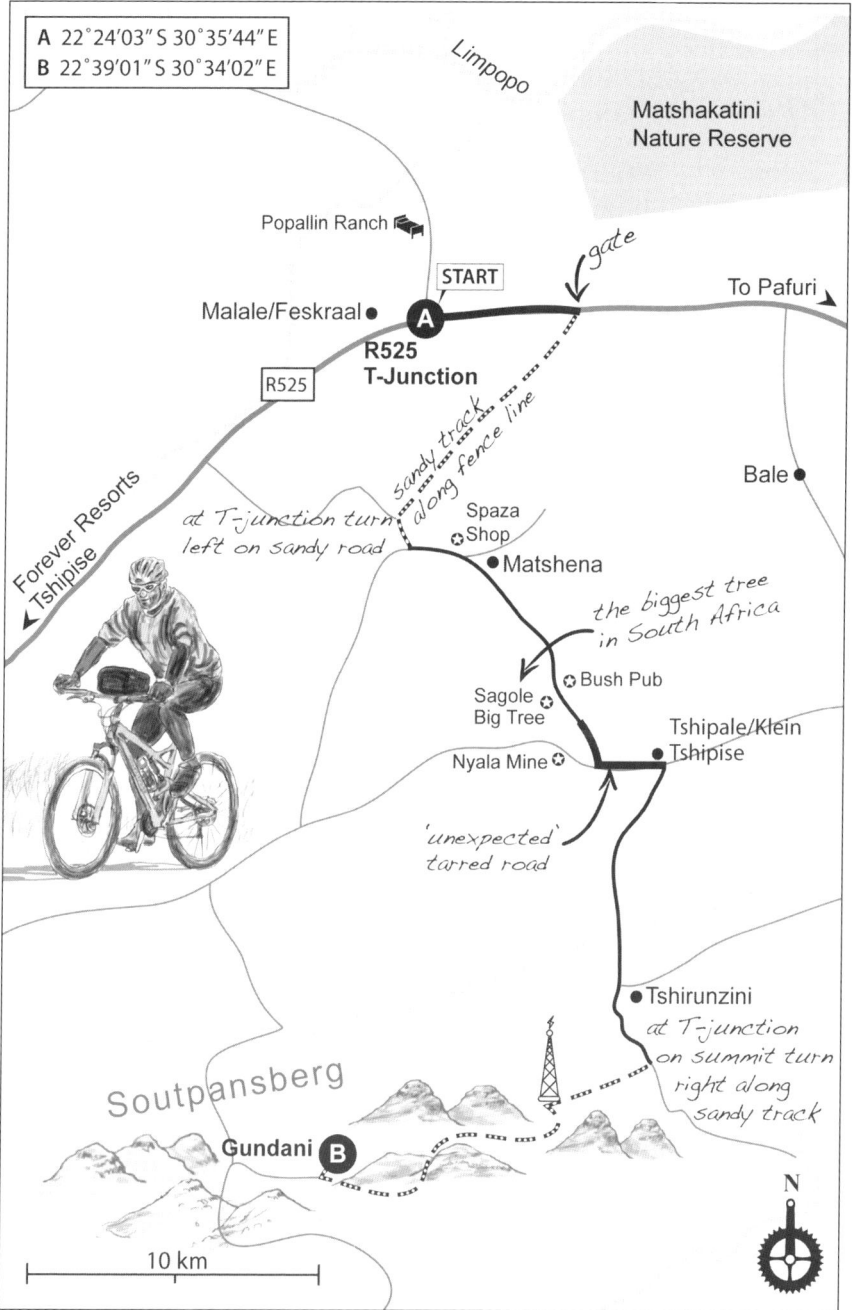

A 22°24'03" S 30°35'44" E
B 22°39'01" S 30°34'02" E

Limpopo

Matshakatini
Nature Reserve

Popallin Ranch

START

gate

To Pafuri

Malale/Feskraal

A

**R525
T-Junction**

R525

Forever Resorts
Tshipise

Bale

sandy track along fence line

at T-junction turn
left on sandy road

Spaza
Shop

Matshena

the biggest tree
in South Africa

Sagole
Big Tree

Bush Pub

Tshipale/Klein
Tshipise

Nyala Mine

'unexpected'
tarred road

Tshirunzini

at T-junction
on summit turn
right along
sandy track

Soutpansberg

Gundani **B**

10 km

N

Baobabs are succulents and don't have growth rings so they cannot be dated accurately. Recent thinking is that, generally, they are not as old as was previously reckoned. Ones like Sagole may be 2000 years old, others seldom more than 1000.

watermelon salesman at the side of the road. The women of Gundani would not cook for us, so we supped on chip buns and beers under a warm half-moon sky.

The route

At the R525 T-junction, ride (on the dirt shoulder) about 2km east along the tar to the first gate and turn-off on the right. This is a little-used track-cum-cattle path heading southwest and following a fence line (called a cut line on some maps). After about 5km you start navigating along back roads and past villages, keeping west of Bale. From there kind of follow our track to the Sagole Big Tree.

There is a nominal cost (R15 at the time of writing) to enter the small nature reserve and picnic site. Giving the tree a hug is not only recommended, it is mandatory (feel the love). Pick up an unexpected tarred road just south of the Sagole Big Tree and take it for 5km to a T-junction. The Nyala manganese mine is to the right – but we go left.

Here, a random network of tarred roads starts and often ends nowhere in particular; 4km more brings you to a village (Tshipale, says Garmin's RoadTrip maps). The road sign under big trees on the left says it's something else – in typically few vowels but lots of Zs, Vs, Ts and Hs typical of the Venda language.

There's a brick spaza shop next to an open-air market on the right (south) side of the road; our route takes an insignificant track to the right through the village and pops out the other side on a sandy road. It's pleasant and easy riding, sticking to an S-shaped route when you come to intersections, crossing an intermittent river with a broken-up causeway, and then climbing slowly but surely towards the mountains.

Where the road starts to ascend noticeably you'll see Tshirunzini village on the left and a nice shade tree on your right with block-size rocks to sit on – the first of what Steve and I came to recognise as 'traveller's trees'. Take your time over lunch here because ahead lies 6km of severe climbing on loose gravel.

It's a north-facing slope and it's likely to be afternoon when you ride it, so this will be a very big sweat: make sure you have enough to drink (also for the flatter summit ride that follows), and take it easy so you don't blow a head gasket.

You're at the top of the Soutpansberg when the track levels off, becomes sandy and you come to a side-junction with directions to Mutele and Gundani, the latter being your route. The track runs west for about 10km; about halfway it goes to the left around a communications mast to Gundani village on the

Soutpansberg summit. There is one excellent downhill run after the mast, but otherwise lots of grinding through thick sand and over sharp rocks.

Water has to be carried in buckets to the Gundani Mutsiwa Campsite, where accommodation is provided in two double safari tents. Ask about getting food, and maybe even beers, in the village.

STAGE 3
GUNDANI TO THOHOYANDOU   60km

GRADING: Medium, moderate
OVERNIGHT: Fig Tree Lodge

IN A NUTSHELL
Other than the confusing proliferation of newly tarred roads, undeveloped tracts of natural bush, bewildering local language and maps with conflicting place names, it can be *moerse* hot riding up north-facing slopes in Venda. On a map it looks cool: just 60km, lots of downhill. But factor in some wind, a beating sun and the fact that the Soutpansberg consists of several ridges all the way to Thohoyandou, and you have yourself a right riding challenge.

Snapshot of the experience
The 2.5km ride out of the Gundani Mutsiwa Campsite on a rough gravel track to the tarred pass road was the toughest part of the day – just the kind to get the lactic acid burning in your cold leg muscles. From there it's a sweeping 8 or 9km in top gear, pedalling not really required, the bracing wind really blowing your ears back.

Then we followed whatever tracks we could pick up along the main road, sometimes detouring into villages, sometimes riding on footpaths or on the shoulder when there was one (the traffic here is a bit hectic). It was fun until two lads shouted 'Kill the Boer' at us. We did a U-turn to ask them why they would say something so stupid to visitors to their area. They jumped about in denial, until one of them leapt in front of a speeding taxi and we had to scream him out of its path. That put an ashen-faced end to their country bumpkin nonsense.

The bonus at the end of the day was Fig Tree Lodge, and ice-filled glasses of Coke, lots of chocolate milks, beer, and a real bushveld *pap-en-vleis* braai.

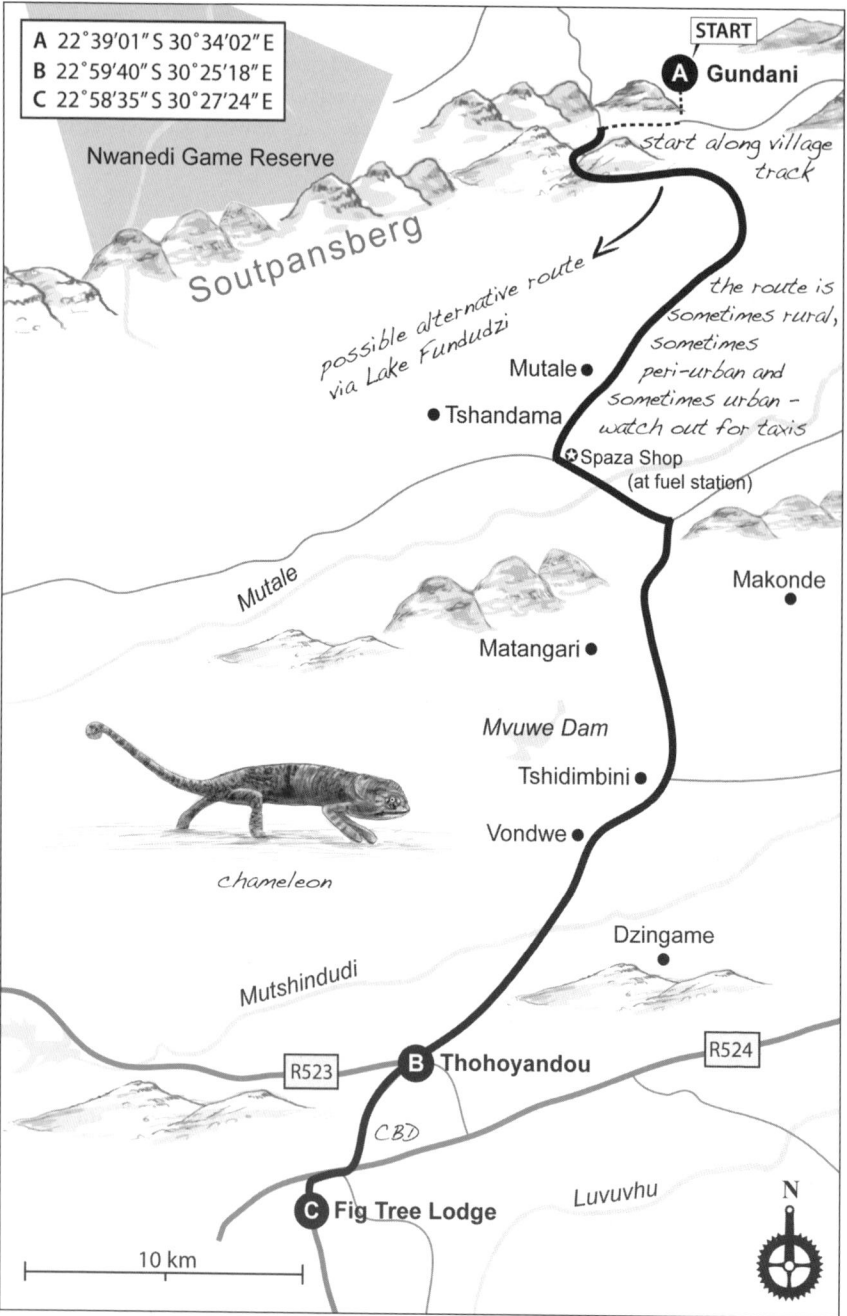

A 22°39'01" S 30°34'02" E
B 22°59'40" S 30°25'18" E
C 22°58'35" S 30°27'24" E

START

Ⓐ **Gundani**

start along village track

Nwanedi Game Reserve

Soutpansberg

possible alternative route via Lake Fundudzi

Mutale●

●Tshandama

the route is sometimes rural, sometimes peri-urban and sometimes urban – watch out for taxis

✿Spaza Shop (at fuel station)

Mutale

Makonde ●

Matangari ●

Mvuwe Dam

Tshidimbini ●

Vondwe ●

chameleon

Dzingame ●

Mutshindudi

R523   Ⓑ **Thohoyandou**   R524

CBD

Ⓒ **Fig Tree Lodge**   *Luvuvhu*

N

10 km

The route

In one respect this route is the simplest (follow the tarred roads just about all the way), as well as the least satisfying (follow the tarred roads just about all the way).

However, as we were going to print, my second cousin Sarah and her man, Casper Venter, of Makhado found a much better alternative (92km) for this stage. The first part of their route, undulating and easy-going, runs through villages and fields along a high mountain plateau of the Soutpansberg range. Then, just before going into the Thathe Vondo plantations, you catch glimpses of the sacred Lake Fundudzi. The final 18km of the route – all very scenic – is on tar through the Vondo Pass, and past the Vondo dam and tea estate. The GPS track for this new route will be posted on Dragon Trax.

Back to our original route. Two significant rivers cutting east–west through the Soutpansberg result in two ridges and two valleys. This 'standard route' runs as follows: from Gundani take the gravel road to the tarred road, turn left (south) and descend the pass. About 8km from the base of the pass, turn left at the T-junction (buy cold drinks at the fuel station shop); 2km further cross the Mutale River, then, another 2km on, turn right at the T-junction. Carry on pretty much straight all the way into Thohoyandou, till you reach the T-junction with the R524; turn right and proceed about 1.5km to Fig Tree Lodge (on the service road on the left) – a really good, well-priced, large-hearted lodging.

Okay, people, it's over to you now to Wiki this route into better shape if you can and post your findings on Dragon Trax.

. . . .

STAGE 4
THOHOYANDOU TO MIDDLE LETABA DAM   57km

GRADING: Medium, easy to moderate
OVERNIGHT: Middle Letaba Resort

IN A NUTSHELL
You pretty much ride wherever you want; fences are only broad demarcations. When you're travelling across communal lands, if you come across anyone, do be courteous and deferential, even though the right of way is pretty much established wherever there is a path. It's great chatting to schoolkids and people in spaza shops, at cellphone kiosks or waiting for taxis. Mentions of Beit Bridge and Cape Town are often greeted with whoops and cheers.

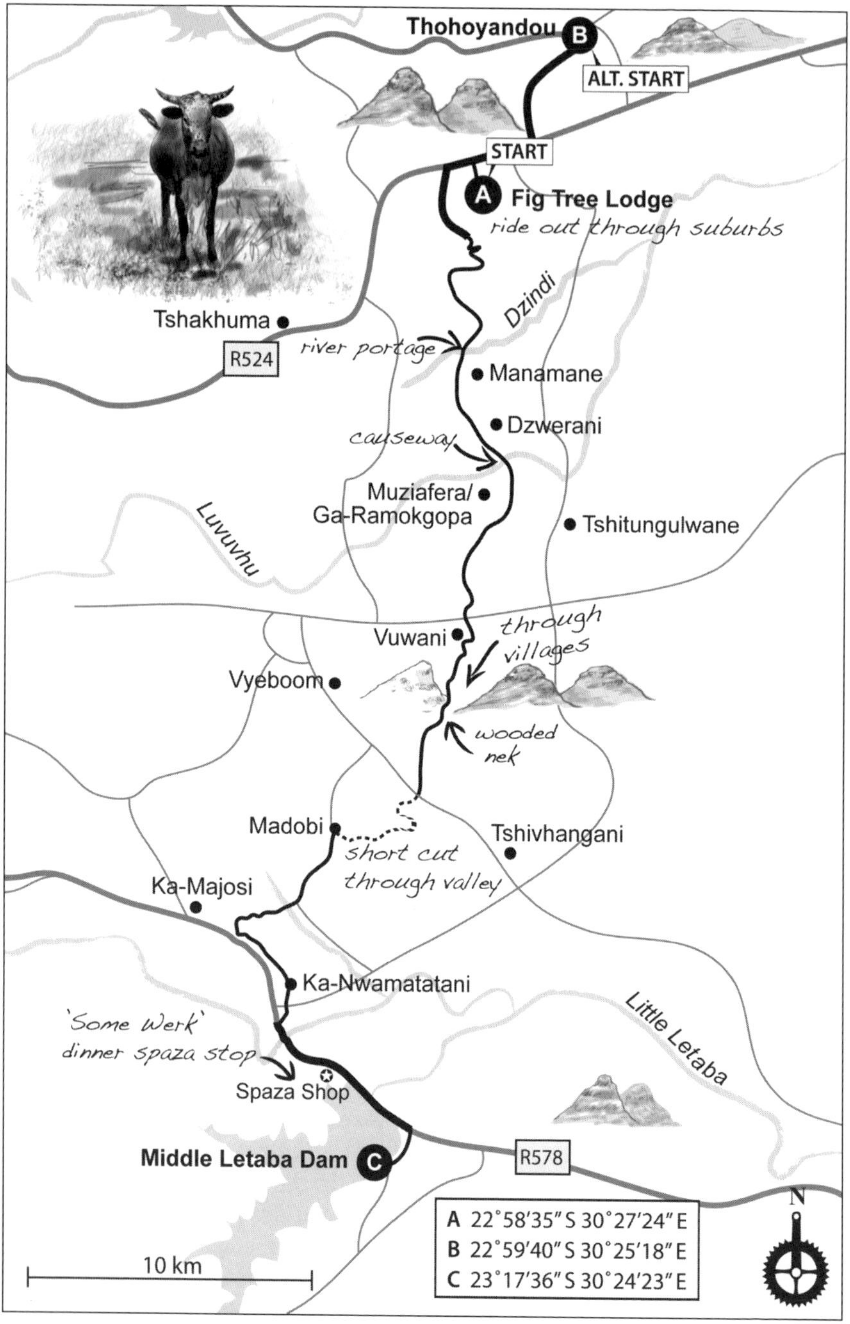

Thohoyandou B

ALT. START

START

A **Fig Tree Lodge**
ride out through suburbs

Dzindi

Tshakhuma •

R524

river portage

• Manamane

• Dzwerani

causeway

Muziafera/
Ga-Ramokgopa •

• Tshitungulwane

Luvuvhu

Vuwani •

through villages

Vyeboom •

wooded nek

Madobi •

Tshivhangani •

short cut through valley

Ka-Majosi •

Ka-Nwamatatani •

'Some Werk' dinner spaza stop

Little Letaba

Spaza Shop

Middle Letaba Dam C

R578

A	22°58'35" S 30°27'24" E
B	22°59'40" S 30°25'18" E
C	23°17'36" S 30°24'23" E

10 km

N

Enjoying the splendours of Middle Letaba Resort – army ants in the hammock, free condoms in the chalets.

Snapshot of the experience

My riding partner goes by many names, among them Henry the Navigator and amaMapper. Today it was a new one, Sho't Left Steve, from his proclivity for saying: 'Hey, let's try that jeep/cattle/foot track …' and shooting off on some seemingly impossible mission. And that made all the difference to a day that turned into one of the finest mountain biking days ever.

Take a few hints for river crossings: any flow deeper than your knees is probably much stronger than you imagine; always keep your bike on the downstream side of your body so it can't push you over; most river bottoms are rocky and you need to tread carefully to prevent mishap; and, finally, make sure everything is tied on securely so you don't do what I did and lose your cycling shoes down the Dzindi River.

In dealing with semi-feral cattle, Eardstapper's strategy was to ride straight at the centre of the herd, bellowing till the cattle gave way (sometimes only just in time). The Daytripper's preferred strategy was to ride up slowly and talk to them. This invariably took longer but was the more personable way of dealing with an African man's most prized possessions.

The route

Big towns are always a problem – to get out of, that is. But, when we studied our GPS track, what we thought had been a totally haphazard ride (10km and an hour-plus later) turned out to have been a pretty adroit case of navigation. So, from Fig Tree Lodge, where we stayed, proceed west along the R524 for about 2.8km to the last traffic light along the busy built-up part, then sho't left to go through Shiyandima district for 12km to the peri-urban Dzindi River.

It's a lovely, undulating ride from there all the way to the Luvuvhu River, through villages and fields, and occasionally patches of thorn bush (two of only three punctures incurred along the entire trail were suffered here). A further 10.5km from the Dzindi River, cross a causeway over the Luvuvhu. For the next 15km, due to the paucity of places to cross the Little Letaba River, you sho't left wherever you feel it's appropriate.

Ride through Muziafera/Ga-Ramokgopa along minor dirt roads, heading south to bypass Vyeboom town. We then found a pathway over a forested hill, and picked up a series of tracks and side roads all the way to a crossing of the Little Letaba on the R578. Do be aware that riding through herds of semi-feral cattle requires a few cunning strategies to get them to give way.

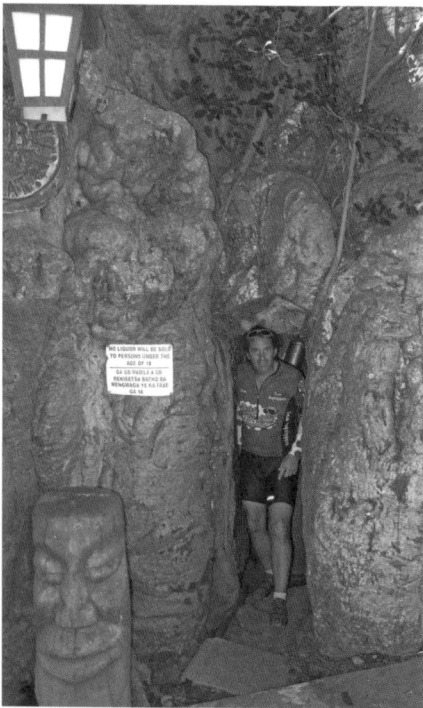

'Never touch the stuff!' Steve exits the amazing Sunland baobab bar.

Here, riding on the tarred road for about 8.5km is the only option, across the arcing Middle Letaba dam wall. Immediately after, take the turn-off to your right that leads to the southern shore of the lake to the resort. Although it is no Sun City, you do need to call ahead to book.

There's no food here; you have to eat at Colbert Mabunda's 'Some Werk' spaza take-away and bar (highly recommended: the grilled chicken with *pap* and chakalaka). And we scored beers.

It was necessary to nuke the area around our chalets (two-sleepers) to discourage the rampant army ants from destroying us. Steve's evening nap on the nearby hammock ended abruptly when the ants found him in about two minutes, tops. Condoms are supplied free, and in bulk.

STAGE 5
MIDDLE LETABA DAM TO SUNLAND FARM   60km (MODJADJISKLOOF)

GRADE: Medium, easy to moderate
OVERNIGHT: Sunland farm

IN A NUTSHELL

The first part starts along footpaths and cattle tracks, many going round in square circles – like us. But the riding is first class: you can pretty much take a line and ride on whatever path you find. Hazard warning: the paths don't all go straight, some end in big dongas, others hard up against impenetrable thorn bush. The second half could be improved by reducing the amount of tar riding were it not for aggressive commercial farmers on the tarred Giyani road.

Snapshot of the experience

Oom Schalk Lourens would well know the many kinds of thorn bushes that are only too happy to embed their long, straight, sharp thorns in a tubeless tyre, arm or leg. Oom Schalk would also advise there are only two you need to worry about around Middle Letaba dam. One is the knob-thorn acacia with its double recurved spines; the other is the buffalo thorn, with its lethal jab-and-hook combination.

We started the day along footpaths and cattle tracks but ended up riding nearly 40km on tar. There is a more direct dirt route from the Giyani road to Sunland farm, but one with the kind of gate that says: 'Go on, punk, make my day!' We suspect one of the farmers here has illegally – or at least immorally – closed off what looks like it should be a public road direct to Sunland farm, near Modjadjiskloof.

You end the day at Sunland, sitting in the shade of a gargantuan baobab that boasts a pub right inside its elephantine trunk. Around it are five four-bed A-frame chalets, a plunge pool, and a large lawn and entertainment covered-deck area.

The buffalo-thorn's botanical name 'Ziziphus' recalls the ancient Greek oke, Sisyphus, trying to roll a big rock uphill: when you try to extricate yourself from the tangle, you just get more deeply entangled. Like us today.

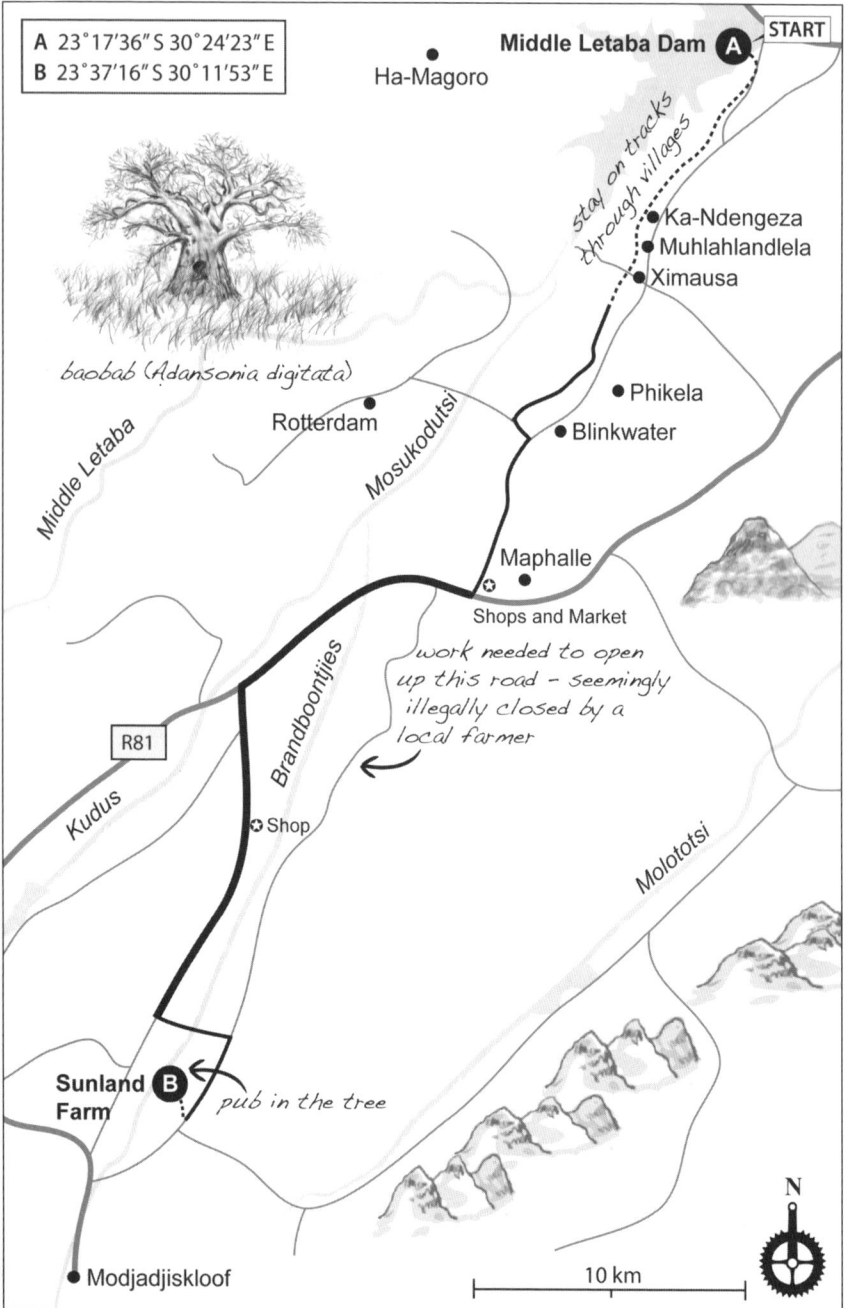

A 23°17'36"S 30°24'23"E
B 23°37'16"S 30°11'53"E

Middle Letaba Dam **A** START

Ha-Magoro

stay on tracks through villages

Ka-Ndengeza
Muhlahlandlela
Ximausa

baobab (Adansonia digitata)

Rotterdam

Mosukodutsi

Phikela

Blinkwater

Middle Letaba

Maphalle

Shops and Market

work needed to open
up this road - seemingly
illegally closed by a
local farmer

Brandboontjies

R81

Kudus

Shop

Molototsi

Sunland
Farm **B** pub in the tree

N

Modjadjiskloof

10 km

The route

From the gate of the resort, take a sho't right to keep parallel to the lake's southeast shore as far as you can on footpaths. You'll resort to roads when passing through or along the edge of interesting villages; always chat to the locals where you can.

The route goes southwest all day, generally towards the Middle Letaba River, then its more southerly tributary, the Mosukodutsi, which some maps mistake for another river, the Koedoes (or Kudus) River. It seems that the Afrikaans and English names could be a case of mishearing the African.

There is nothing difficult about the riding here, which is mostly flat and undulating, but the route-finding is another matter. On the other hand, there is some really nice, even challenging, single-track riding to be done.

If you're following Garmin maps, head for the tall communications mast, then ride through Ka-Ndengeza village, first on village lanes, then on a gravel district road. Once you leave that road, Muhlahlandlela village is next. About 10km from the start you leave village life behind for a while to go bundu-bashing for some 4km, till you come to the back end of Ximausa village: across the vlei-lands on your right is where the Mosukodutsi meets the Middle Letaba.

Beyond the village it's back into thornbush country for 7km till you come to Blinkwater. Take a right onto the gravel district road for a few hundred metres alongside the village, then a left at the side-junction to go due south, then southwest, for about 14km to Maphalle village. Some 2km further is the tarred R81, known as the Giyani road. There's a village market as well as some shops and a fuel station.

You're forced to ride on the shoulder of the tarred road for 24km (there's no way through the commercial farms) and the traffic is ugly. Sho't left when you can onto the lesser Modjadjiskloof road, following it for 13km. Some long downs are followed by long ups between big tomato and fruit farms.

Don't miss the turn-off on your left to Sunland, like we did. It's about 7.5km on rough gravel road to the farm, where chilled beers and a cool dip (or hot shower) await you.

From the bridge Steve peers into a river gorge, halfway up the Magoebaskloof mountains.

RECOMMENDED
6 days

Bushveld and Berg Trail

Sunland farm (Modjadjiskloof) to Pilgrim's Rest
•432.7km

STAGE 1
SUNLAND FARM (MODJADJISKLOOF) 53.7km
TO KURISA MOYA NATURE LODGE

GRADING: Medium, hard
OVERNIGHT: Kurisa Moya Nature Lodge

IN A NUTSHELL

The roads in the Modjadjiskloof area were being upgraded when we rode through there, but the riding from when you set off from Sunland farm through the last section of hot Lowveld bush country is easy-going. Once you go up the Kudus River valley, you face the Great Escarpment, and ascending it entails a great effort – not butt-busting, but long and sustained all the same.

Snapshot of the experience

You start off in fine to mild rolling countryside, till you turn up the Kudus River valley – flat for a while, then pretty much all up, up and up. The mountains get greener, higher and wetter. As the route steepens, rivers race down the sides of the valley creating waterfalls, rapids and pools.

From the concrete bridge spanning the river gorge to the Kurisa Moya turn-off, the sweat will be flowing off you because, at the end of the long up, the final 3km has some vicious ups and downs. With luck a cool wind will blow you into this mountain nature retreat, where afternoon showers are regular as birdsong.

The route

Our plan to ascend the escarpment by avoiding the main Magoebaskloof Pass came together after local knowledge pointed us to the Kudus River valley road. Kurisa Moya Nature Lodge was an overnight option, or we could try Haenertsburg 30-odd kilometres further. A recce showed this to be a pretty tough stretch across unknown territory through the knuckles of the top of Magoebaskloof mountains. The shorter route won.

Kurisa Moya can be translated as 'sacred spirit' or 'enchanted wind', but the winds that frequently blow down, or up, the Kudus River valley as you attempt to breach the heights of the Great Escarpment on the north side of Magoebaskloof can be more vindictive than benevolent.

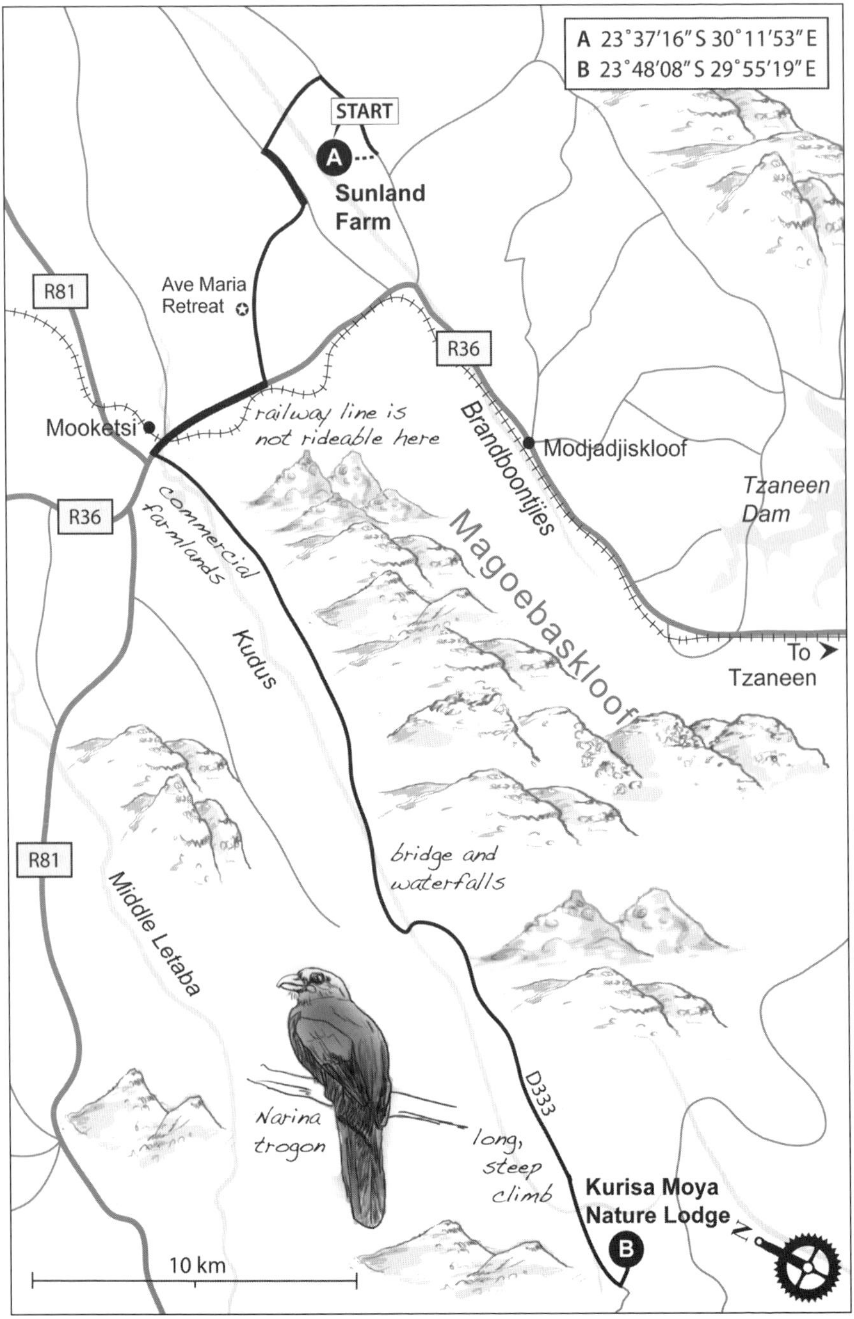

A 23°37'16"S 30°11'53"E
B 23°48'08"S 29°55'19"E

START

A ⋯
Sunland Farm

R81

Ave Maria Retreat ☼

R36

railway line is not rideable here

Brandboontjies

Mooketsi

Modjadjiskloof

Tzaneen Dam

R36

Magoebaskloof

commercial farmlands

Kudus

To ➤ Tzaneen

R81

Middle Letaba

bridge and waterfalls

Narina trogon

D333

long, steep climb

Kurisa Moya Nature Lodge

B

10 km

From Sunland, retrace your route for about 7km on rutted dirt road back to a tarred road (the short cut across the Brandboontjies River is both a seasonal vlei and private land with no right of access). At the tar, turn left for 2km, then take a right onto a gravel road running west for 7km past Mooihoek and the Ave Maria retreat.

There you hit the busy R36 Tzaneen–Polokwane road. Keep well clear of the traffic. Finding a way along the railway line to Mooketsi (the old Duiwelskloof) is hopeless. Luckily after about 5km you turn left onto the Kudus River valley dirt road, just before crossing the Kudus River and entering Mooketsi.

The road is more or less flat for about 10km, mostly dense thornveld and bushveld trees on your left and commercial farmlands on your right. Look out for wildlife here: warthogs, monkeys and small antelope, including common duiker. Then the long climb begins, easy enough for 7km, but it really announces itself as you climb from around 800 to 1600m, the last part in the full glare of the afternoon sun.

Around 28km up the valley, at 1400m altitude, you cross the concrete bridge where the river, in invigorating cascades, tumbles into churning pools before it races off to the Lowveld. The final 3km to Kurisa Moya is the steepest, but the rewards from this famous 'green' birding reserve's hospitality – and the mountain and valley views – are more than worth it. Lodging (self-catering or catered) consists of Thora Baloka cottage at the escarpment edge, two A-frame forest chalets and an old farmhouse.

STAGE 2
KURISA MOYA NATURE LODGE TO HAENERTSBURG

30km

GRADE: Short, hard
OVERNIGHT: maGriet's Bed & Breakfast

IN A NUTSHELL
Although there are extensive indigenous forests in the mountains, our route sticks to the upper ridges and plateaus of the Magoebaskloof, a combination of large timber plantations, some small commercial farms, and plots of the comfortably retired (think Hogsback).

The previous day's climb up the Kudus River valley had left us a bit knackered – but nothing that couldn't be cured with a cold Castle or Windhoek, a slap-up meal, red wine and a blazing fire at Kurisa Moya.

Snapshot of the experience

It had rained *tokoloshes* and samango monkeys the previous night, so instead of being able to let our downhill momentum carry us up each hill, we had to negotiate chocolate-mousse tracks and big puddles in each trough of the road.

There's a fair network of back roads and forestry tracks along here, but we tried to keep to as much of the high ground as possible, which meant more climbing in the first half of this stage followed by a long descent down to the quaint village of Haenertsburg.

So, a short but sharp day, with almost three hours of riding time versus the six or so we got used to on our ride. If you're ending your ride here, you might choose to make an early start at Sunland and press on through to Haenertsburg in one big push – but big it will be if you do.

The route

Depending on where you're staying, it's about 1 to 2km back to the Kudus River valley road. Take a left; you will soon encounter tar. It's up-down-up past the turn-off to Houtbosdorp (erstwhile capital of Limpopo) for 3.5km, then turn off to the left towards Dap Naudé dam and Haenertsburg. Mist and cold wind usually envelop this high ground, so go prepared.

Although on tar, it's a stiff climb for 3.6km from the turn-off to the crest of the ridge – but don't expect this to be the last! (Riding directly south through the Kurisa Moya reserve up to the ridge will cut out this tar section, but it's *terra incognita*, so first person to post a new route gets a Dragon Trax scouts badge.)

For 9.5km you ride a roller-coaster dirt road mainly through timber plantation – most likely undergoing some logging operation somewhere, with resulting churned-up roads. Ignore the sharp left turn to Kromdraai/Broederstroom; keep right for 1km or so, then bear left **not** taking the right turn to Veekraal/Mankgaile.

Mist on top of Magoebaskloof was so thick, Steve kept on appearing and disappearing like a lighthouse.

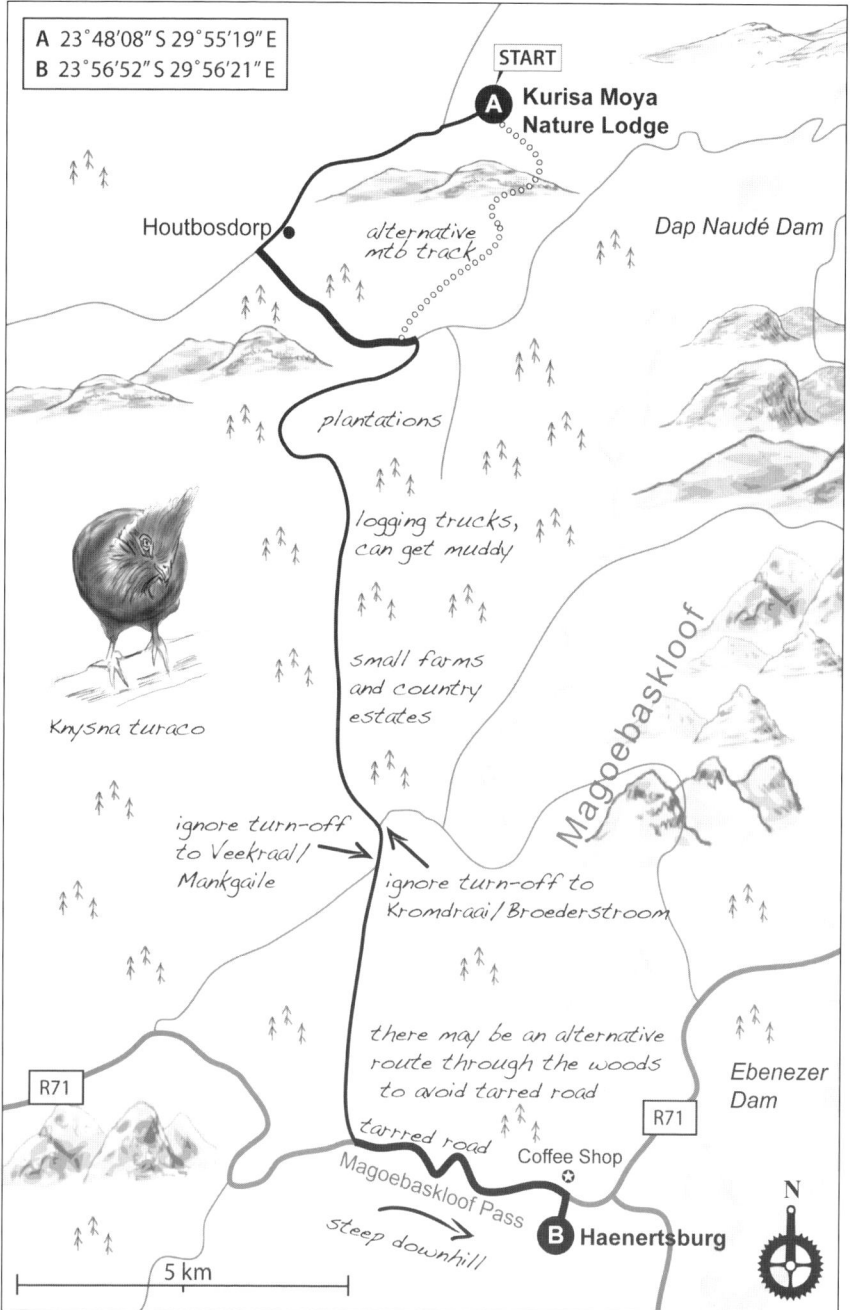

A 23°48'08"S 29°55'19"E
B 23°56'52"S 29°56'21"E

START

A **Kurisa Moya Nature Lodge**

Houtbosdorp

alternative mtb track

Dap Naudé Dam

plantations

logging trucks, can get muddy

small farms and country estates

Knysna turaco

ignore turn-off to Veekraal/Mankgaile

ignore turn-off to Kromdraai/Broederstroom

Magoebaskloof

there may be an alternative route through the woods to avoid tarred road

R71

Ebenezer Dam

tarred road

Coffee Shop

R71

Magoebaskloof Pass

steep downhill

B **Haenertsburg**

5 km

N

There are several private estates amid the natural grassland, timber plantations and small farms. About 2.4km from the previous junction is the first of four tracks going off to the left; the next is about 400m on, then 600m, and finally another 200m. It's possible this one goes downhill, parallel to the tarred road, emerging in the vicinity of Haenertsburg (after Carl Ferdinand Haenert, a big-game hunter who came to the area in the 1850s and found gold here around 1880). The safe option (but for the traffic) is to continue for another 1km to meet the tarred Magoebaskloof Pass road at a high point, turn left and follow it steeply down the pass for 4km to the village.

This dinky tourist-friendly village has quite a few accommodation options; we opted for maGriet's and were roundly and soundly spoiled.

- -

STAGE 3
HAENERTSBURG TO CHUENESPOORT   79km

GRADE: Long, hard in places
OVERNIGHT: Molapo-Matabele Resort

IN A NUTSHELL
Problems with the several routes forging across the Wolkberg are toughness and length, river crossings, crocodiles, up-and-back versus up-and-over options, and lack of accommodation. And the previous night it had rained and rained and rained. For us, the Chuenespoort dam option it had to be. We suspect this section might yield a veritable Rorke's Drift of Dragon Trax bravery badges in the future.

Snapshot of the experience
The weather will play a very big part in dictating which route you take over, through or around the rugged Wolkberg mountain wilderness. Because of declining weather, downpours forced us to stick to the muddy back roads of Sekhukhuneland (our original Option Three) and we headed through rural villages for Chuenespoort; pity the last

'O waar, be-waar, Bewaarkloof!' could be the theme of this tale. The Wolkberg and the Bewaarkloof attract storm clouds like black-jacks to sheep. That's why there are forests in this area.

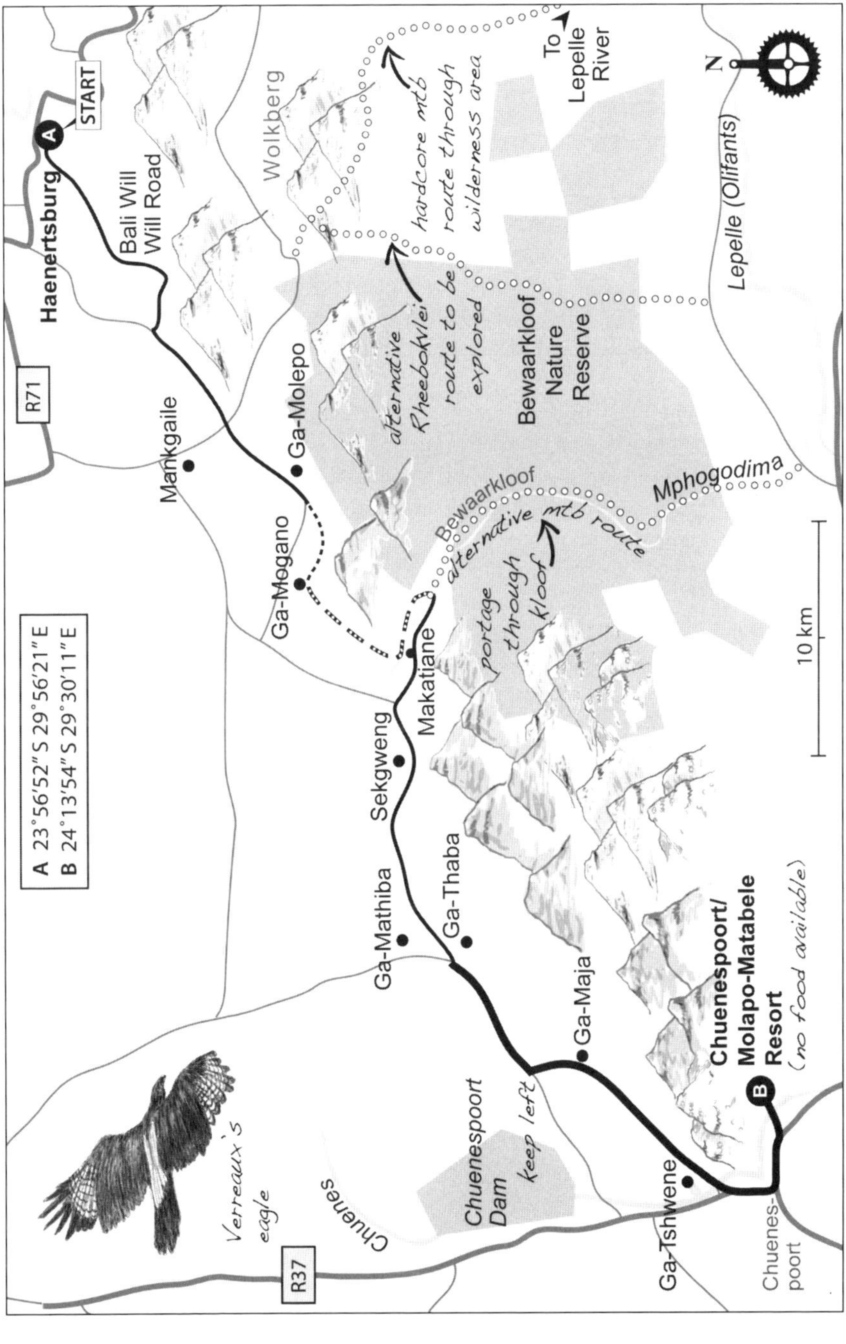

A 23°56'52"S 29°56'21"E
B 24°13'54"S 29°30'11"E

R71

Haenertsburg

START

A

Bali Will Will Road

Mankgaile

Wolkberg

Ga-Molepo

hardcore mtb route through wilderness area

To Lepelle River

Lepelle (Olifants)

N

alternative Rheebokvlei route to be explored

Bewaarkloof Nature Reserve

Ga-Mogano

Mphogodima

Bewaarkloof alternative mtb route

Makatiane

portage through kloof

10 km

Sekgweng

Ga-Mathiba

Ga-Thaba

Ga-Maja

Chuenespoort/ Molapo-Matabele Resort (no food available)

B

Chuenespoort Dam

keep left

Ga-Tshwene

Chuenes- poort

Chuenes

Verreaux's eagle

R37

20km was on tar wending through the kloof. For the second time on our trip we learned 'motel' here means an old apartheid-era resort for the 'separate but equal' *plaaslike bevolking* – now a drive-in 'bonk' place with loads of free condoms in the bungalows.

The route

Heading for the Wolkberg, the Bali Will Will (go figure) road on the northwest side of town starts as a slow ascent through plantation, then rises a few times through very steep steps, past Black Forest where there appears to be a tea and cake stop on a private farm. After about 5.5km of ascent you reach the high point at around 1650m, and then begins a nearly 8km downward run along good gravel road.

At a T-junction, with the Mankgaile settlement ahead, turn left here, keeping the mountains on your left. For the next 5.5km skirt around the left-hand side of the sprawling settlement, taking a variety of tracks and roads. Carry straight over the gravel main road that goes left to Klipdraai and Wolkberg, angling towards the mountains.

After about 15km of riding alongside, in and out of villages, a jeep track leads towards the mountains and the obvious gap of the Bewaarkloof. This route leads down the Mphogodima River – the Bewaarkloof – then to the R37 and the only reliable place to cross the Lepelle (Olifants) River.

Lost again! Steve seeks directional aid from the medical corps of Sekhukhuneland.

The Bewaarkloof is the preferred option, but **our** track proceeds for another 33km, starting along footpaths for about 8.7km, then bearing left onto a gravel road past some of the mines that have sprung up recently. Bear left at a further two intersections, keeping the mountains as close as you can to your left. Eventually you meet the tarred R37 Chuenespoort road; turn left again with the Chuenespoort dam on your right.

The only way to proceed now is along the busy road through the poort for about 16km, going south, swinging southeast, then due east past the Lebowa-Goma turn-off till you reach the Molapo-Matabele Resort, the only place we could find to overnight. There is, unfortunately, no food available here (but we did manage to rustle up some beers).

STAGE 4
CHUENESPOORT TO BURGERSFORT   157km

GRADE: Very long, hard (1 days); Long, hard (2 days)
OVERNIGHT: Kusile Guest House

IN A NUTSHELL
This is a 4000-plus-calorie day, requiring extra stops at spaza shops to share 1.25-litre Cokes. Because of the burgeoning mining activity in the area, the rate at which roads are being tarred here might either impress or distress you. The final 22km to Burgersfort is all on tar – the nasty, narrow, busy R37. If you can find accommodation in or near Steelpoort (we couldn't), an option is to reconfigure this stage into two: a 90km leg and a much shorter one. Then you'd probably push straight on to Ohrigstad (a 65km stage), incorporating stage 5.

Snapshot of the experience
If you want to see South Africa on the move, this is the place to come and watch it happen – literally right before your eyes. Huts are transforming into houses, complete with ornate pillars, as if a vast army of worker ants were busy. Old dirt tracks are transforming into proper tarred roads and towns are springing up all over the place that was once the dirt-poor 'homeland' of Lebowa. And it's all due to the chrome-, platinum- and copper-rich rocks of the Bushveld Igneous Complex that cover this part of the country.

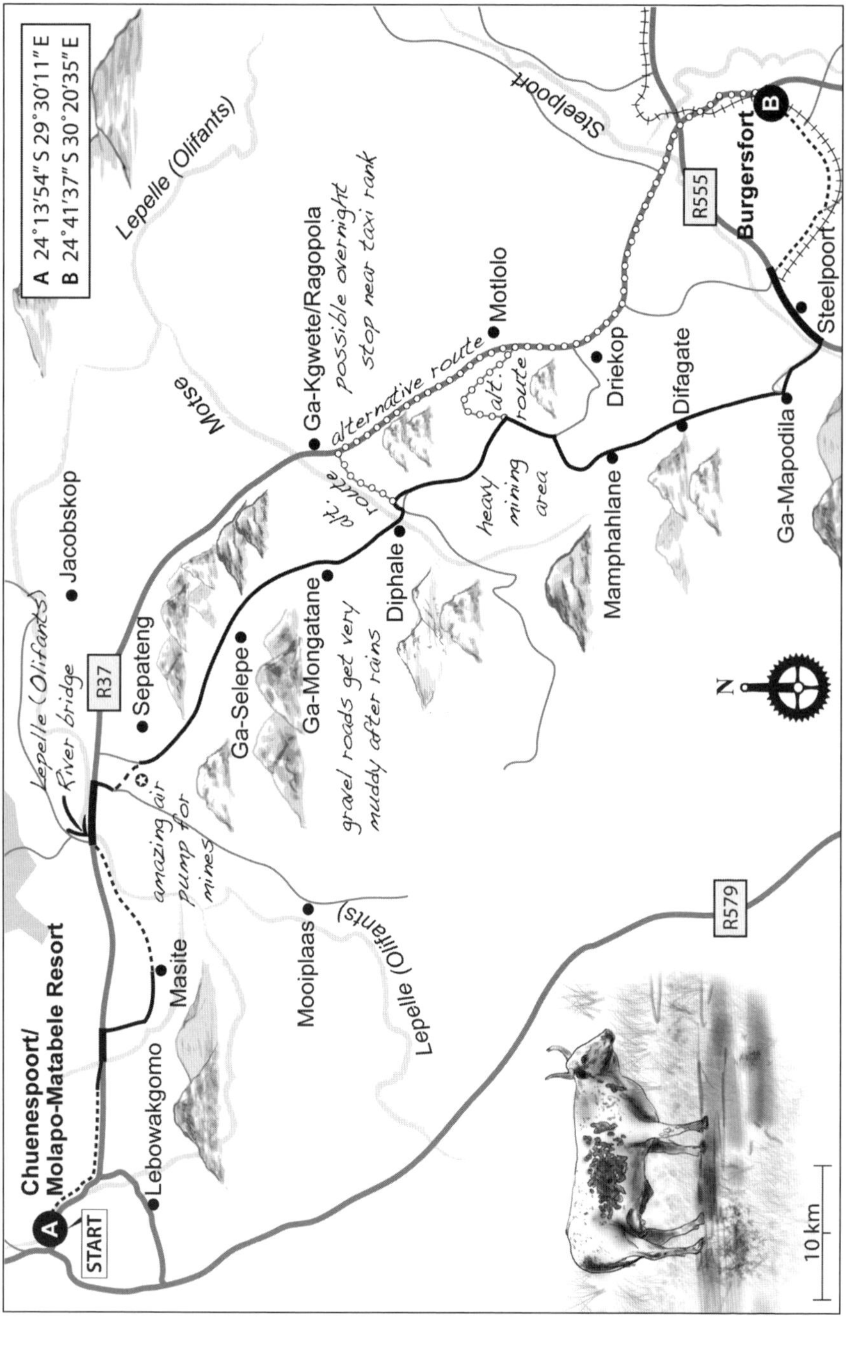

A 24°13′54″S 29°30′11″E
B 24°41′37″S 30°20′35″E

Lepelle (Olifants)

Steelpoort

Ga-Kgwete/Ragopola
possible overnight
stop near taxi rank

Motlolo

alternative route

alt. route

alt. route

heavy
mining
area

Burgersfort

R555

Steelpoort

Driekop

Difagate

Ga-Mapodila

Mamphahlane

B

Motse

Jacobskop

Diphale

N

Lepelle (Olifants)
River bridge

R37

Sepateng

Ga-Selepe

Ga-Mongatane

gravel roads get very
muddy after rains

amazing air
pump for
mines

Masite

Mooiplaas

Lepelle (Olifants)

R579

Chuenespoort/
Molapo-Matabele Resort

Lebowakgomo

A

START

10 km

The route

This is a complex section to unpick because ground conditions dictated that what we wanted to do differed substantially from what we were able to do.

Next to the tar road we found a rough jeep track, then crossed over to the right (south) side of the R37 to ride from village to village for 20km to the Lepelle (Olifants) River bridge. From there we headed south again, following gravel roads and occasional footpaths through a shattered landscape of volcanic hills, the sprawling rural expansion fuelled by an explosion of platinum and chrome mines. After you cross the Lepelle and break right along dirt roads through the rural sprawl, you come across a noisy geo-industrial-looking lung contraption: the air pump for the platinum mines (a thumping pump station that looked and sounded like a gargantuan alien).

If you could ignore the environmental degradation, this region, amazingly, carries an air of prosperity. *De rigueur* are the candy-twist pillars of new suburban-style houses next to mud or iron shacks. The quality of life among this newly emerging black middle class is unexpectedly high.

The copious rain had left abandoned cars on the road; all around were churned-up veld and mud puddles. The volcanic rock erodes to a thick, glutinous clay that's hard to get off your bike and feet. Such conditions made riding hard on what otherwise would have been a lovely day. But we realised that, for any normal cyclist, we'd still have to split the 122km distance in two.

Glorious mud – the area's volcanic soils rendered unrideable by torrential rains.

A truck-stop-style inn we'd heard about around the halfway mark, near a taxi rank in Ga-Kgwete/Ragopola on the R37, eluded us so we pressed on instead along back roads until we were forced back to the tar, about 15km northwest of the Steelpoort River.

On the outskirts of a seemingly random Burgersfort, we tracked down Kusile Guest House, a superbly appointed (if quite expensive) establishment offering fine dining – and Driekie, the wife half of the owner-couple, is something of a serious road and mountain bike rider.

· ·

STAGE 5
BURGERSFORT TO OHRIGSTAD   45km

GRADE: Short, easy
OVERNIGHT: Iketla Lodge

IN A NUTSHELL

It is uphill most of the way, on a stony, loose track where you can never get any momentum so the hard-pedalling is relentless; and it can be *bliksems* hot and humid. The amphitheatre-like mountain topography of the Apiesdoring and Kromkloof valley area creates a natural hothouse that sucks the moisture from soft-shelled creatures like us. I wouldn't want to ride it in midsummer.

Snapshot of the experience

Our accommodating hosts (Driekie joined us on this stage, which to her was a short training ride; husband Pieter helped out with the logistics) showed us the preferred railway service-track route to Ohrigstad, and let us in on the fact that it runs all the way from Steelpoort to the west (we hope to re-route the Spine track from the Chuenespoort road to there).

The previous day we'd ridden twice the distance and finished with energy

After a great dinner at Iketla Lodge, our host, Albert, generously doubled the day's bar takings and donated them to Operation Smile. Later, trying to sleep, night-owl Steve summed it up: it's the great people of South Africa who make this ride amazing.

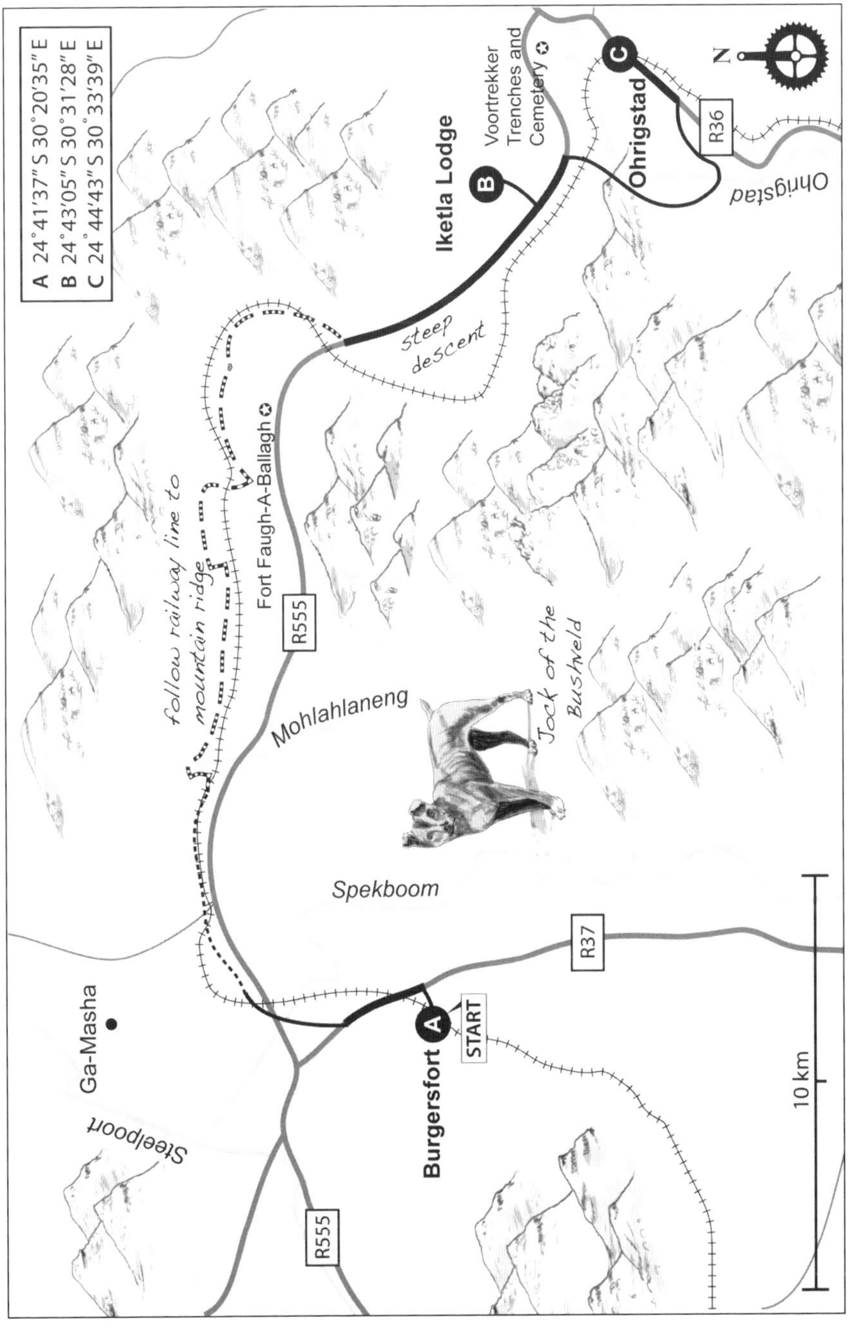

A 24°41'37"S 30°20'35"E
B 24°43'05"S 30°31'28"E
C 24°44'43"S 30°33'39"E

N

Voortrekker Trenches and Cemetery ✪

Iketla Lodge

B

Ohrigstad

C

R36

Ohrigstad

steep descent

Fort Faugh-A-Ballagh ✪

follow railway line to mountain ridge

R555

Mohlahlaneng

Jock of the Bushveld

Spekboom

R37

Ga-Masha

Burgersfort A

START

Steelpoort

R555

10 km

to spare; this stage really took its toll, probably more psychologically than physically. The total distance was 13km more than we'd anticipated, and, in the heat, both Steve and I ran out of water. Not surprisingly, Driekie was clearly bored holding back for us plodders.

The route

Wherever you stayed, it will still involve riding the Iron Rooster, as the Chinese call it. That's a railway line to you and me, *stimela* to others. It appears to be an easy 32km (or so we thought), following the service track along the railway line between Burgersfort and Ohrigstad.

From Kusile Guest House, head north for about 1km before ducking off right through an industrial area on the northeast side of town, and then outlying middle-class suburbia, to the railway track. You have to veer right again onto the tarred R555 for about 1km, through a peri-urban workers' area, before finding a side road leading, for another 1km, back to the railway line.

Rising gently at first, the track periodically dips, ducks and dives to ford stream courses on the steeper slopes – and loop round larger river courses (such as the Mohlahlaneng about 4.5km along the railway) – making for more strenuous riding than you'd expect. The track ascends steadily, from around 800m to nearly 1400m at its highest point.

Just past the point where you swing to the left, away from the tarred road, are the remains of a small Anglo-Boer war fortification, Fort Faugh-A-Ballagh, accessible along a steep footpath.

From here the track goes bumpity-bump for another laborious 8km. Over the final few kilometres, the track executes several rather cruel dips clearly not made by a cycling road engineer. Follow the side road on the left-hand side of the R555 for about 2km, before hitting the tar for a fast and exhilarating 8km downhill rush into the Ohrigstad River valley.

Roughly 4km down on the left is the turn-off to Iketla Lodge, our recommended overnight stop. If you plan to ride into Ohrigstad itself (as we did for hamburgers and drinks), continue for another 2km, taking the gravel road that, together with the surrounding farmlands, follows the slowly left-curving sweep of the valley for just short of 7km into the small one-time Voortrekker capital (Ohrigstad was abandoned for Lydenburg because of rampant malaria).

Iketla Lodge, perched on the edge of a tree-fringed canyon, surrounded by Black Reef quartzitic sandstone crags and with awesome vistas of magnificent wild bushveld, more than made up for the day's grind. A naturalists' delight, the lodge teems with plants, birds and beasts. Iketla might be a bit larney for back-to-basics trail riders, but after the rigours of Sekhukhuneland, you might feel like a bit of First World game-lodge luxury.

STAGE 6
OHRIGSTAD TO PILGRIM'S REST   68km

GRADE: Medium, moderate to hard
OVERNIGHT: Royal Hotel

IN A NUTSHELL

This is pioneer country with its reminders of the Voortrekkers –
cemeteries, redoubts, small monuments and tracks, some of which have
become roads. We were elated to be able to follow the path of that crusty,
bearded old pioneer Casper, Paul Kruger's father, deep into back-country
– through Caspersnek, the passage through the Strydpoort mountains, up
the very poort that gave the entire Mpumalanga escarpment its name.

Snapshot of the experience

We left Iketla Lodge feeling pretty relaxed, with clouds clinging to the high
escarpment ridges like rusk crumbs to a Voortrekker's beard. For a while
now we've been deep in pioneer country. Now we were headed for gold-rush
territory, but the trekkers who searched for passages over the escarpment had
no inkling of what riches lay beneath those antediluvian rocks.

The ride up Caspersnek was not as dire
as we'd expected, with the previous day's heat
dissipating into mist and drizzle, and the
pass road was so enchanting, the end point
so alluring. After 1km of climbing – the final
400m ever so steeply – to the mountain crest,
we met the kind of wind you remember well
after the labours of the day are forgotten.

And the warnings about the poor state
of historic Pilgrim's Rest were, we found,
not so much greatly exaggerated as totally
unfounded. Our warm welcome on a
drenched afternoon at the Pilgrim's Pantry
was matched later by the fire-warmed
reception at the Royal Hotel – now a heritage
site – and the promise of being tucked up
under goose-down duvets in our Victorian
cottage annex.

*Steve and I share a
feeling for those things
that imbue a landscape
with meaning that goes
deeper than trees and
rocks: psychic marks in
the landscape like the
telltale scars of the
steel rims of wagon
wheels passing 175 years
ago ... and an elephant
that leaves footprints
in the mud along the
same track a thousand
years before that ... and
a dinosaur a hundred
million years earlier.*

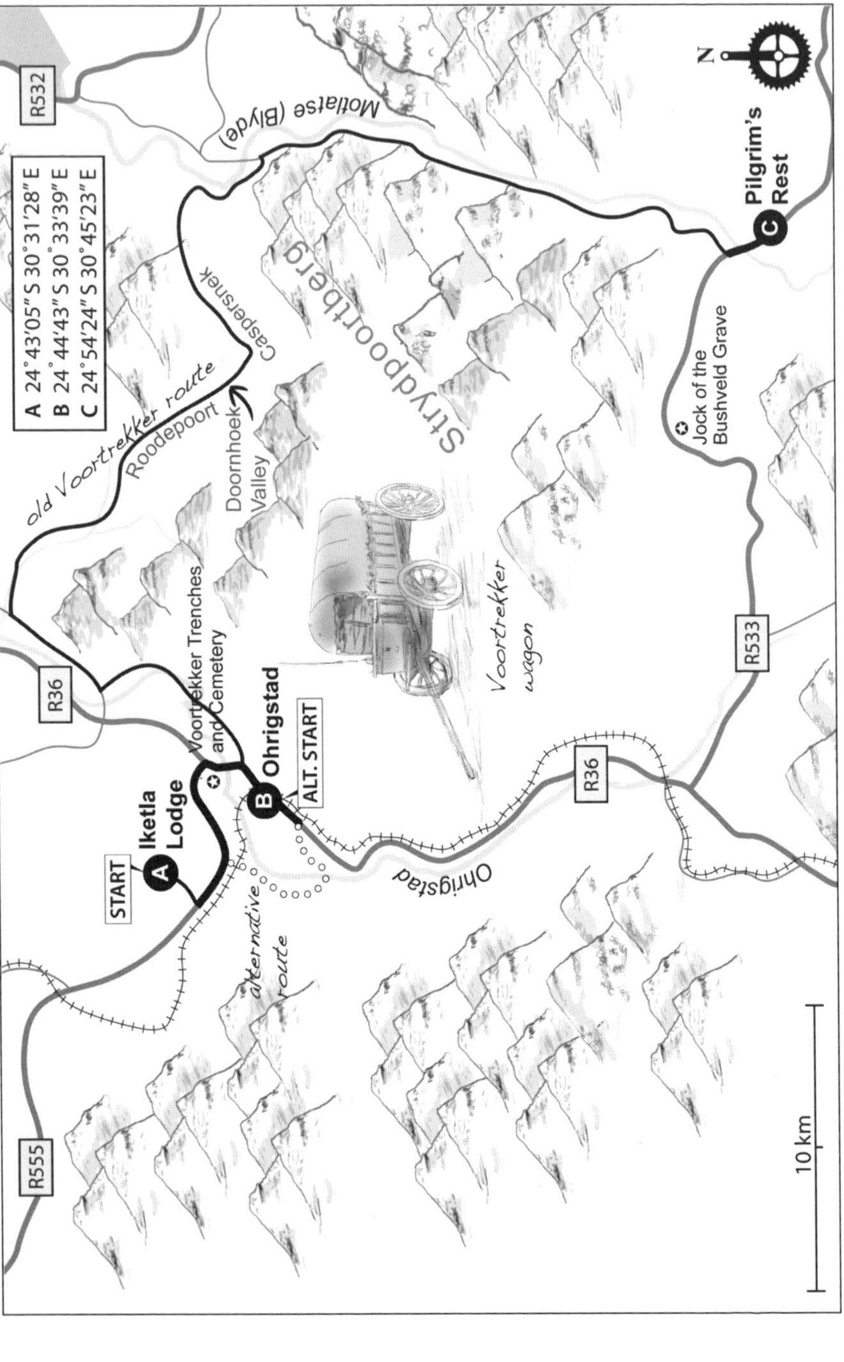

A 24°43'05"S 30°31'28"E
B 24°44'43"S 30°33'39"E
C 24°54'24"S 30°45'23"E

R532

Mottatse (Blyde)

Pilgrim's Rest
C

N

Caspersnek

old Voortrekker route

Roodepoort

Doornhoek
Valley

Strydpoortberg

Jock of the
Bushveld Grave

Voortrekker Trenches
and Cemetery

Voortrekker
wagon

R533

R36

R36

START

Iketla
Lodge

A

B Ohrigstad

ALT. START

Ohrigstad

alternative
route

R555

10 km

The route

On the surface, in this bucolic farmland of the rich alluvial Ohrigstad valley, the only sign of past suffering is the Voortrekker cemetery we stopped by at the bottom of a 6.5km sweep down the R555 from Iketla Lodge.

At the intersection, turn right onto the R36 and cross the Ohrigstad River. Soon after, turn left onto a gravel road that, after some distance, ramps up towards Caspersnek – a vital passage for many years, until the age of better roads could create more direct paths. Follow the river for

A friendly trekker brings hot drinks and lunch in the Amarok on Caspersnek.

some 13km, mostly under a canopy of tall bushveld thorn trees reminiscent of trail sections along the Limpopo River. For now it's flat and easy cruising.

But, in mountain biking, all things flat must eventually go up (if only to go down on the other side). At around 1000m altitude, turn right up the old Voortrekker route where the valley road begins to steepen, very gradually at first and then more noticeably when the river splits after about 5km, where you follow a stream from Roodepoort and into Doornhoek valley.

This valley is quite intensively farmed, in appearance a prosperous and benevolent corporate-type operation. Passing a quasi-bush-lodge setup, you need to keep those wagon wheels rolling as the road climbs past 1100, 1200 to 1250m at the base of the pass. It's only 1.5km of steep climbing from there till you reach the summit turn at around 1400m. Then you can tuck in and fly down the other side of the pass for 10km without turning the pedals till you reach the Motlatse (Blyde) River.

You've gone from harsh bushveld deep into montane habitat, with tree ferns replacing acacias. At the bottom of the pass, turn right to follow the general course of the Motlatse River. Over 21km the landscape rises a mere 200m to Pilgrim's Rest but the road, running mainly due south now, is a roller coaster so you'll need to push quite consistently to the end – and more so if there's a headwind, and maybe some rain.

Over the stone arch bridge and up the short but lung-pumping hill to the village, it is custom to steer your bike into the first comely-looking store for convivial sustenance – the beer-and-burger fare appears first, the tea-and-scones type a little further. Cheers, dears.

RECOMMENDED
8 days

Timberlands Trail

Pilgrim's Rest to Natal Spa (Paulpietersburg)
• 491.9km

STAGE 1
PILGRIM'S REST TO LONG TOM PASS 51.4km

GRADE: Medium, hard
OVERNIGHT: Misty Mountain

IN A NUTSHELL
If, unlike us, you ride this section north to south as we'd originally planned, and it's wet outside, carry a change of clothes and consider taking a pair of wet-shoes (the Motlatse [Blyde] River crossings come at the beginning). Spare riding shorts (maybe even longs) will carry you through the second half of the ride and a daunting family-bear trio of climbs. Luckily for you, the fire at the Misty Mountain lodge will be blazing and the bar most welcoming.

Snapshot of the experience

When, before tackling this stage, we decided to contact Trent Sinclair who runs mountain bike trails on Mount Anderson private reserve, it was a case of reverse polarity. Given that the ghostly weather had turned a whiter shade of pale, he reckoned we'd be riding not so much along the spine of the dragon as through its stomach. Also, given that a side elevation of the Long Tom Pass resembles the Alps, our suggested routing would involve the Mother Of All Climbs. We were happy to make use of local knowledge and took up his offer to join his rowdy, hairy biker group, riding from Long Tom Pass to Pilgrim's Rest. Our only quandary was, did this change in direction contravene some unspoken code of long-distance riding, given that those following our route would most likely be sticking to the general north–south direction? You decide. Whichever way you go, you'll be able to make sense of our map's north–south directions.

The Long Tom Pass tops out at around 2200m and the trail drops to 1400m; in between there are quite a few ass-hauling sections and some very steep climbs. We took a look out of the condensation-frosted window at a scene that resembled the bridge of a fishing boat in a perfect storm, and reckoned we'd be wise to take Trent's 'downhill' option.

The route

Our reverse ride starts at Hops Hollow micro-brewery and guest house at the

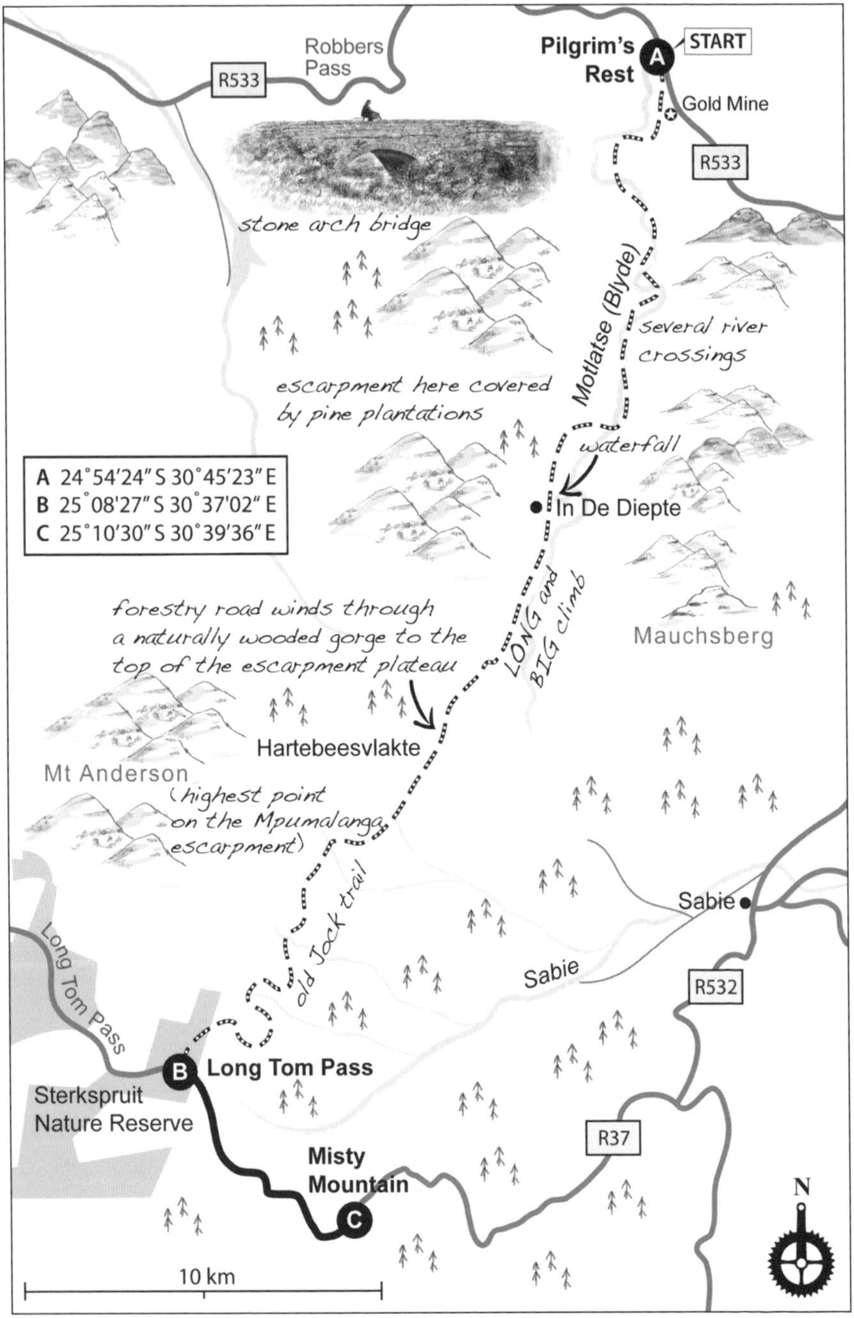

Robbers Pass

R533

Pilgrim's Rest Ⓐ START

Gold Mine

R533

stone arch bridge

escarpment here covered by pine plantations

Motlatse (Blyde)

several river crossings

waterfall

● In De Diepte

A 24°54'24" S 30°45'23" E
B 25°08'27" S 30°37'02" E
C 25°10'30" S 30°39'36" E

forestry road winds through a naturally wooded gorge to the top of the escarpment plateau

LONG and BIG climb

Mauchsberg

Hartebeesvlakte

Mt Anderson

(highest point on the Mpumalanga escarpment)

old Jack trail

Sabie ●

Long Tom Pass

Sabie

R532

Ⓑ **Long Tom Pass**

Sterkspruit Nature Reserve

Misty Mountain

R37

Ⓒ

10 km

N

summit of Long Tom Pass, where there's a secure place to park and get yourself together. You're entering timber territory and you need a permit*; access is not permitted during logging operations. Cross over the tar road and hop over the gate to get onto the old wagon road made famous by *Jock of the Bushveld*.

We forded the Motlatse (Blyde) – five chilly times.

At an altitude of 2200m, the first kilometre is through the Sterkspruit Nature Reserve. Then you begin a fast, tricky descent through plantation for about 3.5km along a rutted and very loose stony track that can be treacherously slippery.

The next 9km or so is through old pine plantations, crossing three tributaries of the Sabie River. If not logged, this area is usually quite wet underfoot, deteriorating to downright slushy. Nice descents are followed by taxing climbs, some requiring walking unless you're racing fit.

You're now at about 1800m, riding along the grassy montane southeast slopes of Mount Anderson (2285m), looking into the Sabie River gorge. After about 2km, the jeep track levels out onto the Hartebeesvlakte, rising gently to 1900m before twisting and turning and ducking down to cross the upper waters of the Motlatse River.

The path descends to the river, then climbs out again, well away from and above the river, before starting the mother of all descents. The track drops 300m over some 4km, levelling off at In De Diepte (a small forestry settlement). The river executes a number of tight hairpins down to the right. For a short while our track follows a footpath (more of that if conditions permit), then the track does a tight right–left and drops to the base of the falls, at In De Diepte where it picks up a gravel road for a short distance. For the next 10km the track closely follows the Motlatse River, on both well-defined track and through rank riverine bush and tall grass (or you can stick to the gravel). You will need to wade across the river several times; if it's full you'll get soaked to your waist.

After the final crossing it's about 3.8km to the outskirts of Pilgrim's Rest, where the gravel road skirts the old mine to the tarred road, the old stone arch bridge on your left.

***You need two permits:** one from Komati Land Forests for the upper Tweefontein and Hartebeesvlakte area; one from York Timbers for the lower In De Diepte area. (See the table 'Additional Contacts' on page 206–207.)

STAGE 2
LONG TOM PASS TO ALKMAAR/N4   56km

GRADE: Medium, moderate; one big ascent
OVERNIGHT: Eric's Chalets (Alkmaar); Die Rots Guesthouse (Schoemanskloof)

IN A NUTSHELL

James, our host at Misty Mountain, ended up blazing a trail for us on his quad bike to Rhenosterhoek. The route then heads up into the plantations. It's hellishly steep but that is, we kept reminding ourselves, where the 'mountain' part of mountain biking is derived: we go up to come down. And come down you certainly do over the other side of the Gunyatoo valley, then over the Rooiwal ridge and into the Stats River valley that leads towards Sudwala Caves. Mankele and the caves are famous mountain biking areas; unfortunately you have no choice but to give them a miss to get in a decent day's riding. On this stage, we rode no more than 50m on tar.

Snapshot of the experience

After 10 days of rain, we awoke to golden sunshine and a hint of last-autumn warmth. We were also needing to dodge another conspiracy: the overwhelming kindness of our hosts that kept us from making early starts. Eggs Benedict, a third cup of coffee and shooting sunbeams with the lodge owners easily added an extra hour to our breakfast.

    At the end of our ride, we hit the N4 where we found lovely, comfortable lodgings near Alkmaar, with tables and umbrellas al fresco round an inviting swimming pool.

Time and again, it's finding the start of a route that's the trickiest part. We looked deep down into the convoluted confluence of the Alexanderspruit, Houtbos and Nels streams, and the labyrinth of forestry tracks, and wondered how we'd get from A (Misty Mountain) to B (over the stacked ridges) without having to go via C and maybe Z.

We dunked in up to our heads – helmets, glasses and all. The beers were chilled, sarmies well toasted and the chips … well, you can imagine what they tasted like after we'd been five hours in the saddle.

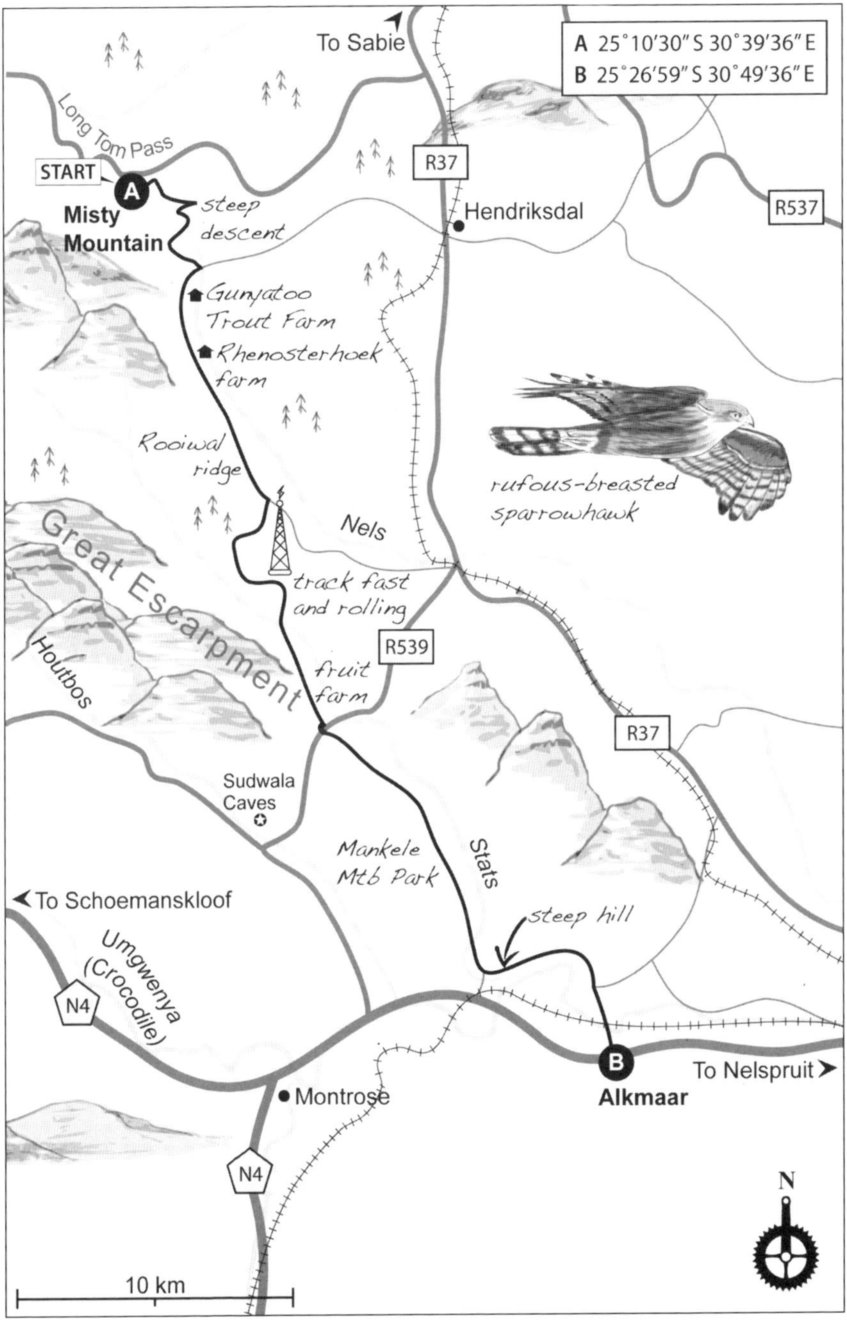

A 25°10'30" S 30°39'36" E
B 25°26'59" S 30°49'36" E

To Sabie

Long Tom Pass

START

Misty Mountain

A

steep descent

R37

Hendriksdal

R537

Gunyatoo Trout Farm

Rhenosterhoek farm

Rooiwal ridge

Nels

Great Escarpment

Houtbos

track fast and rolling

rufous-breasted sparrowhawk

fruit farm

R539

R37

Sudwala Caves

Mankele Mtb Park

Stats

◀ To Schoemanskloof

steep hill

Umgwenya (Crocodile)

N4

Montrose

B

Alkmaar

To Nelspruit ▶

N4

N

10 km

The route

Starting at the reception at Misty Mountain, at 1650m, you take a track for about 800m east (up) and parallel to the tarred road, then turn sharp right through young pine growth in a wide-arc boomerang down the left-hand side of the upper Nels valley. After roughly 5km, you hit the stream at around 1350m, then head straight down the valley floor for 6km to a T-junction. Keep right and continue down the valley on a good gravel road, past some scattered buildings at Rhenosterhoek, 4km from the junction, then take a lesser logging track uphill to the right, into the plantations.

After about 5km of ascending towards tall communication towers on the ridge, cross over the Rooiwal ridge, keep on the flat awhile, then bomb down an old track with deep ruts and sharp rocks in places, making for excellent riding. Descend further till the now-maintained track flattens and crosses the Stats River, proceeding down the valley (south) through a big commercial fruit farm for 11.5km to the tarred R539. Do a quick right for less than 100m, then sho't left down the gravel road towards Mankele and Sudwala Caves.

There follows a fast 12km run into the Umgwenya (Crocodile River) valley, pine having given way to Lowveld bush and big trees. Just where you cross a stream, with the N4 in sight, you sho't left again, up a steep hill, and follow a gravel road for roughly 7km (take a left turn at the junction). You emerge at the N4 at a cluster of agri-industrial buildings, and Alkmaar. Cross the Umgwenya, then the railway a short way downstream of Montrose – once famous for its falls and now-ruined hotel.

There are quite a few accommodation options around here, including a backpackers. We decided to go far from the madding national-road crowd, and bussed up the Schoemanskloof branch of the N4 to Die Rots Guesthouse. It did mean that in the morning we'd have to bus back down to Alkmaar, but our amaDriver Philippe never tired of testing the Amarok on the open road.

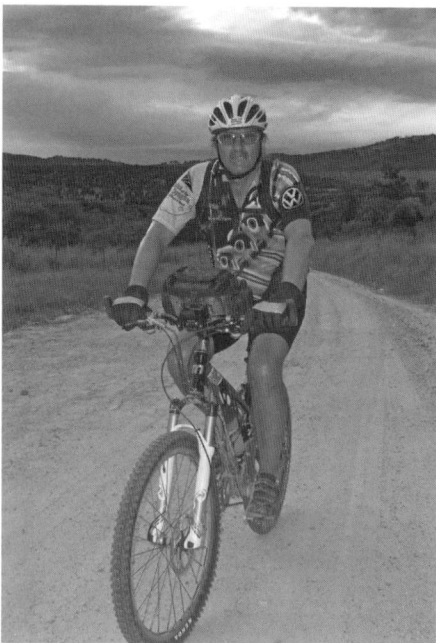

Near Alkmaar, where one road looks like any other.

STAGE 3
ALKMAAR/N4 TO KAAPSCHEHOOP   30.5km

GRADE: Short, moderate to hard
OVERNIGHT: Kaapsehoop Guesthouse

IN A NUTSHELL

Don't be fooled by the short distance – this day's route involves some 1177m of climbing from the Lowveld to the top of the escarpment (luckily the *padkos* from Die Rots was great: bacon and cheese sarmies on Ellie's amazing fresh-baked *potbrood*). It is helluva pretty, though, if you care to peer over your sweat-stained glasses.

   If you've got any oomph left, the taxing uphill is followed by 13km that's rolling, fast and a lot of fun as you more or less follow, in reverse direction, the route of the Kaapschehoop hiking trail just in from the edge of the escarpment.

Snapshot of the experience

We took a wrong turn only a few kilometres into the day's ride, which led to some forward-back, forward-back riding along back roads till the locals started to look at us askance. We also – before we had to haul ass and bike across a thorn-entangled stream by way of a fallen tree – inadvertently stumbled on either a right-wing *vergadering* or a *snor* and two-tone-khaki-shirt gay gathering in the bush.

   Quaint Kaapschehoop village, not long ago an old mining ghost town, is a bit of a secret artists' getaway, with some new holiday houses, restaurant-pubs and several B&Bs.

The route

Start at the Alkmaar/N4 junction; cross to the south side of the freeway and take the gravel road up-valley for about 800m. Follow it where it swings left (south) and at the fork take the left-hand prong. For the next 4km or so you ride through bush and small fruit farms,

The Kaapschehoop area is one of the last outposts of endangered blue swallows, which once nested on the escarpment grasslands before these were pretty much all planted with timber. (Your books, magazines and toilet tissue have to come from somewhere – just pull out any bits of blue swallow you might find pressed into the paper.)

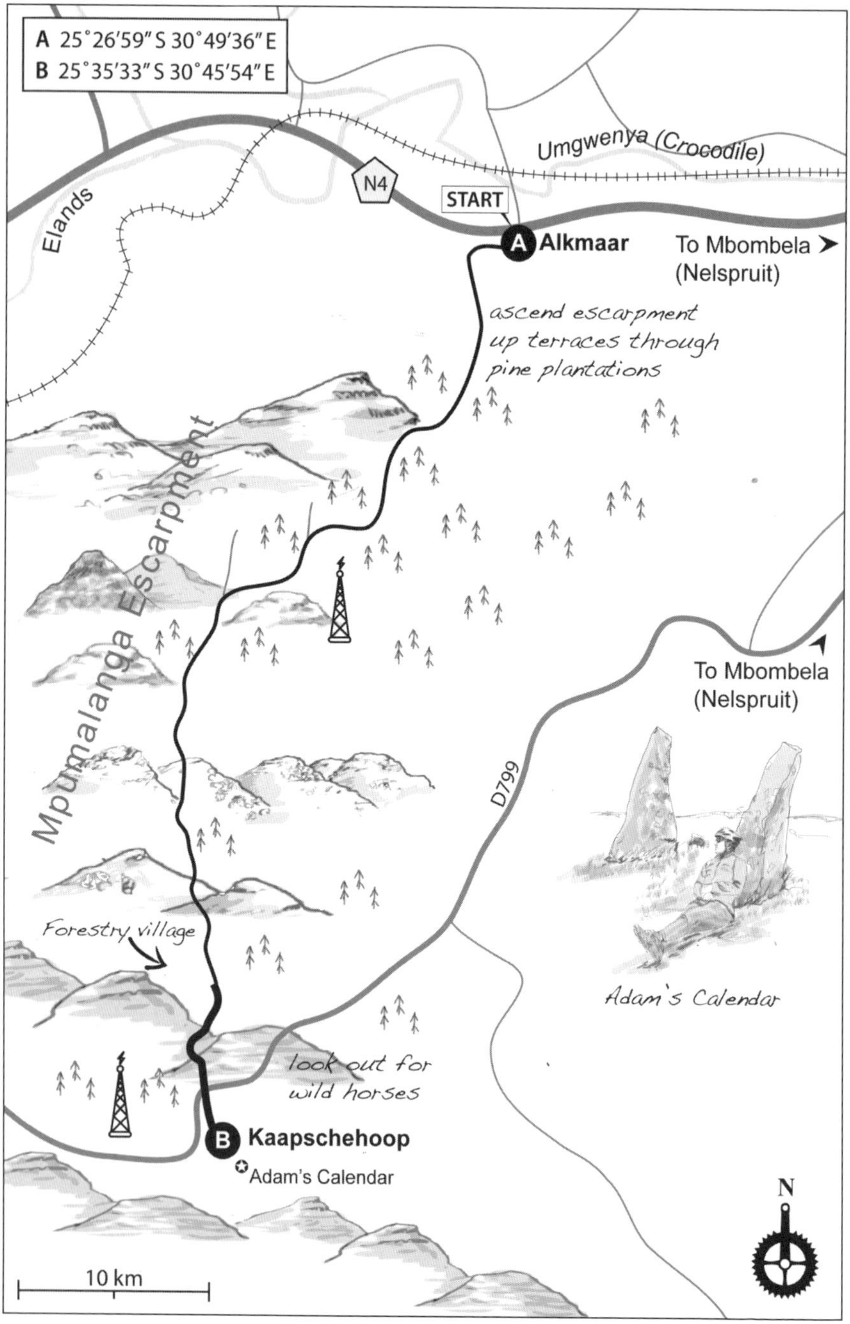

A 25°26'59"S 30°49'36"E
B 25°35'33"S 30°45'54"E

Umgwenya (Crocodile)

N4

Elands

START

A Alkmaar

To Mbombela ➤
(Nelspruit)

ascend escarpment
up terraces through
pine plantations

Mpumalanga Escarpment

To Mbombela ⤴
(Nelspruit)

D799

Adam's Calendar

Forestry village

look out for
wild horses

B Kaapschehoop

Adam's Calendar

N

10 km

then you swing sharp right. The private lands end, riverine forest covers the road and you start the big climb.

All too soon you are deep in pine plantation and equally deep in one of the very big ascents of this section of the Spine of the Dragon route. For much of the day the ranks of commercial trees seem to haunt you like dark ghostly battalions. A sense of a post-nuclear holocaust persists as you ride through landscapes of freshly lumbered tracts of mountainside, where now and again you're rewarded with views over the edge of the escarpment, the Lowveld and, on a clear day, all the way to Mozambique.

For 10km you drag your butt and bike up 800m. At around 1500m a boom and menacing sign (an old one) across the road – courtesy of the local timber consortium – implies that if you proceed you risk torture and your bike being thrown over the escarpment. (We ignored it and took a breather there instead, before taking a left turn. It turned out okay.)

You ride out of the last section of forest at around 1600m and reach a T-junction with a larger gravel road that generally follows the escarpment edge (going wide around gully heads) in a general southwest/south direction. For 10.5km it's more or less level, superfast riding on gravel roads. Around 4.5km from that first summit T-junction, the road forks – you can take either, the right-hand track going towards the forestry village but swinging back. The route, still a very minor road, is tarred in places to keep dust down.

Back in the plantations, and nearing the village, the route reverts to tar. The famous feral horses here have the freedom of Kaapschehoop, so you're likely to see them sometime during your stay, munching on roses and the like. You pop out on the D799 Mbombela (Nelspruit) tarred road – watch out for flying traffic – then ride into town. It's straight ahead.

We recommend you outspan instantly at the Bohemian pub and restaurant, the quieter, more refined place when the town hops on weekends. After a full pasta meal there, we retreated to our annex cottage of the immensely hospitable Kaapsehoop Guesthouse.

En route to Kaapschehoop, this minor stream caused major problems and thorny encounters.

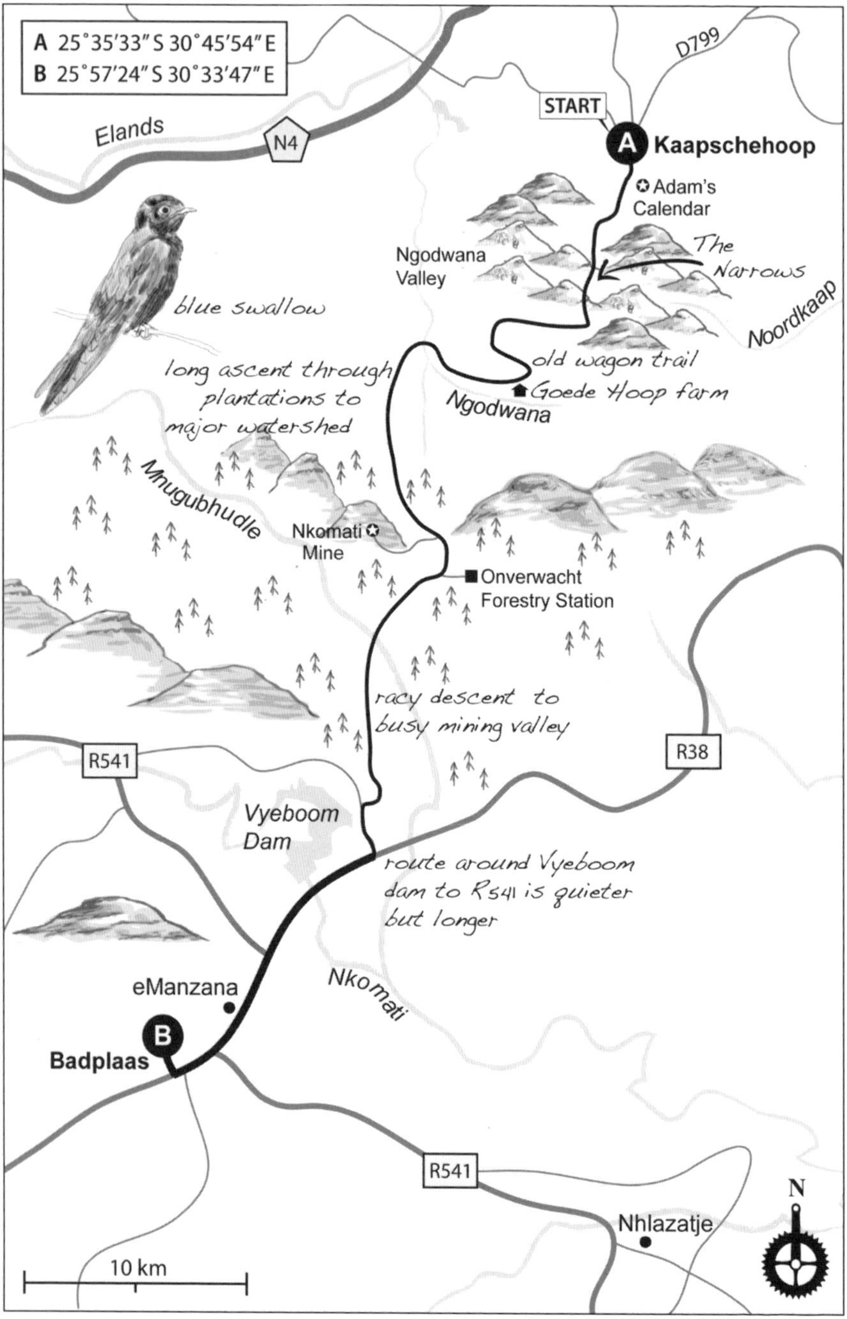

A 25°35'33" S 30°45'54" E
B 25°57'24" S 30°33'47" E

D799

Elands   N4

START
A Kaapschehoop

✿ Adam's
Calendar

The
Narrows

Ngodwana
Valley

Noordkaap

blue swallow

old wagon trail
🔺 *Goede Hoop farm*

*long ascent through
plantations to
major watershed*

Ngodwana

Mnugubhudle

Nkomati ✿
Mine

■ Onverwacht
Forestry Station

*racy descent to
busy mining valley*

R541   R38

Vyeboom
Dam

*route around Vyeboom
dam to R541 is quieter
but longer*

Nkomati

eManzana •

B

Badplaas

R541

Nhlazatje •

N

10 km

STAGE 4
KAAPSCHEHOOP TO BADPLAAS   75.5km

GRADE: Long, hard
OVERNIGHT: Forever Resorts Badplaas

IN A NUTSHELL

This stage has developed something of a reputation for sucking you in and spitting you out. It's not for sissies. There are plenty big hills (some very big), equally big downhills, and some torturous long hauls when done in the midday sun. But the riding is among the best mountain biking we've done so far, starting along forestry tracks, old wagon roads that have not felt the arc of a rubber wheel over their rutted, overgrown surfaces for years, farm tracks, and a district road with not one vehicle all day. The pull up from the Ngodwana valley to the top of the Nkomati ridge stands out months after the fact.

Snapshot of the experience

Although we'd done our homework, at the start of our day it was a pretty labyrinthine task to unlock the mystery of the Ngodwana valley. We were grateful to our host, Neels, eager to give his Land Rover a spin through the rockeries and timberlands of the escarpment.

I spent most of the day singing that old Blood, Sweat & Tears number, you know the one ... 'What goes up must come down, Spinning wheel gotta go round...'

Here, natural beauty abounds, especially along the Kaapschehoop escarpment with views over the Lowveld all the way across Barberton to Swaziland. The upper Ngodwana valley is the jewel, tucked between proud, dolerite-fringed spurs, where we found Saaiman, his wife, Saartjie, and their son, Skoffel, leading an idyllic life in this green, bucolic valley with gurgling streams converging at the valley mouth.

The route

As you leave the village on the tarred D799, hop the first gate on the left to pass the monolith in the veld on the right of the jeep track. Way over the marshland to the right you should make out the ruin of a miner's home up against the pines. Where the main track swings hard right after about 2.25km, carry on south for 1.7km to find one of South Africa's most intriguing landmarks,

Adam's Calendar, believed to be one of the world's oldest celestial calendars – and a place of immeasurable cultural and spiritual significance.

From there, swing right (west) and follow the track along the edge of the tree line across the upper Noordkaap River and the head of The Narrows to find your way back onto our GPS track – the key to unlocking the Ngodwana valley route. The trick is to pick the right line through The Narrows canyon, then follow an old wagon track that clearly has not seen much traffic since the last wagon came this way, down a steep spur.

In the valley below, to the right is a scattering of farm buildings but only the old Goede Hoop homestead is still occupied. You should stop to pay your respects and ask directions. From there, keep well to the right above the swampy river, then cross the river where you see a track and fence gate. The river is shallow but still good for a refreshing dip, as the way ahead is long. As the old James Thurber poem says, '…uphill all the way and even further'.

From here it's all up for the next 12km, where you crest the Limpopo/Vaal-Orange watershed and proceed, on a reasonably level gradient, to the Nkomati mine turn-off to your right at about 1500m. Then brace yourself for the big downhill of the day.

Around 2.8km into the descent, bear hard right, not left to the Onverwacht forestry station. Then you swoop down to cross the Mnugubhudle River, where a dip is advised (you may hear timber trucks rumbling in the very distance). From the river it's an 8km ride to a T-junction on a busy dirt road (lots of mine traffic), with one big climb, then a further 3.5km alongside the Vyeboom dam on the Nkomati River to the tarred and even busier R38.

The 13km roller-coaster plod into Badplaas is no joy ride. It's worth looking for an alternate route around the north side of Vyeboom dam to avoid the tar (at 700m resolution, RoadTrip shows a network of paths around the dam).

The old wagon road after The Narrows – the crux of the route.

STAGE 5
BADPLAAS TO CHRISSIESMEER   58km

GRADE: Medium, moderate to hard
OVERNIGHT: Just Country (self-catering)

IN A NUTSHELL

The day starts at around 1174m altitude and you spend the first 26km climbing to 1700m. The route follows a quiet gravel back road all day; when we did it, four vehicles constituted the Badplaas morning rush hour. Most of the riding is across wide, open veld with timber plantations on the high ground starting about midway.

Snapshot of the experience

Leaving Forever Resorts Badplaas, a real *oord* of the old order, but decent and just right for our needs, we headed straight into fast-driven clouds and a chill wind blowing strongly into our faces. It made even the downhills feel like uphills. We spent the first part going up, up – down; up, up – down; repeat. Then repeat again.

This is a little-known corner of the country, particularly around Chrissiesmeer, which has the country's only natural inland lakes – around 230 of them. There are so many lakes here it looks more like a landscape carved by sheet glaciers than by running water. The biggest lake was named after Christina, daughter of the South African Republic's President Pretorius, when the original Scottish settler took a fancy to her.

If the powers that be have their way, the Chrissiesmeer lake district will soon be laid waste by opencast coal mining. We are a growing nation and need that energy, I guess. So, if you want to save this place, go solar.

The route

If you camp near water, chances are the following day's trip is going to start uphill. And so it is with Badplaas: the route starts almost immediately opposite the resort entrance, heading due south on a gravel road.

Over the next 15km the road climbs steadily from 1100m, past 1200, 1300, and so on, just nudging 1600m. It drops back to nearly 1400m, then over the next 10km climbs again, cresting out at 1700m where it pretty much levels off for the rest of the ride.

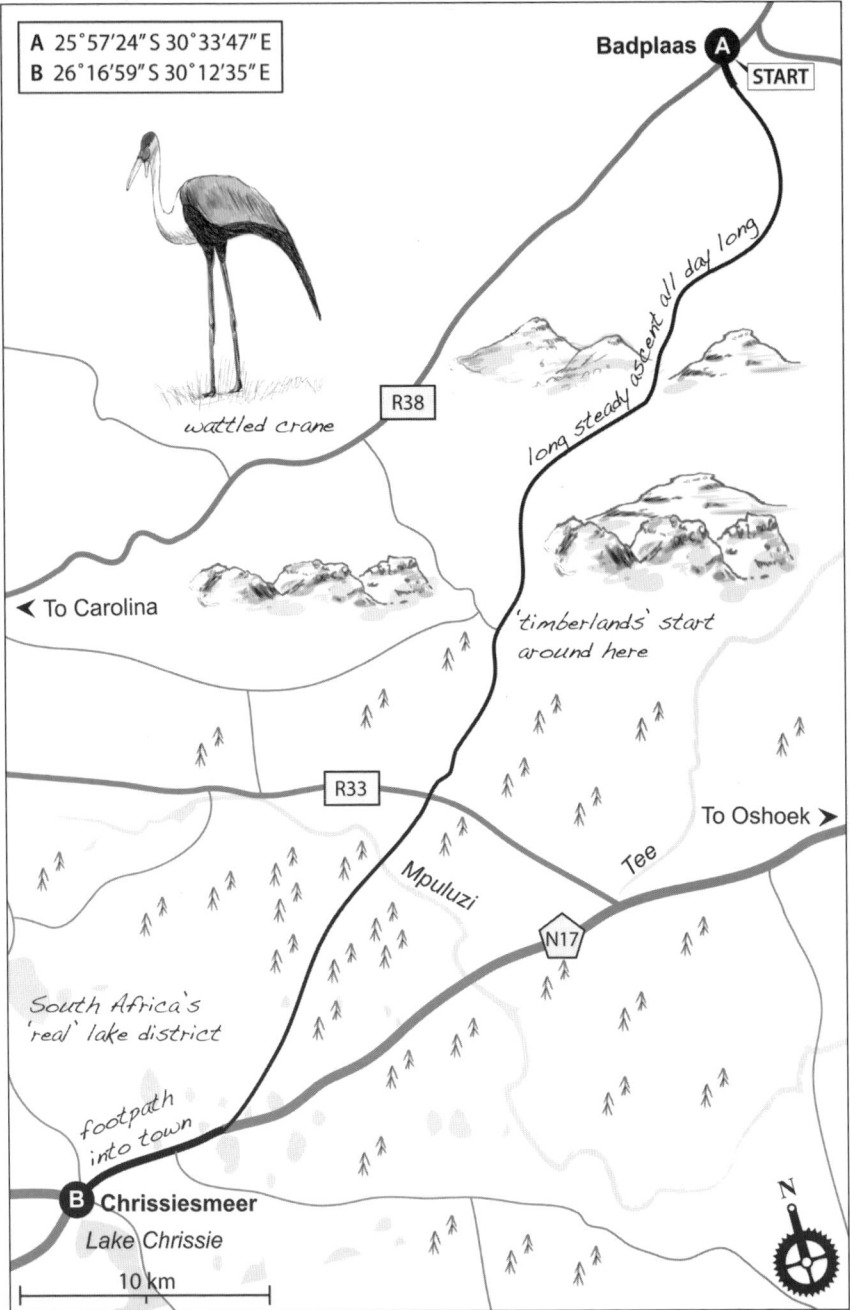

A 25°57'24" S 30°33'47" E
B 26°16'59" S 30°12'35" E

Badplaas **A**
START

long steady ascent all day long

R38

wattled crane

◄ To Carolina

'timberlands' start
around here

R33

To Oshoek ►

Tee

Mpuluzi

N17

South Africa's
'real' lake district

footpath
into town

B Chrissiesmeer
Lake Chrissie

N

10 km

At around 25km you hit the first timber plantations of the day, newly planted areas alongside older lots. That the road 'levels off' is a relative term – it gains some 100m in altitude over the next 7km to a high point of 1785m, but it's the kind of riding that requires hard pedalling on gravel without respite (other than stopping, no sobbing permitted).

The road does descend to 1740m over 7km to the tarred R33, but rises again to 1770m. It's all very energy-sapping. When you get into the zone, however, it's a very Zen-like experience and the reason we get addicted. For the next 15km to the tarred N17, the gravel road crosses several water courses, a few streams and passes through a few small plantations, the ups and downs never severe.

When you see the hand-painted sign advertising 'gabagges' for sale, you are near the end but with one small sting in the tail: you have to ride on a very tenuous footpath alongside the narrow national road (leading to Carolina) or risk becoming road kill.

It's not a pretty end to a big-sky Highveld day, but regain your good cheer by making a turn at Ben's coffee shop (western end of town). You'll find the Just Country cottage, overlooking the *meer*, on the town's southernmost street (same one as the old jail).

· ·

STAGE 6
CHRISSIESMEER TO AMSTERDAM 72km

GRADE: Long, moderate
OVERNIGHT: Glen Oak Lodge

IN A NUTSHELL
The landscape is lovely, with lakes and streams, happy cows making milk and contented sheep growing wool in the lush fields. There are wattled cranes on some of the bigger wetlands and coveys of spur-winged geese, herons, egrets and ducks. It's an amazing, little-known corner of the country. And, for the first time since leaving Beit Bridge, the general lay of the land is pretty much downhill.

Snapshot of the experience
Chrissiesmeer awoke with the first frost of winter sleeping softly on the Highveld grass and mist lying on the lake like a duck-down duvet (just a very

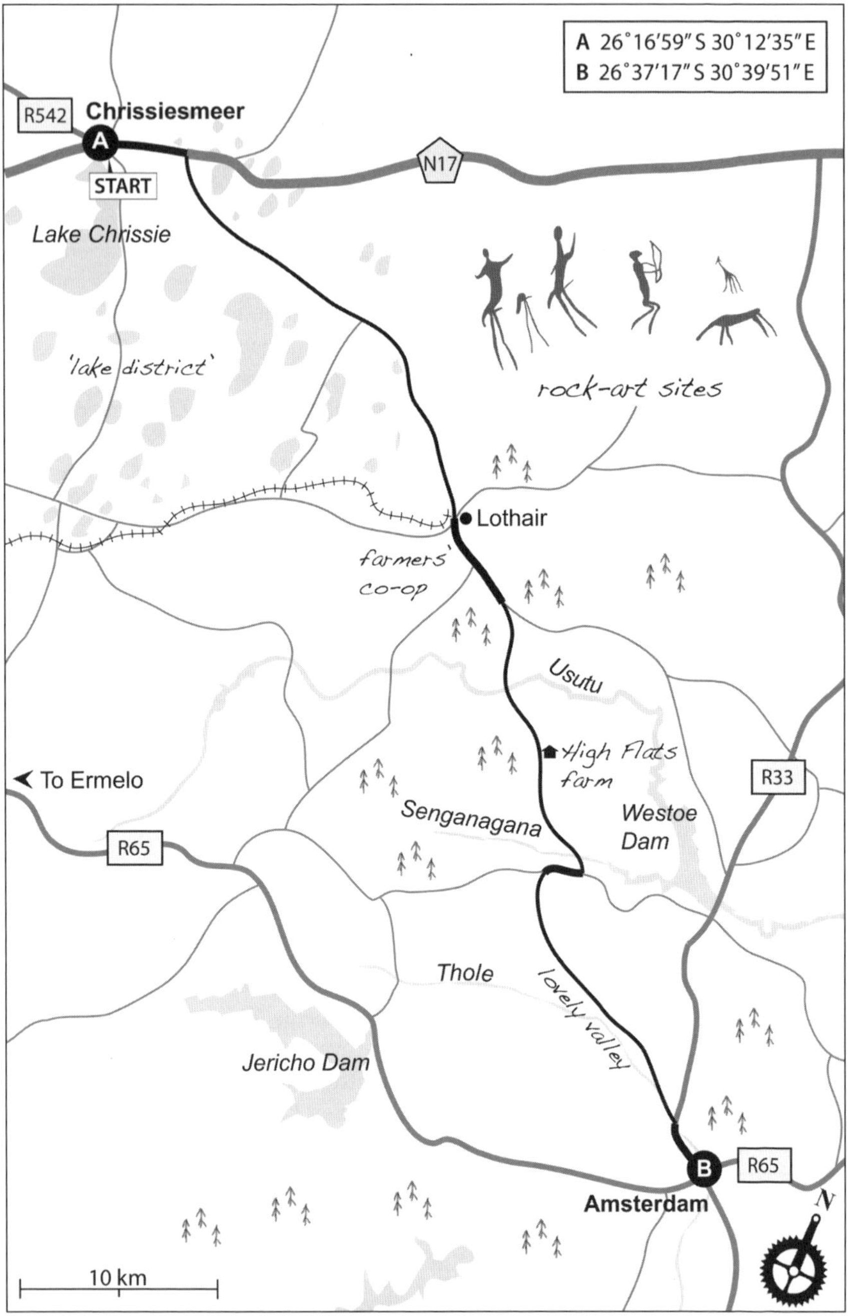

A 26°16'59"S 30°12'35"E
B 26°37'17"S 30°39'51"E

R542 **Chrissiesmeer**
A
START
N17
Lake Chrissie

'lake district'

rock-art sites

● Lothair

*farmers'
co-op*

Usutu

▲ *High Flats
farm*

Senganagana

R33

R65

*Westoe
Dam*

◄ To Ermelo

lovely valley

Thole

Jericho Dam

B R65
Amsterdam

N

10 km

cold one). It was hard to get going before nine, with our hostess, Heather, heaping up pots of oats with honey.

By the end of the day, Amsterdam, well, there's not much you can say about the place other than that it is there. Except, as always, you find your way into the caring hands of exceptional hosts. The decent Italian-style coffee, really good pizzas and expansive gardens of Glen Oak turn a dump (the town) into a really nice experience. When you turn down the covers of some of the less-well-worn country towns, you often find the most unexpected pillow gifts.

Steve sang most of the day, 'Even the uphills are down....' We flew into Amsterdam like leaves on an autumn wind. Well, that's how it felt.

The route

From Glen Oak Lodge, ride east out of town along the N17 for 4km, then take the gravel road to the right, passing close by Mullersrus wetland after 1.5km. From here you ride through the heart of the Mpumalanga lake district – really most exhilarating; the riding is so easy and the lie of the land so gentle on the eye, lung and legs.

About 2km off to your right you pass the second-largest lake in the area, Eilandsmeer, then Knock Dhu, Lake Banaghar and, before you know it, after little more than 27km you are in the 'town' of Lothair. The last 5km is through commercial timberlands; stop in at the farmers' co-op to stock up on cold drinks and Milkreem (you can never have too much on a ride like this), and the locals are very sociable.

At Lothair turn immediately right into town, ride for 1km, then sho't left (a corner-cutting short cut) to head out east to southeast along a tarred road. Follow the tar (good shoulders on both sides) for 4.8km, then take the gravel road south (right) through plantation country, gliding into the Usutu valley and crossing the river after an uplifting 3.5km downhill run.

Soon after passing the Lion Match Co. plantation, where timber gives way to grassland, you wonder how many boxes of friends can be made from a single pine tree. You're now in the land of fairly substantial rivers, meaning you descend and climb out, descend and climb out….

You crest out of the Usutu valley at High Flats farm; here lines of trees offer respite from sun or wind. Descend again through smaller plantations into the Seganagana River valley and, 11.2km from the Usutu River crossing, head into an exhilarating downhill rush. After a roughly 1.5km uphill pull to a T-junction, the route takes you west (right).

About 2.5km later, take a sharp left (south) at the corner of a plantation to the right, and head slowly downwards into the bowl that captures the headwaters of the Thole River. For a scintillating 14.2km you swoop along the left-hand side of the valley through mixed grassland, maize fields and pine plots. There are the inevitable down-up-and-over intervals to cross tributaries or side gullies; otherwise you drop from 1570m to 1270m, where you hit the tarred R33. Swing sharp right towards Amsterdam town.

You hit the outskirts after 2.8km; cross the intersection with the R65, take the first right into Crewel Street, first left into Lanyon, and Glen Oak Lodge is on your right (ring the bell and tell 'em we sent you). The lodge also delivers the best meal in town. For recovery snacks, there's a decent take-away in Lanyon Street, en route to the lodge, where we found excellent fresh pies.

. . . .

STAGE 7
AMSTERDAM TO PIET RETIEF/MKHONDO   64km

GRADE: Medium, moderate
OVERNIGHT: LA Guesthouse

IN A NUTSHELL

This is as dense a concentration of timberlands as you will see anywhere in this country; the ride to Piet Retief/Mkhondo is pine, pine, pine just about all the way. There's no other way to say it, the day's ride is ... well, boring: not too long, not too short, not too hard, not too easy, just an endless vista of pine battalions where once there was rolling grassland. That's not to forget the riding down into, then climbing out of, valleys on loose sand (drudge or fun-fest, depending on your preference).

Snapshot of the experience

It occurred to us there are three kinds of fitness: leg-muscle strength, aerobic performance and backside endurance. Finally, at day 18 on our ride all three seemed to be in sync – although the 25km climb out of Badplaas will always threaten to unseat our equilibrium by creating extreme butt friction. Along with momentum, Bactroban, Milkreem and aloe cream are our friends.

This ride shows up many things about South Africa you don't always see: the good, the bad and the ugly. We would argue there is far, far more of the good. However, it does also show up the glaring gap between 'us' and 'them', the haves and have-nots, the hads and will-haves.

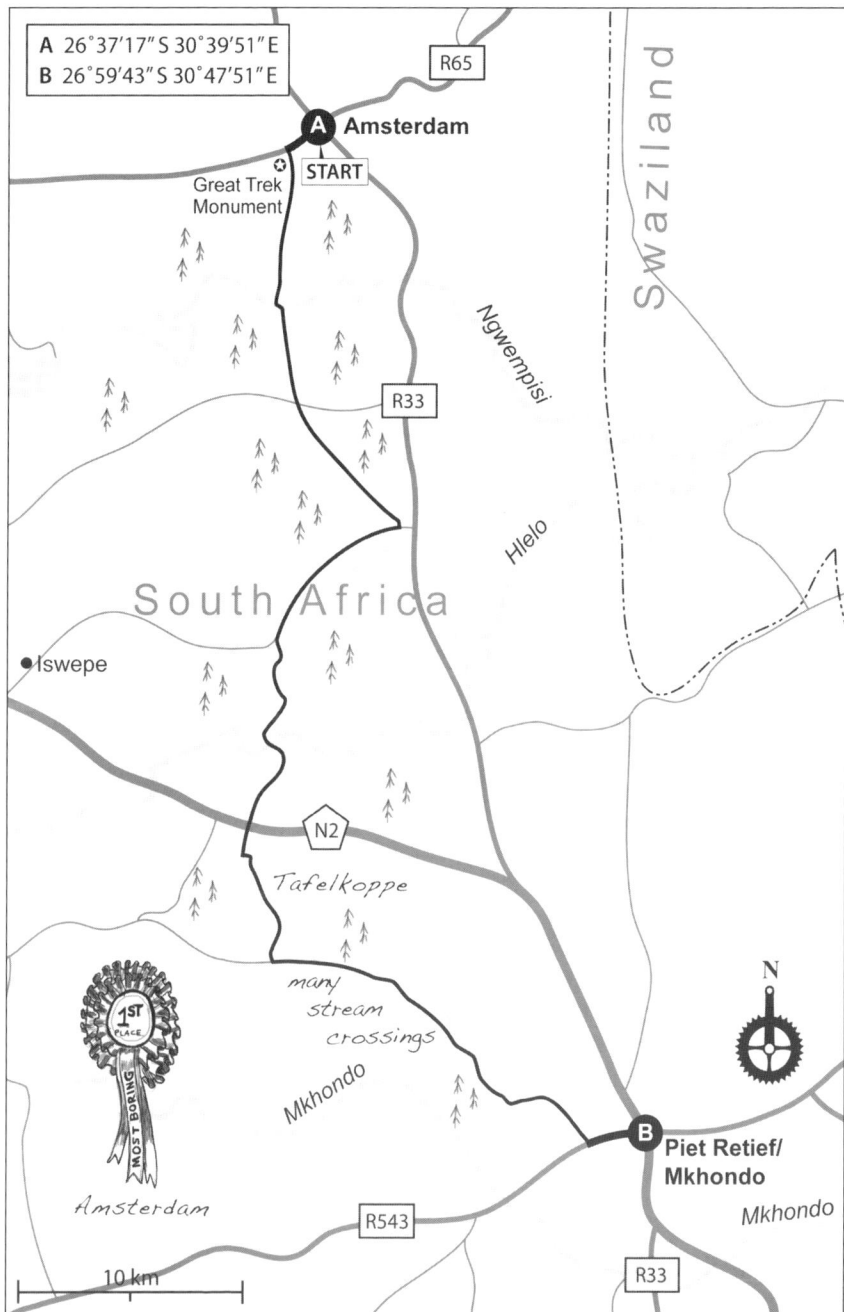

A 26°37'17"S 30°39'51"E
B 26°59'43"S 30°47'51"E

R65

Swaziland

A Amsterdam

START

Great Trek Monument

Ngwempisi

R33

Hlelo

South Africa

Iswepe

N2

Tafelkoppe

many stream crossings

Mkhondo

1ST PLACE

MOST BORING

Amsterdam

N

B Piet Retief/ Mkhondo

Mkhondo

R543

R33

10 km

The route

Leave town on the R65 (southwest), then swing around the shanties to the left on the edge of town (there's an Ossewa Trek monument at the turn-off). Head down into the Ngwempisi River valley, crossing the river after 7.4km and executing a neat left-right manoeuvre. Then it's an easy 5km climb to reach a skew intersection where timber, ploughed fields and grasslands all meet. Carry on straight across (southeast) and head into the Swartwaterspruit valley.

Mkhondo, as we will likely get to know the town of Piet Retief, is the name of the local river. It means assegaai, and it predates the arrival of Piet and his Trekkers, so it's fitting.

It's about 2.8km to the river, and another 4km to a T-junction where you're confronted by heavily ranked battalions of timber. The route sneaks a right here, timber to the left, open fields to the right, heading slightly uphill, parallel to the Hlelo/Tweespruit headwaters. Shortly your vision is filled again with plantations that make for a long, undulating ride over 13.5km, down increasingly steep slopes to the Hlelo River. Watch out for logging machinery along here, especially when approaching the river. Give way; they're bigger and tougher than you.

Climb steeply up the valley for 1.5km till the road swings right (the gradient lessens), then swings left and evens out as you approach the N2 crossing, 4km from the river. Ride over a concrete railway bridge, then cross over the national road; you're surrounded now by timber. Head along and down plantations on the right for 4.5km to cross the first of several tributaries of the Mkhondo River, on which Piet Retief lies 20km away.

After crossing the first stream, climb for 2.5km up to a T-junction and turn left (east). More stream crossings come after 2.1km and 3.5km. The road swings from east to southeast, opens onto a patchwork of timber and fields, and after 7.3km crosses another tributary.

The gravel road climbs out the valley for about 1.5km, swings east and then reaches the Blouberg settlement on a crest 3.8km from the last river crossing. This is a satellite village of Piet Retief (2km on). When you reach the R543, the 'have-nots' part of town is to your right, the 'haves' live to the left. Turn left, dip down and then up to cross the railway line, and ride up Market Street to the LA Guesthouse near the top of the street.

On your way you might choose to stop at the fish-and-chips shop next to the filling station (turn left from Kruger into Church [N2]; it's on your right). They advertise the best chips in the country, and we could find no reason to disagree.

Without getting too heavy, it was election time when we arrived and there was clearly a tussle between the old and new guards – good roads or redistribution. Taking a country ride sure makes you think about things.

STAGE 8
PIET RETIEF/MKHONDO TO NATAL SPA   84.5km
(PAULPIETERSBURG)

GRADE: Long, moderate to hard
OVERNIGHT: Natal Spa Hot Springs & Leisure Resort

IN A NUTSHELL
Don't imagine that because you're following a railway line, and trains cannot negotiate severe inclines, it's going to be a breeze. Gear yourself for lots of short, sharp ups and downs (sometimes not so short ones) across rivers where you cannot cross by railway bridge. You'll also need to do some creative route-finding where the service road suddenly ends against a steep embankment.

Snapshot of the experience
This is one of those days that seem bigger than others of the stage – there were several big river crossings (by bridges), some big bridges that we ducked under, and a landscape that was generous in its vistas and its 'furniture'. We could feel the terrain changing from tranquil timberlands to more dramatic battlefields and started to gird our loins for the adventures ahead. Also distinguishing this stage from most others was the fact that nearly the entire distance is on or along the busy Richards Bay railway line.

The route
You need to backtrack east along Kruger Street, under the railway bridge, turn left to get onto the tracks at the station and you'll soon pick up the service road. This takes you through the 'township' part of town, following a tributary of the Mkhondo River on your left till you cross the river after about 7.3km. The only

From the Hinze family we learned that in 1947 the royal White Train stopped at Commondale so the king and queen of some past empire could meet the local giant. He believed he was 6 foot 6 inches, but the king thought otherwise, ordering that a tape measure be produced. This was when the giant discovered he'd been, all the while, an astonishing 7 foot 3 inches. Some say he fought in the Anglo-Boer War; he must have had a problem finding a horse he could fit on.

way across is on the bridge, which you should mount above the wetland, and then ride-push your mountain bike across.

Pick up the service road where the railway crosses a gravel road, and follow it down the Mkhondo/Assegaai valley, parallel to the R33; 7.2km past the Mkhondo crossing, one leap gets you across the road and Swartwater River. Watch out for snakes between the timber plantations, cutting a path between the R33 and N2. About 6.8km from the previous bridge, where two railway lines converge, you have to go around and over the railway to pick up the track again on the far side of the bridge, crossing from left to the right of the line.

For the next 4.6km it's down-up-down across three tributaries of the Wit River. As the railway line approaches the R33, veer off down to the right 150m before the bridge. Ride down the tar till just before the bridge and pick up the service road again to the right. The track takes a wide loop around to the right to cross and then rejoin the line.

About 4km on is the first of some amazing post-and-lintel-style railway bridges. The service road does a few snake-bends around, under, around and over to regain the line level, crossing the *spruit* by causeway. It's worth taking a break here to catch the view and maybe a photo.

After 16km of the usual up-and-down riding through this water-lined land, detour off left to go under and around the second of the two magnificent railway bridges, this time crossing the Sikube River, a tributary of the Langfonteinspruit, which then flows into the Phongolo. About 1km further is Commondale, where we popped into the Hinze farm (The Cycad B&B) for much-needed succour, coffee and a local history lesson.

Just before reaching the Phongolo, the line splits: right to Paulpietersburg, left around Dumbe ridge (1356m), which hides the town from view. This is our line. It's the loveliest part of the ride, with big mountains ahead and the railway snaking off into the distance. It's a 15km pull from the Phongolo to the end of the climb, but no blood-and-guts stuff.

KwaZulu-Natal railroad workers hard at work on a Sunday near the Phongolo River bridge.

Duck off the railway at an overhead bridge, then take the gravel road left to pick up the P221 (tar), turning left (southeast), up and then down into the Bivane valley. It starts with a toughish 9km pull up along the shoulder, followed by a 9km hell-for-rubber descent. Take it easy because taxis ply this route and it's easy to overshoot the corners.

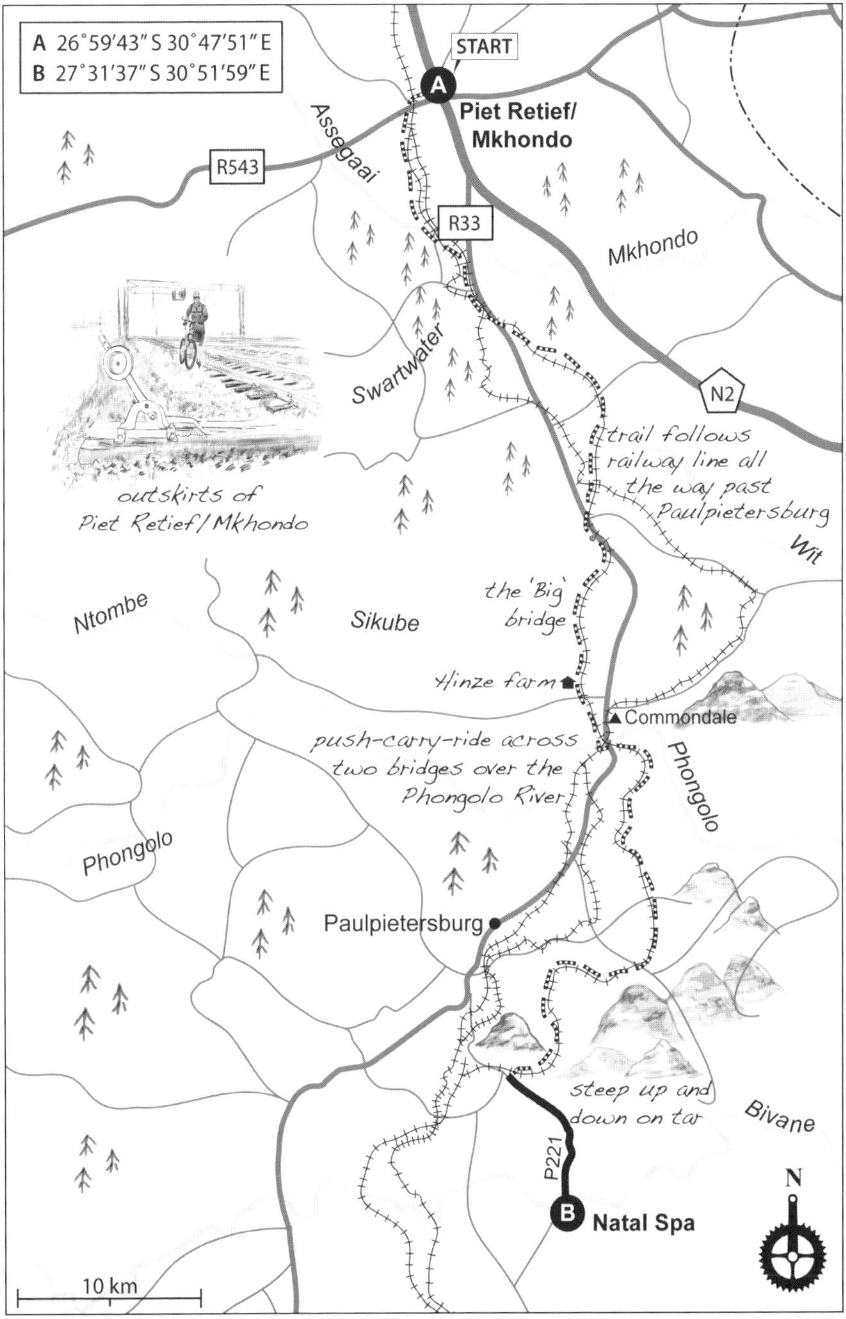

A 26°59'43"S 30°47'51"E
B 27°31'37"S 30°51'59"E

R543

START

Piet Retief/
Mkhondo

Assegaai

R33

Swartwater

Mkhondo

N2

trail follows
railway line all
the way past
Paulpietersburg

outskirts of
Piet Retief/Mkhondo

Wit

Ntombe

Sikube

the 'Big'
bridge

Hinze farm

▲ Commondale

Phongolo

push-carry-ride across
two bridges over the
Phongolo River

Phongolo

Paulpietersburg

steep up and
down on tar

Bivane

P221

B Natal Spa

N

10 km

RECOMMENDED
5/6
days

Battlefields Trail

Natal Spa (Paulpietersburg) to Phuthaditjhaba •
453km (recommended) or 488km (alternative)

©Steve Thomas

STAGE 1
NATAL SPA (PAULPIETERSBURG) TO BLOOD RIVER

105km

GRADE: Long, hard; strenuous to severe
OVERNIGHT: Blood River Heritage Site

IN A NUTSHELL

All around, the intensely green hills of Zululand seem to echo with the sounds of history. The entire area around Vryheid, location of an early Boer 'republic', is littered with Zulu-Boer, British-Zulu and Boer-British battle grounds. The route, over the back of the Skurweberg and through Blood River Poort, is tough – but hoo boy, what countryside and great riding tracks! The ride down from the summit is one of the great descents of the entire route, so engage your big chain-ring, crouch, touch and engage. The second half is easier, but you still have to turn those cranks over 105km of testing, dusty Zululand, a place that is many things but never flat or boring.

Snapshot of the experience

The route we mapped offers amazing riding – and the spirits of history. At the Holkrans Anglo-Boer War battle site on the Skurweberg, a Zulu impi overcame a party of 56 Boers taking cover from the British under an overhang. Decades earlier, before the battle at Blood River, Sarel Cilliers stood on a small cannon and declared that, if God granted the several hundred Voortrekkers and camp attendants victory over Dingane's Zulu army of some 15 000 warriors, they would forever keep the day and the place sacred. And so some of them have.

The route

Leave the Spa going south on the tarred P221, head uphill for 3.5km through plantation and cross the P34, then take the forestry roads heading eastward. After a 7km straight run through timberland, take a sharp left, emerging in farmland; turn right (east) onto the D24. You cross

Taking a spear to a gunfight proved the Zulus' undoing at the Battle of Blood River: 3000 lay dead at the end of the day's action, with three or four Boers wounded. On the west side of the site is a circle of 64 replica bronze wagons. It's a stirring spot.

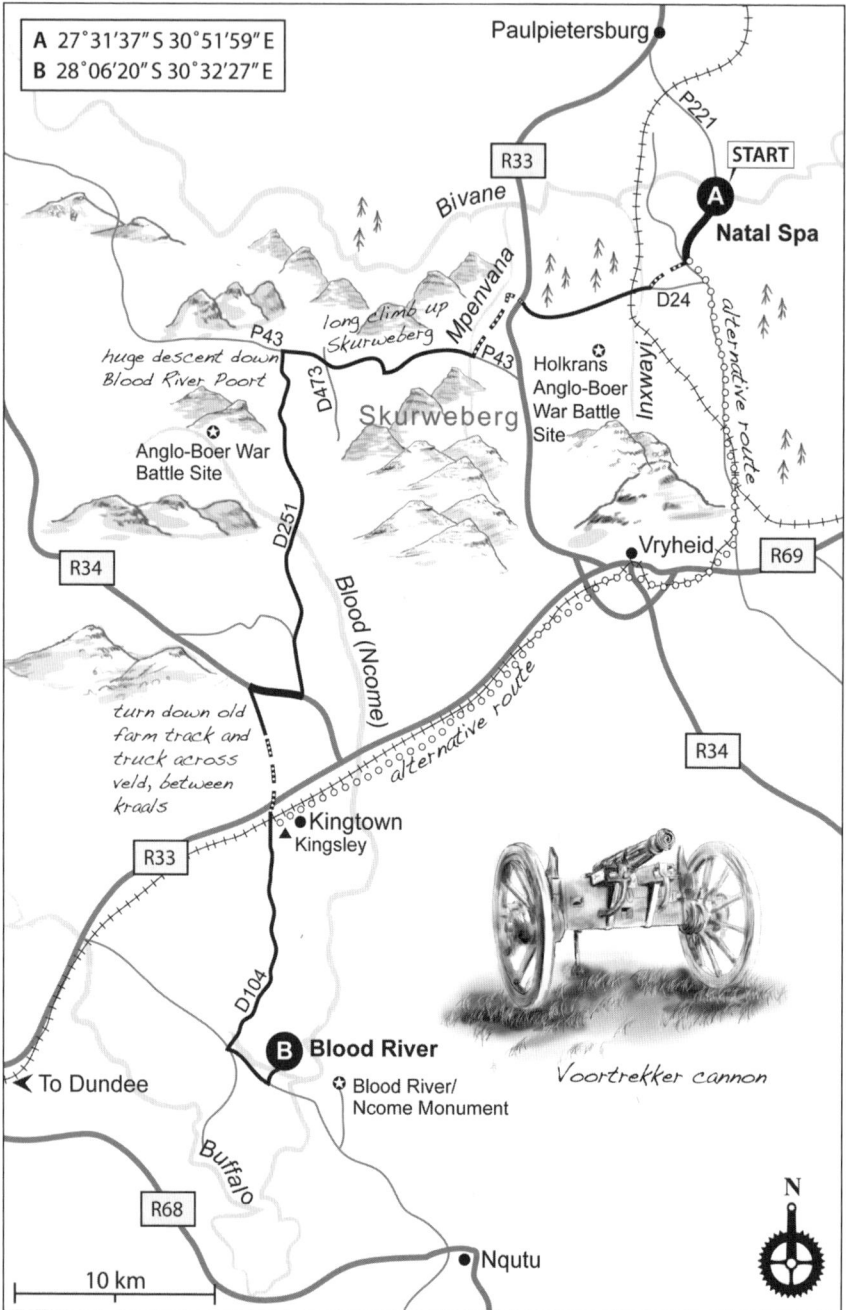

A 27°31′37″S 30°51′59″E
B 28°06′20″S 30°32′27″E

Paulpietersburg

P221

START

R33

Bivane

A

Natal Spa

D24

alternative route

Mpenvana

long climb up
Skurweberg

P43

P43

Holkrans
Anglo-Boer
War Battle
Site

Inxwayi

huge descent down
Blood River Poort

D473

Skurweberg

D251

Anglo-Boer War
Battle Site

R34

Blood (Ncome)

Vryheid

R69

alternative route

R34

turn down old
farm track and
truck across
veld, between
kraals

R33

Kingtown
Kingsley

D104

B Blood River

To Dundee

Blood River/
Ncome Monument

Voortrekker cannon

Buffalo

R68

Nqutu

N

10 km

two railway lines – the first over, the next under – then the Inxwayi River, after which is a 16km slog up and around the Skurweberg, passing the Holkrans monument on your left (the battle site is on a private farm).

An alternative, to turn this long stage into two shorter ones: don't stay at the Natal Spa, but overnight in Paulpietersburg. Ride to Vryheid along the railway line, continue to Blood River along the railway running parallel to the R33, southwest out of Vryheid, picking up our track 5.5km after crossing the Blood (Ncome) River at Kingsley station.

Back to our track: about 5km downhill, cross the tarred R33 (left to Vryheid). Then it's southwest through more plantation for about 5km. Swing south for another 5km into farmland, then head straight down to the Mpenvana River, following it down to the gravel P43, where you swing right (west).

About 3km on, cross the Mpenvana River, then start a 9.5km slog up to the **real** summit of the Skurweberg (from 350m to 1600m). Plantation gives way to open veld; once you get onto the plateau the views are way too grand to worry about the slog. Taking comfort in the knowledge that what goes up must go down, you're headed for a 2.5km down-run on loose gravel. Where it flattens out, pass the turn-off to the gravel D473 and continue west for 2.5km. This is the Blood River Poort (an Anglo-Boer War site) road, a 12km downhill rush through the poort, which peters out into rural Zululand. From Blood River it's an increasingly flat, tedious and corrugated 14km to reach the tarred R34, where you turn for about 2.5km, then left onto a gravel road (hop the fence if needs be).

The next 9.5km are more fun, along a series of seemingly quite random rural tracks (lots of gates) to get you back to the R33. Beware: this area can become exceedingly boggy at times. On reaching the tarred road, do a right-left, right-left, over the railway lines around Kingsley station and Kingtown (not much of a town) to reach the gravel D104.

Head south from here to Blood River; it's a gently rolling run for 23km, as the sun lowers its eyelids over the golden-green grass-tops glinting like the assegaai tips of a massed Zulu impi. If there's still light, and it's warm enough, it's worth taking a walk from the Information Centre down to the laager of 64 replica Voortrekker wagons – then imagine you're a Boer or a Zulu warrior, preparing for the impending morning attack.

A giant sandstone 'castle' requiring circumnavigation.

©Steve Thomas

STAGE 2
BLOOD RIVER TO RORKE'S DRIFT LODGE 68km

GRADE: Medium, moderate to hard
OVERNIGHT: Rorke's Drift Lodge

IN A NUTSHELL
This section of the route is brilliant: not one smear of tar, only a procession of connecting district roads, jeep tracks, cattle tracks and footpaths. For those of us out on the long haul, it seemed as if the hills of Zululand had finally flattened out when in actual fact they do present something of a riding challenge.

Snapshot of the experience
You've got to empathise with the Zulus – everyone wanted a piece of their green, hilly, river-braided countryside. First up were the British settlers from Port Natal, then the Voortrekkers, and later the entire British Empire, in the form of Lord Chelmsford's conquering army of 1878/79.

Not everyone gets excited about history, I know, but it's hard not to imagine the various armies, columns of settlers or other invaders, crossing these hillsides with their patchwork Nguni cows. Here on the left, Dingane's impis took up their ox-head formation on the side of Blood River Hill, spying the circle of 64 wagons in the valley, ready for easy plucking.

There, the red line of Chelmsford's army crossed the Buffalo River to make camp at an ominous looking keel-shaped mountain. And as you ride, you sing, like a young Zulu man walking across the hills to visit a maiden, the words of that Juluka song, 'Impi':

Impi! wo 'nans' impi iyeza. Obani bengathinta amabhubesi?
[War! O, here comes war. Who can touch the lions?]

The route
Heading out of the Blood River battle site area, turn left and loop around to the south, passing the Ncome museum, which gives an alternative account of the battle (like, it never actually happened). Cross the river, riding east for a few kilometres, then swing south

You can argue history all you want – but, let's face it, if a whole bunch of people with muskets and field guns suddenly started pouring into your backyard, you'd get a bit tetchy too.

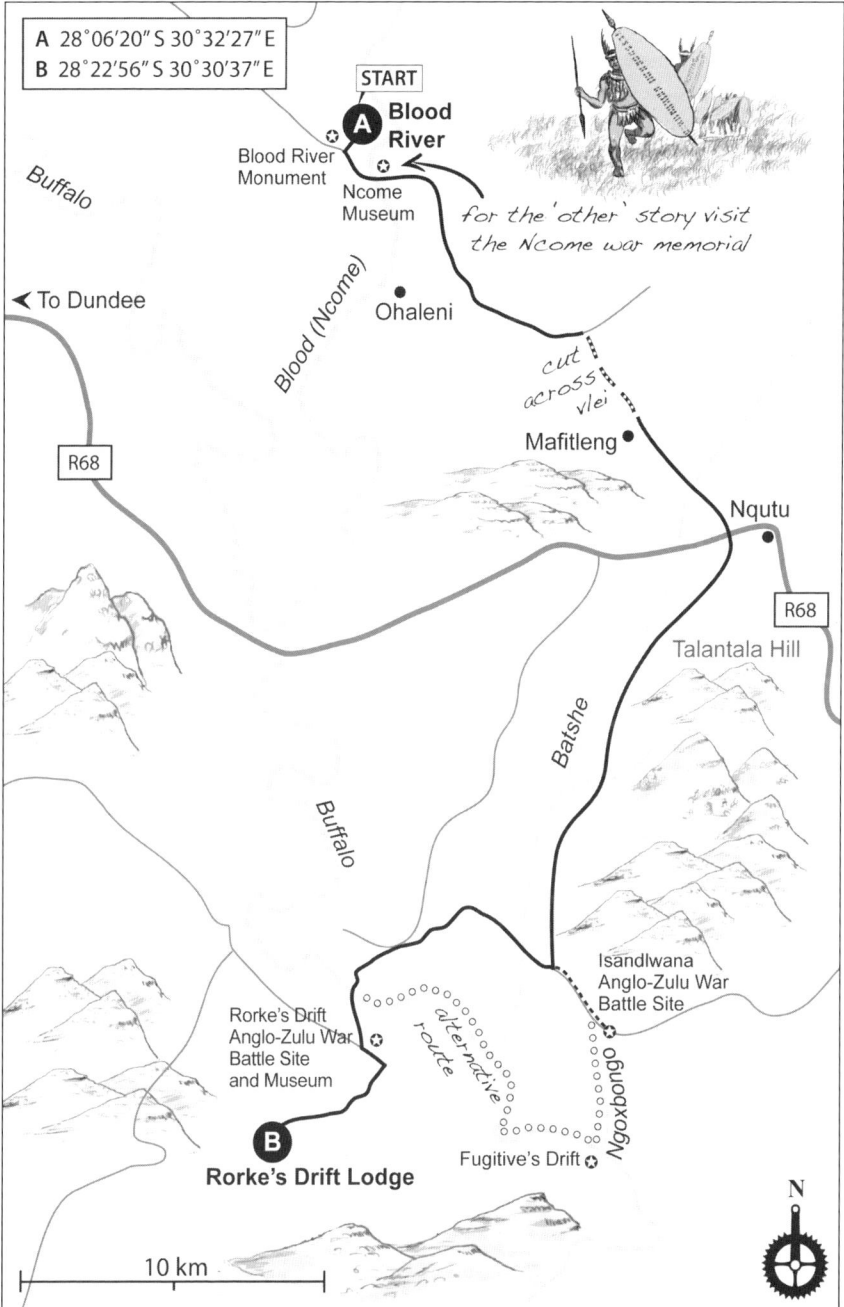

A 28°06'20" S 30°32'27" E
B 28°22'56" S 30°30'37" E

START
Blood River

Blood River Monument
Ncome Museum

Buffalo

for the 'other' story visit the Ncome war memorial

◄ To Dundee

Blood (Ncome)

● Ohaleni

cut across vlei

Mafitleng ●

Nqutu ●

R68

R68

Talantala Hill

Batshe

Buffalo

Isandlwana Anglo-Zulu War Battle Site

alternative route

Rorke's Drift Anglo-Zulu War Battle Site and Museum

Ngxoxongo

B
Rorke's Drift Lodge

Fugitive's Drift

N

10 km

through village-dotted grazing lands. The first 12km are on gravel road, with its pedestrians, donkey carts, goats and cattle.

The route takes a right turn, along a footpath, down to cross a vlei, then up the opposite slope where it joins a gravel road after about 3km. Pass through a village into open, well-cultivated lands and cross the Batshe River to reach the built-up outskirts of Nqutu town straddling the R68 route (about 21km from the start). You'll find small and large shops here, including some large chain stores.

From Nqutu there's a fast, straight downhill run on a well-surfaced road, crossing the Batshe River again and into increasingly rural lands. Keeping the river on your right, the road climbs steadily up towards Talantala hill, skirting around its western flank. At about the 30km mark, near the cliff face, we found our traveller's tree for a lunch break.

At the southwest tip of the hill (you've been riding quite hard up against the cliff line), take a sharp right turn (west) downwards to cross the Batshe yet again and climb up the other side of the valley. The gravel road turns from northwest to southwest as it crests the rise, then takes a rolling descent down to the Buffalo River. Along this stretch, way over to your left, is the sharp outline of Isandlwana breaking the skyline.

To include the Isandlwana battle site on your ride, don't take the previous right turn; continue around the back (south side) of the hill and bear east for about 10km. From there, ride south, then along the Ngxobongo stream to where it joins the Buffalo River. Turn right (west) to ride along the northern bank of

A 'traveller's tree' near Rorke's Drift where, perhaps, soldiers dallied on a fateful day on their way to battle back in 1879...

the Buffalo. Soon you pass Fugitive's Drift; from there continue on a bridle path until you reach a low concrete bridge. This marks the spot where a Zulu impi, blooded at Isandlwana, crossed the river to meet its Waterloo at Rorke's Drift.

Across the river to the left is the new Rorke's Drift Hotel (a thatch lodge, actually). The Rorke's Drift battle site and museum complex is just up and over the hill and it's well worth a linger.

From the museum complex, take the gravel road south for 100m and turn right (west) along what looks like a farm road, passing a windmill that's turned by a merry-go-round. The Rorke's Drift Lodge is well signposted, just about 5km along this road through several farm gates. It's worth the extra pedal.

STAGE 3
RORKE'S DRIFT LODGE TO ELANDSLAAGTE   93km

GRADE: Long, hard
OVERNIGHT: Mawelawela Lodge

IN A NUTSHELL

After a hard slog up from Rorke's Drift, we've devised for you a sneaky short cut across to, and then down, the awesome Van Tonder's Pass, along which the British made a hasty withdrawal (you can't do otherwise) from Dundee to Ladysmith after the Anglo-Boer War battle of Talana Hill. This is followed by a 20km cruise on tar into Wasbank. From here you follow the railway to Elandslaagte, but it's a hard slog, crunching and grinding most of the way on loose aggregate.

Snapshot of the experience

Things did not go well for the Boers at Elandslaagte (the battle site lies in Nambiti Private Game Reserve, 3km from the station, on the hillside to the southeast), where they were put to flight and to the sword by a squadron of British 5th Lancers regiment. This showed that the British could, with intelligent strategy, match the Boers' withering fire power.

Our own 'battle of Elandslaagte' was tucking into *slap* chips and pies in the sorry little settlement of Wasbank. As with the British's first assault on Spioenkop, it seemed like a win until an hour later, when we had to evacuate the meal next to the railway line.

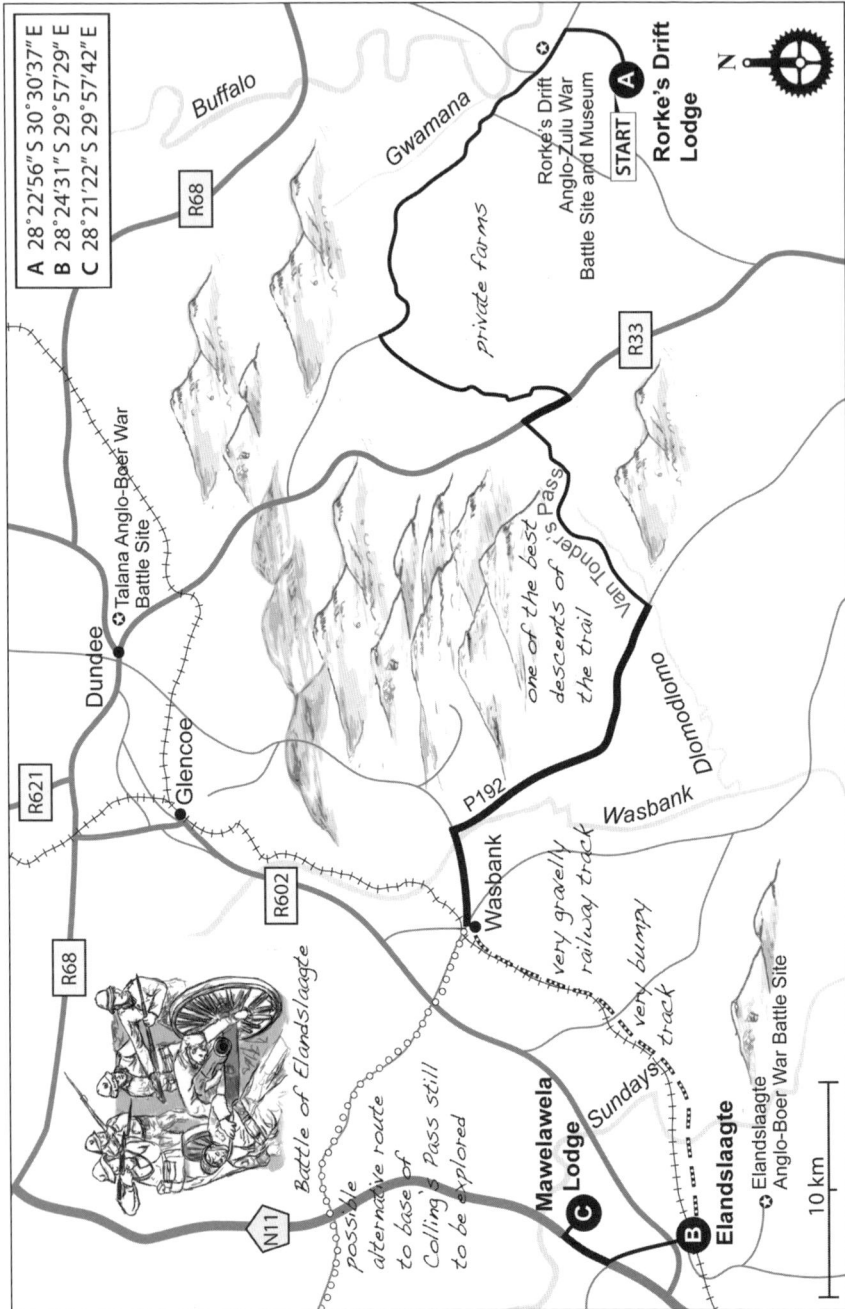

A 28°22'56"S 30°30'37"E
B 28°24'31"S 29°57'29"E
C 28°21'22"S 29°57'42"E

N

Buffalo

Gwamana

R68

Rorke's Drift

✪ Rorke's Drift
Anglo-Zulu War
Battle Site and Museum

START — A

**Rorke's Drift
Lodge**

private farms

R33

✪ Talana Anglo-Boer War
Battle Site

Van Tonder's Pass

one of the best
descents of
the trail

Dlomodlomo

Dundee

Glencoe

R621

R68

R602

Wasbank

P192

Wasbank

Battle of Elandslaagte

very gravelly
railway track

very bumpy
track

Mawelawela

**Mawelawela
Lodge**

C

N11

possible
alternative route
to base of
Colling's Pass still
to be explored

Sundays

B **Elandslaagte**

✪ Elandslaagte
Anglo-Boer War Battle Site

10 km

At the real Battle of Spioenkop, the British mistook a minor point for the summit, were soundly shot down, counter-attacked and forced the Boers off the summit, only to retreat in disarray, allowing the Boers to reoccupy the strategic vantage point. The Kop stand at Anfield Stadium in Liverpool commemorates this battle.

So many things happen every day on a long ride: riding into large herds of cattle, dodging potholes and taxis on the roads, getting lost down decreasing tracks that terminate at rivers or hard up against mountains, ending up with 'gippo guts' from bad pies.

The route

If you're able to tear yourself away from the overwhelming generosity of the 4-star lodge's chef and host, retrace the 5km back to Rorke's Drift battle site. Swing a left (northwest) to ride roughly parallel to the Buffalo River for about 7km, till the main course of the river veers northeast. Continue northwest, following the Gwamana tributary for 7km.

From climbing gently upstream, where the route now swings west, the incline steepens and you top out at around 1400m, before swinging northwest again (an alternate route is blocked by private farms and there's no visible way through). For a while pastoral Zululand gives way to formal KwaZulu-Natal-style farms where the route turns sharp left (southwest).

After some kilometres of roller-coaster riding, you climb slowly for about 10km where you reach the tarred R33; here, do a sharp right for 2km towards Dundee. Turn off the tar to the left, where begins the best part of the day's ride – a 13km sweeping, swooping, turning, tumbling ride down Van Tonder's Pass, dropping 350m into the Dlomodlomo River gorge.

There you hit the sort-of tarred P192, heading right (west) on tar for 34km to the sad settlement of Wasbank, where the Voortrekkers stopped to wash before taking up position for the impending battle of Blood River.

There is absolutely nothing redeeming about the 20km ride along the train line from Wasbank to Elandslaagte stations, passing several ruins of stations where steam trains once ran. The service road is a bed of sharp gravel that makes riding rather unpleasant. In summer it becomes an overgrown gauntlet run of slapping buffalo grass and thorn branches. There just doesn't seem to be a decent alternative. If there is, it lies within the Nambiti Private Game Reserve that seems to occupy a vast tract of virgin veld in these parts.

There was no-one home at the Elandslaagte backpackers where we'd intended to stay, which leaves no other place thereabouts. To reach Mawelawela Lodge, ride about 5km up the N11 (north) towards Newcastle. You pass an old coal mine on the right and then a farm stall; the lodge is in an old mining village a few kilometres further on.

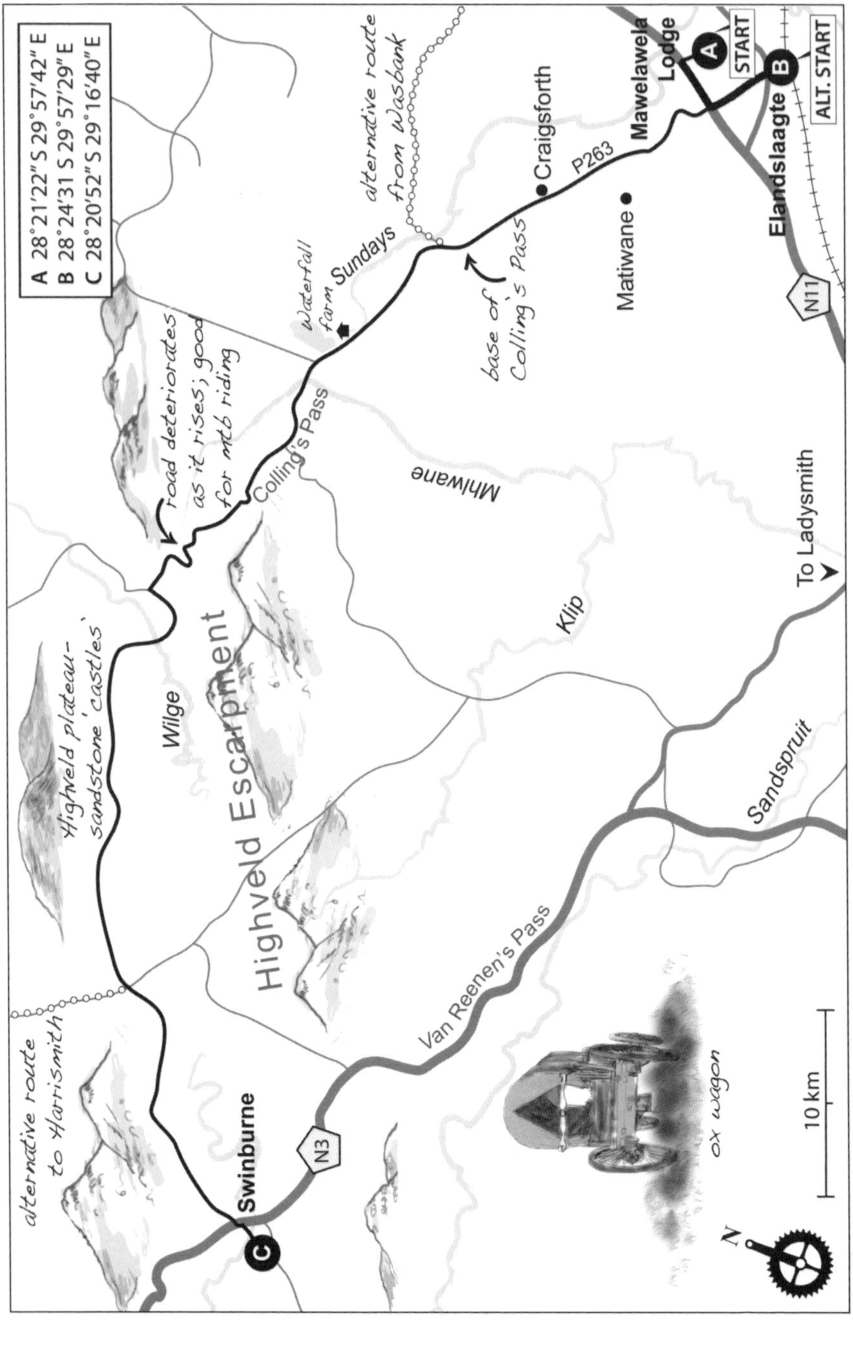

A 28°21'22" S 29°5742" E
B 28°2431 S 29°5729" E
C 28°20'52" S 29°1640" E

START
A
B
ALT. START

Mawelawela Lodge
Craigsforth
P263
Matiwane
Mhlwane
Elandslaagte
N11

To Ladysmith

alternative route from Wasbank

Waterfall farm
Sundays
base of Colling's Pass
Colling's Pass

road deteriorates as it rises; good for mtb riding

Highveld plateau – sandstone castles

Wilge

Klip

Highveld Escarpment

Sandspruit

Van Reenen's Pass

Swinburne
C
N3

alternative route to Harrismith

ox wagon

10 km

N

STAGE 4
ELANDSLAAGTE TO SWINBURNE   93km
ALTERNATIVE ROUTE: ELANDSLAAGTE   114km
TO HARRISMITH

GRADE: Long, hard (to Swinburne); Long, hard (to Harrismith)
OVERNIGHT: Waterfall Farmstead B&B (Colling's Pass); Mount Olive Stables Cottage (Swinburne); Various options (Harrismith), see Useful contacts (p. 202)

IN A NUTSHELL

This and the next stage sound more complicated than they are, because we offer alternative routes (for those who do and those who don't want to ride the gnarly western route around Sterkfontein dam). This is where you have to scale the Great Escarpment, which is why, as Steve puts it, 'This is one bite-the-bullet day, or two bite-the-ham-sandwich days.' The routing on the next three days is open to discussion and alteration, depending on the abilities of your group.

Snapshot of the experience

The day's route-finding problems were compounded by the tempting passes to choose from. In short, our route took us from Elandslaagte, up Colling's Pass to Swinburne. Instead of staying over, we decided to press on to the top of Oliviershoek Pass where we overnighted at Windmill Lodge (formerly the Caterpillar and Catfish Cookhouse) – making it a very long day. The next day's route took us around the south and west sides of Sterkfontein dam to Phuthaditjhaba.

The poet AC Swinburne (after whom this little outpost of a long-lost empire might well be named) wrote some vile anti-Boer poetry, notably 'Transvaal', from which even some of his own countryfolk shrank in shame. At the other extreme stands Thomas Hardy, denounced as a pacifist (a dirty word at the time) for his anti-war sentiments. His poem 'Drummer Hodge' is one of the finest of the period.

The route

Altogether, our initial route made for a very challenging two days, but perhaps not the best for mountain bike touring. It was more like mountain bike warfare. Hence, we've reconfigured this part of the route. The recommended option is to ride straight through from Elandslaagte to Swinburne, a tough 90-odd kilometre day. Alternatively, if you want to avoid the next day's strenuous ride around Sterkfontein dam, you can reroute via Harrismith (114km), overnighting at Waterfall farm, 30km up Colling's Pass, to give those legs a rest.

Back to the day's route: From Mawelawela Lodge, near Elandslaagte, back-pedal about 4km south, past the lodge's farm stall (where you'll want to stock up if you plan to overnight at Waterfall farm) to where the gravel P263 crosses the tarred N11. Turn right here; this is the Colling's Pass road. After about 7km of steady ascending through a bucolic pastoral area named Matiwane (after a Zulu warlord around the time of Shaka), the road branches to the right. Then cross the Cwembe stream, a tributary of the Sundays River that flows into the Thukela.

Continue ascending through the Craigsforth area of scattered dwellings. The road dips and crests as it follows the general course of the Sundays River. At about 30km the Waterfall farm sign appears on the right (for the 'ham sandwich' option, turn in here). If you're pushing on, continue further upstream to about 40km from the tarred road (altitude 1140m), past a large dam on your right. From here the route follows a windy-windy track along the Mhlwane tributary till you reach the Free State border on the watershed, at around 1800m altitude.

The district gravel road steadily gets narrower, becomes less frequently used and its condition progressively worse (we would say it improves). It's all high grassland as you descend towards the Wilge River. The road splits and you do a big loop around to the left to cross the river by narrow causeway. This is where you begin to see 'giant's castles' – sandstone bastions looming out of the grasslands like fortresses. They are the eroded remains of a landscape that once supported a thick slab of Drakensberg basalt. Interspersed are wetlands where you might see congregations of waterbirds in spring and summer.

Ride around Nelson's Kop, one of the impressive sandstone castles, then reach a crossroads – and a decision: keep left to overnight in Swinburne or push on to the Windmill Lodge in Oliviershoek Pass, and then ride round Sterkfontein dam to Phuthaditjhaba the next day; or go right to overnight in Harrismith (keep left, swing left again onto the tarred R34 to town), with the next day's ride taking you to Lesotho via Kestell and the Golden Gate Highlands National Park.

©Steve Thomas

Approaching Phuthaditjhaba – farmers just don't provide gates where you most need them!

On your marks, get ready ... two intrepid mountain bikers stare down the 'old regime' military road under Beit Bridge. (*Baobab Trail*)

Okay, won't be needing these old klonkers anymore ... Steve throws his Zula over a farm gate along the Limpopo River. (*Baobab Trail*)

The Eardstapper doesn't know it but he's seconds away from losing his cycling shoes in the Dzindi River. Rule 1: strap 'em on. (*Baobab Trail*)

Whoa there, big guy! The Daytripper figures how he's going to get around or through morning rush hour in Venda. (*Baobab Trail*)

The now-famous 'Some Werk' (*saamwerk*) food emporium at the Middle Letaba dam wall – the only diner in the district. (*Baobab Trail*)

Our friends Adrian and Robyn arrived with a large bucket of KFC and joined us at Kurisa Moya. (*Bushveld and Berg Trail*)

Sekhu-who? This region in the old Lebowa 'homeland' was named after a chief who gave the Voortrekkers the runaround. (*Bushveld and Berg Trail*)

Evening closes shop near the Lepelle (Olifants) River ... and still we have not found a place to sleep. So we pedal on to Burgersfort. (*Bushveld and Berg Trail*)

Steve holds forth to the youths of Sekhukhuneland on the wonders of travel and other sage things – as is his wont. (*Bushveld and Berg Trail*)

Lovely Iketla Lodge in the hills above Ohrigstad, which we found to be a most relaxing place, with the most generous hosts. (*Bushveld and Berg Trail*)

This little memorial commemorates the Voortrekkers who died of malaria, before they trekked back up to Lydenburg (now Mashishing). (*Bushveld and Berg Trail*)

Approaching Pilgrim's Rest along the upper Motlatse (Blyde) River where it has tumbled down from nearby Long Tom Pass. (*Bushveld and Berg Trail*)

Taking a break on the Hartebeesvlakte, below Mount Anderson, with the Sabie River gorge beckoning below the clouds. (*Timberlands Trail*)

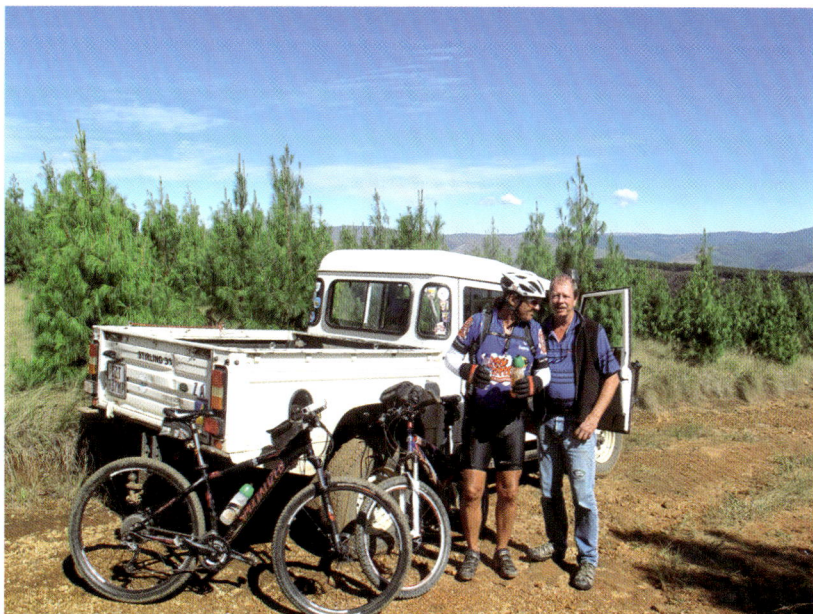

Taking directions at The Narrows, a critical waypoint between Kaapschehoop and the Ngodwana valley. (*Timberlands Trail*)

As winter frost tiptoes across the Mpumalanga lake district, Lake Chrissie rises from a cover of Highveld mist. (*Timberlands Trail*)

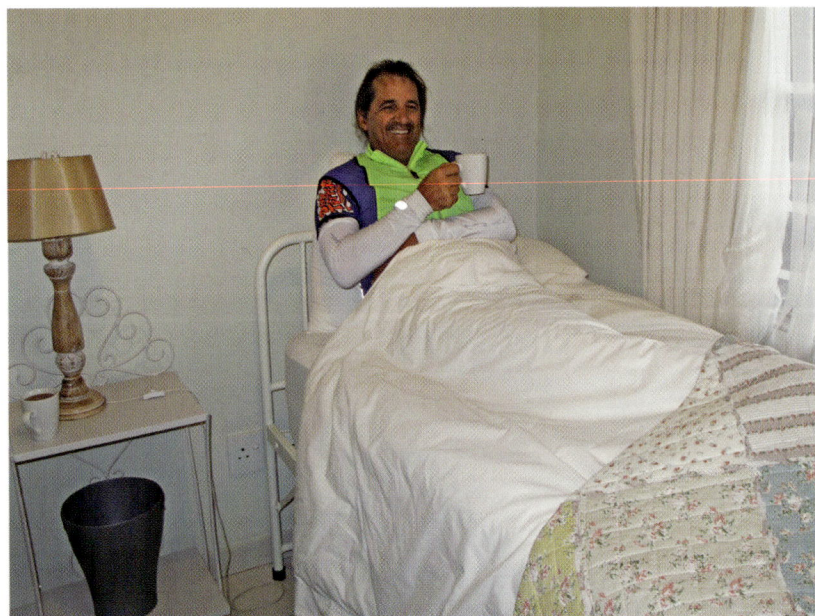

You can ride hard or you can ride soft: Steve psychs himself up to leave his warm bed at LA Guesthouse and hit the cold road. (*Timberlands Trail*)

One of two magnificent bridges near Piet Retief/Mkhondo that are seen only by mountain bikers and railway maintenance workers. (*Timberlands Trail*)

'Excuse me, sir...' Our nonexistent Zulu was good for a laugh while we were asking directions on the Skurweberg near Vryheid. (*Battlefields Trail*)

Steve does his best to chew gum and cycle, all the while conducting peaceful negotiations with the locals near Blood River. (*Battlefields Trail*)

Eating our Waterloo outside Wasbank's finest eating house: two hours later we were retreating in dishonour. (*Battlefields Trail*)

Washing day at Mawelawela Lodge, before the trail tackles the mighty escarpment via Colling's Pass near Elandslaagte. (*Battlefields Trail*)

A lovely scene above the Windmill Lodge near the top of the Oliviershoek Pass – great fun until the route-around-Sterkfontein-dam part. (*Battlefields Trail*)

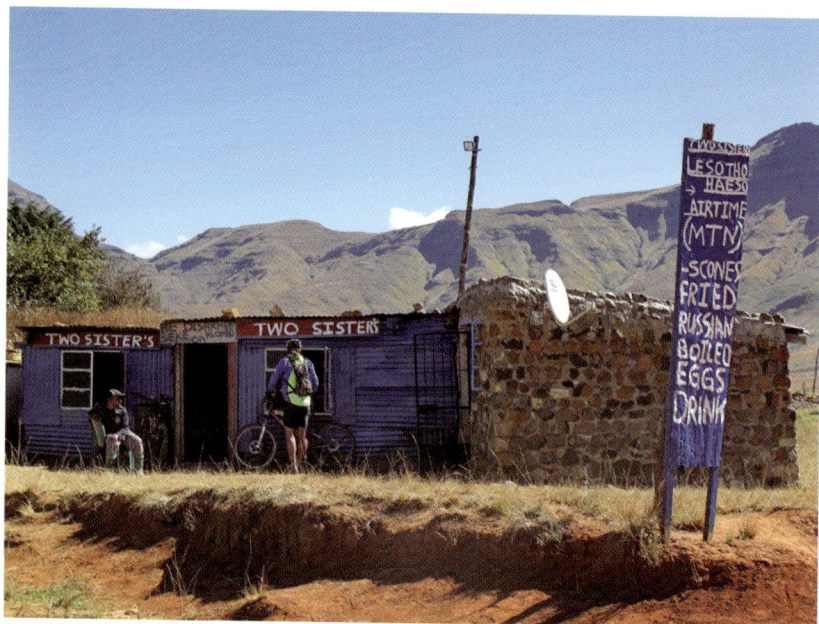

The menu at this spaza in the upper Little Caledon River valley promised much but delivered a whole lot less. (*Roof of Africa Trail*)

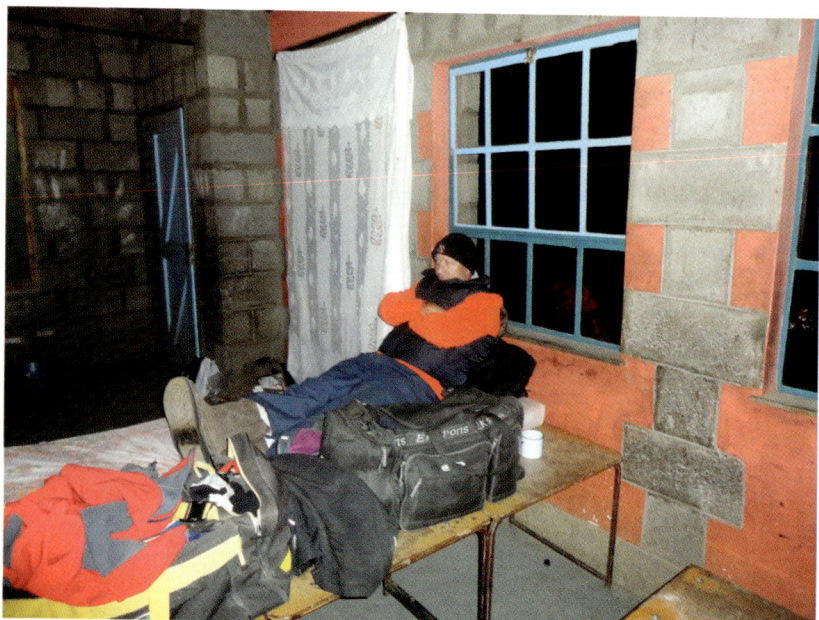

David making the most of the board and lodgings at Motete Primary School, while a storm rages outside. (*Roof of Africa Trail*)

©Steve Thomas

Motete morning – it was early June and winter had come fast to central Lesotho. But life goes on, and so did we. (*Roof of Africa Trail*)

You *can* ride up and over the Maluti watershed, topping out at around 3000m – or you can do it the local way. (*Roof of Africa Trail*)

Crossing the Malibamatso River for maybe the seventh or eighth time on the canyon ride down from Oxbow. (*Roof of Africa Trail*)

Many helpful scouts await your descent into the Senqunyane valley – pray your brakes are in good working condition. (*Roof of Africa Trail*)

The road from Semonkong rocks and rolls and sometimes the easiest way is to push; there are no medals to be won here. (*Roof of Africa Trail*)

In just one hour those fleecy clouds developed into an afternoon storm that chased us down the Maletsunyane valley. (*Roof of Africa Trail*)

While we contemplate the daunting descent to Riverside, a mom and her daughters saunter off to church. (*Roof of Africa Trail*)

From Ketane to Ha Qiqita/Bethel there is one monster climb, but then it's all downhill to the solar capital of Lesotho. (*Roof of Africa Trail*)

STAGE 5
SWINBURNE TO OLIVIERSHOEK PASS 48km + 46km
TO PHUTHADITJHABA
ALTERNATIVE ROUTE: HARRISMITH 53km + 55km
TO KESTELL TO HA NAPO/HA MPHAKHA

GRADE: Short, moderate (Swinburne to Oliviershoek Pass); Short, hard (Oliviershoek to Phuthaditjhaba); Medium, moderate (Harrismith to Kestell); Medium, hard (Kestell to Ha Napo/Ha Mphakha)
OVERNIGHT: Windmill Lodge (Oliviershoek Pass); Hae@home Guest House (Phuthaditjhaba); Qwantani Berg & Bush Resort (Sterkfontein dam, Kestell)

IN A NUTSHELL
Some local Winterton riders joined us on this day to help us find a route around the southwest side of Sterkfontein dam to Phuthaditjhaba, our gateway into northeast Lesotho. Discovery: there is no easy way around this side of the dam. But it took six hours of really hard slog to work that out. This route will be far too hard for riders looking for a more sociable touring route, so a better option for nontechnical riders is to go from Colling's Pass to Harrismith and Kestell.

Snapshot of the experience
For having earlier taken the easy way out of Pilgrim's Rest to Long Tom Pass, we were punished on this day. The first 10km after leaving Windmill Lodge took us more than three hours, bike-hiking sometimes on paths, sometimes not, through rank veld, dongas and vleis, and over sandstone ridges. It was as tough as any mountain bike ride has any right to be.

The route
From Swinburne
At Swinburne, from the N3, duck around the back of the Shell Ultra City, then take the first left onto a gravel road, heading in a southwest direction. This road will take you all the way to the summit of Oliviershoek Pass and Windmill Lodge. About 2km from Swinburne the road does a dogleg, then carries on southwest. After about 7km you swerve south–southwest, and another 7km later you pass a side-junction (Tintwa Pass road) to the left. Carry on to the

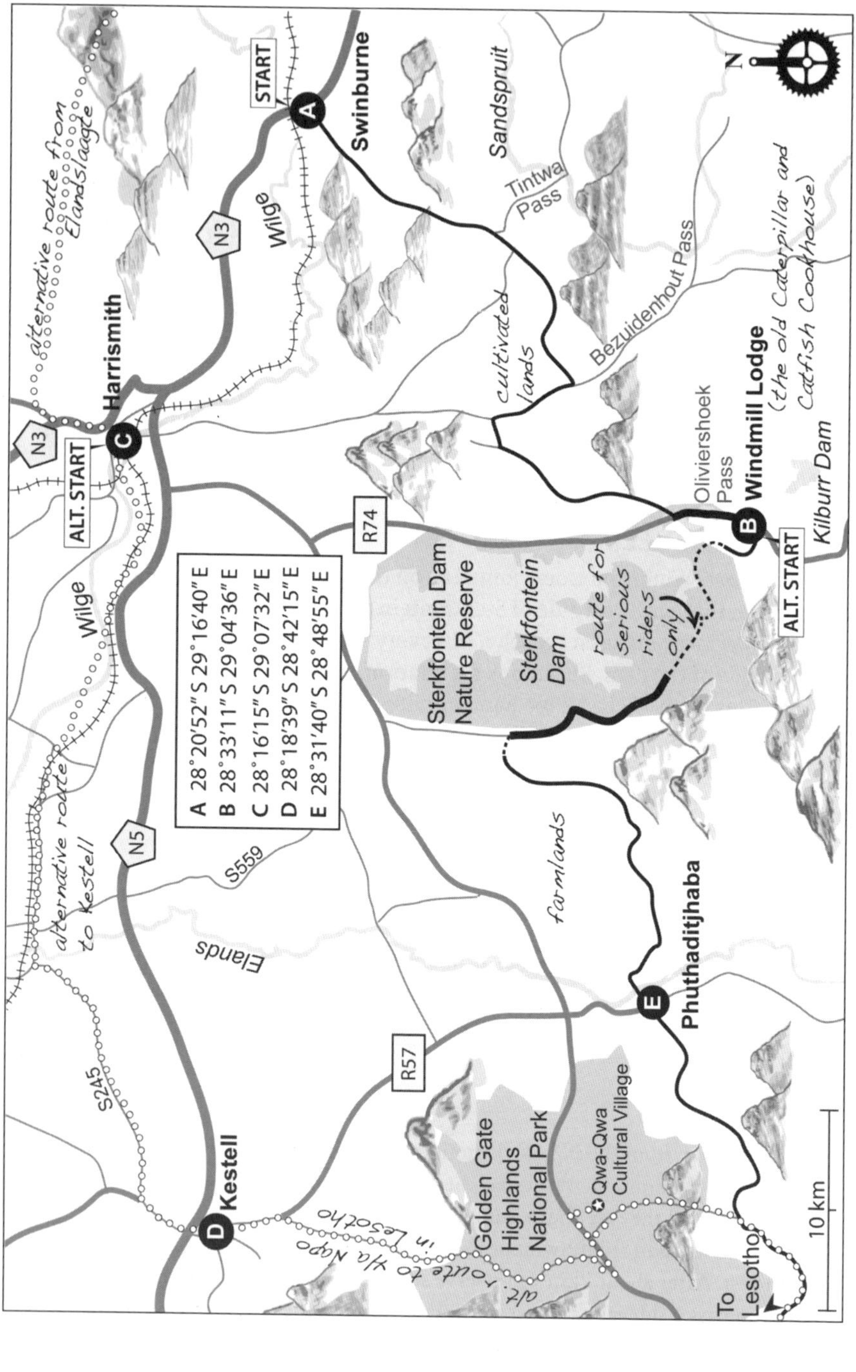

START
A
Swinburne
Sandspruit
Tintwa Pass
Bezuidenhout Pass
N3
Wilge
alternative route from Elandslaagte
Harrismith
C
ALT. START
cultivated lands
Olivershoek Pass
B
Windmill Lodge
(the old Caterpillar and Catfish Cookhouse)
Kilburr Dam
ALT. START
R74
Sterkfontein Dam Nature Reserve
Sterkfontein Dam
route for serious riders only
Wilge
A 28°20'52" S 29°16'40" E
B 28°33'11" S 29°04'36" E
C 28°16'15" S 29°07'32" E
D 28°18'39" S 28°42'15" E
E 28°31'40" S 28°48'55" E
N5
S559
alternative route to Kestell
Elands
farmlands
Phuthaditjhaba
E
R57
S245
Kestell
D
Golden Gate Highlands National Park
Qwa-Qwa Cultural Village
alt. route to Ha Napo in Lesotho
To Lesotho
10 km
N

next turn-off, where you go right, now riding in a northwest direction for about 8km through cultivated lands. Turn left at the next side-junction, following the road until you hit a T-junction, where you turn left to ride parallel to the tarred R74 for 10km. A mere 3km south from where the gravel road joins the R74 lies Windmill Lodge.

While it's not very long, the route from Oliviershoek Pass is severe and will take most of the day. Start off on the track behind the cottages at the lodge, ride up and past a holiday fishing cabin on a small dam, passing through a few stock gates. Swing to the right and the fun begins. The first half of the route follows the southern and southwestern shore of the Sterkfontein dam – not close but always high above. There are paths (sometimes not), but, even where there are, the ground is extremely broken, often marshy, and always hard to ride.

Twice you go through or over game fences or gates. At times, the path, where there is one, goes up quite close to the sandstone cliffs on the left, and here the terrain is very rough. Where the track comes to a small farm and it feels like Phuthaditjhaba is just a hop and a skip over the ridge, you have to take the road north to continue along the lake shore on a roller-coaster profile. Eventually you pick up a tarred road and swing away from the lake, first through farmlands and then into town. Watch out for taxis; ride on the sidewalk where you can.

From Harrismith

From town, hit the railway and follow it west as it gets squeezed between the N5 (left) and Wilge River (right). Where the line turns right (northwest), pick up a nice farm road lined with gum trees on the north side of the railway, although it doesn't run exactly parallel to the line. Wetlands and pans make this route prettier.

The line crosses the Wilge twice via attractive arched bridges where you might have to *pundamatenga* (pick up and carry), but you can ride alongside the track in between. About 3km from the second bridge, the railway follows a gravel road; you can follow either (where the road runs north of the line). About 12km further you have to leave the railway; take the second of two gravel roads to the left (south) – the Elands River runs between them so you can't go wrong.

The railway goes under the first road, then over the river on a bridge, then over the second road. Turn left here and follow the S245 for 15km to the tarred R57. Turn left (south); the road follows a stream for the first 4km, then goes through cultivated lands. At the tarred road turn left. Pretty Kestell is 5.5km further.

A final word on routing: if you go via Oliviershoek Pass, you might want to overnight at Windmill Lodge before tackling the tough ride to Phuthaditjhaba; if you go via Kestell, you'll probably want to do one push of about 55km directly to Ha Napo/Ha Mphakha in Lesotho – otherwise it will be one easy day of 32km to Qwa-Qwa cultural village in the Golden Gate Highlands National Park, and another, more challenging, 33km to Ha Napo/Ha Mphakha beyond.

RECOMMENDED
11 days

Roof of Africa Trail

Phuthaditjhaba to Holy Cross Mission • 544km

STAGE 1
PHUTHADITJHABA TO HA NAPO/   35km
HA MPHAKHA

GRADE: Short, hard; severe riding
OVERNIGHT: Chief Napo's household cottage

IN A NUTSHELL

From the time you leave Phuthaditjhaba and head for the Mountain Kingdom of Lesotho, the normal measures of distance begin to lose their meaning among the towering basalt ramparts of the Maluti mountains. Monantsa Pass is the big issue of the day; riding up it is just a warm-up, if you like, for the huge haul to the top of the range that awaits tomorrow. From the border post (don't forget your passport), you race down the Little Caledon River valley and suddenly the life you know seems to fade away behind the golden sandstone promontories, like gates that open onto a magical kingdom then shut behind you.

Snapshot of the experience

The Two Sisters spaza shop at the bottom of the real hair-raising downhill side of Monantsa Pass promised us airtime, scones, hot Russians and other delights… Promises, promises. We settled for cold drinks and a game of pool instead. As for the airtime, you can buy some, but you won't be able to use it here.

Chief Napo, in whose village you'll overnight, is a delightful old man with kind authority; he's also a keen supporter of the new Trans Lesotho trail we were helping to ride, to sort out the wrinkles. We were already tucked into our rondavel when our local guide Tumi Taabe (organised by Trans Lesotho founder David Waddilove) arrived after a 10-hour taxi ride from Maseru. Mountain bike champion of Lesotho, Tumi was tasked with shepherding us through his country and sorting out trail logistics. Without his interpretation skills, we would certainly have become lost – and maybe unstuck.

The route

The ride out of Phuthaditjhaba is on tar until you reach Monantsa Pass proper at a hairpin bend about 12km from the start (1700m altitude). So far you've been in built-up areas but now the outskirts look more like Rwanda than South Africa.

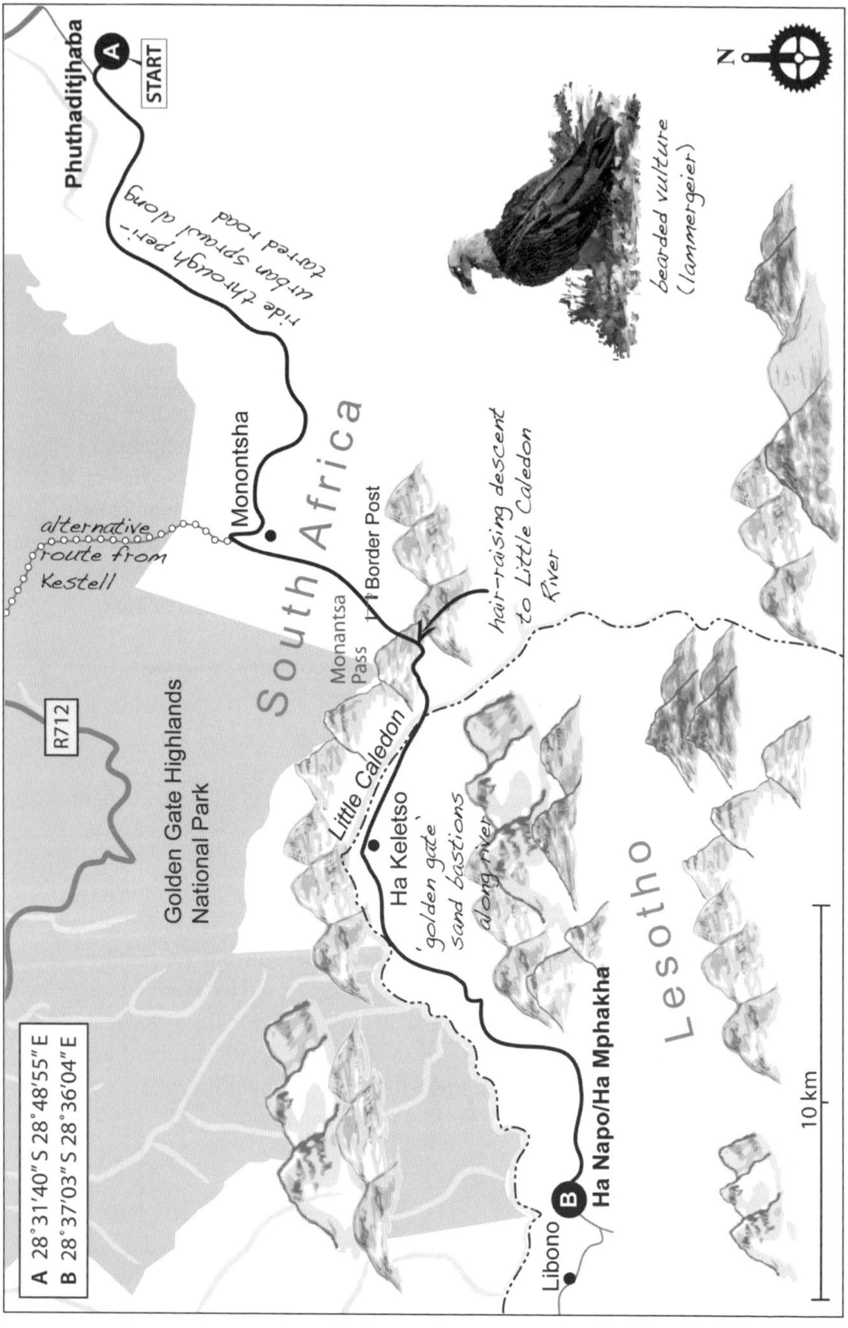

A 28°31'40"S 28°48'55"E
B 28°37'03"S 28°36'04"E

N

START

Phuthaditjhaba

ride through peri-
urban sprawl along
tarred road

Monontsha

South Africa

alternative
route from
Kestell

Border Post

Monantsa
Pass

R712

Golden Gate Highlands
National Park

Little Caledon

Ha Keletso

hair-raising descent
to Little Caledon
River

'golden gate'
sand bastions
along river

Lesotho

bearded vulture
(lammergeier)

Ha Napo/Ha Mphakha

B

Libono

10 km

Slogging up to the border post: whoever Monantsa was, he must have been one fit geezer.

The hairpin bend is at altitude 1900m, and over the next 6.5km, on gravel, you will ascend to an altitude of just over 2200m at the border post. More than likely a chill wind is pummelling the place. (That hairpin bend is where you would rejoin the route on a path up from Kestell via Qwa-Qwa cultural village.)

From there, for nearly 5km you bomb down into, and then along, the upper valley of the Little Caledon River forming the border between South Africa and Lesotho. You'll notice much of the land, even the steepest ground, is heavily cultivated, villages and homesteads dotted all over the mountains.

At the base of the pass proper, a place called Ha Keletso is where you find the Two Sisters spaza shop and pool emporium, where you should stop for some R&R (don't expect too much!). The valley floor then flattens out, although you're still travelling down a young stream's course. The road, due to the rugged topography of interlocking spurs, ascends and descends frequently, which of course means a need for leg and lung power. But the magnificent landscape really takes the sting out of the ride, even if you are gravity-challenged.

A little more than 3km from the spaza shop, the road slowly moves away from the river to keep an average elevation of around 2000 to 2200m. It crosses many tributaries, each of which demands a swift descent followed by a stiff ascent.

The final 7km to Chief Napo's is theoretically 'flat' if you average out the route, but it's a tough ride at the end of the day (more so if this is a long day for you, from Kestell). The overnighting homestead Ha Napo is located on a slight rise (on Google Earth it's shown as Ha Mphakha).

If the chief is not about, anyone there will help you. Firing up hot water is sure to be your priority – as is organising horse backup for the following day if you think you might need it (it's well worth the small price – about R50 – believe us).

STAGE 2
HA NAPO/HA MPHAKHA TO OXBOW LODGE 26km

GRADE: Short, hard; extreme riding
OVERNIGHT: Oxbow Lodge

IN A NUTSHELL

What a ridge, what a push, what a crest! Who would think that a mere 26km ride could be such a big adventure, taking just about all day (seven hours' riding). What starts as a very steep road out of the village soon regresses to a mishmash of sheep and horse tracks on the slippery slopes of the high Malutis. It's a hard three-hour slog to climb the 920m to the top of the ridge, cresting at 2920m.

Snapshot of the experience

Two bearded vultures – *ntsu* in the local lingo – soared over the impressive basalt bastions as we millimetred our way up the … 'tormenting' is the only word that comes to mind … ridiculously steep mountainside.

And then, as I was taking a wide sweep across a shallow stream bed, the back wheel of my bike kicked out, throwing me onto some sharp rocks and a broken bottle, which compromised my next few days of riding. New motto: be prepared for the worst here and make sure you have a plan B for emergency evacuation, if necessary. I managed to get a passing local to lend me his horse while he pushed my bike (for a fee) to the top of the next ridge, from where I freewheeled down to Oxbow. What a day.

'It was an incredible adventure,' reckoned Steve. By which he meant slogging across rivers and vleis, bouncing over tufty Afro-alpine slopes, flying over rocky runnels, racing after wild horses, racing away even faster from Basotho herd dogs – the furry ones that look like bears, not your common or garden thin-ribbed 'Canis africanis'.

The route

You start directly across the road from the hut, head up a steep bank, across a soccer field and onto a track leading up the Pitseng valley. It rounds a spur and starts to climb steeply up the right-hand side of the valley – a horseshoe-shaped amphitheatre surrounded by ridges reaching nearly 3000m.

A 28°37'03"S 28°36'04"E
B 28°46'16"S 28°38'23"E

START

A Ha Napo/Ha Mphakha

Libono

long, steep ascent to the summit of the Maluti mountains – a good place to hire a pony

Magokoeng

Pitseng

3000m

2920m at nek

3000m

freeride descent through broken grass slopes where wild horses roam

Tsehlanyane

alternative route

hairpin corners

A1

Malibamatso

B

Oxbow Lodge

N

5 km

It's a climb of about 9.5km, ascending 920m, to a nek far ahead across the bowl of the amphitheatre. The air gets thin up there and it's a hard push (you can ride only short sections or not at all along broken goat tracks). We hired Basotho guides and their ponies, first riding them but then allowing the ponies to carry our bikes while we walked. Pushing a bike up these narrow tracks has the pedals inflicting constant knocks against your shins.

From the nek the path turns southwest down towards the Tsehlanyane River, keeping to the less steep ground to the left before veering right along the left-hand bank, but still high above the river. Another good reason for a local guide is that the route-finding is tricky and will consume much time and energy.

Higher up there is no real path, although you pick it up in places, only to lose it again as you go bouncing over thick tufts of grass and swampy, stony ground. The track (as in GPS rather than road) weaves in and out of the side-valleys and gullies, descending parallel to the river but still high above it for about 4km. As the valley broadens, you move closer to the river and pick up a more defined path for 2.5km. With 2km to go in the valley, the floor flattens out; there is an army post and hydrological station up ahead. Take care not to go too fast here as wet ground can be extremely slippery.

Here you reach the tarred A1; turn left on it, heading due south for a few hundred metres. Where the road swings left, you have a choice: take the tarred road steeply up, then hair-raisingly down, or cross the road and follow the track that connects the villages along the steep slope below the road. Where this track

In Lesotho the hoof is still often mightier than the carbon and titanium wheel.

©Steve Thomas

touches the tarred road at the apex of the hill, it's best to ride on the tar to the lodge to avoid attacks by vicious village dogs.

By road it's about 7km to the lodge, with one steep and sustained ascent followed by an even longer, dangerous descent with successive perilously tight hairpin corners and local traffic that doesn't stick to any particular side of the road (mostly dictated by potholes and cutting corners). The Oxbow is a comfortable, modern facility but a touch pricey (we negotiated a special Trans Lesotho cycling deal so do insist on it).

STAGE 3
OXBOW LODGE TO MOTETE   36km

GRADE: Short, extreme; lots of portage and river crossings
OVERNIGHT: Motete Primary School

IN A NUTSHELL

The landscape, the scenery, the wildness of the place cannot be surpassed. But remember this is Lesotho, and everything is up. You could – like us – cover the first 20km in seven hours but the next 20km in just two hours (the seven hours are a whole story in themselves).

Once the river valley narrows you are seldom able to ride more than 200m at a time without having to uncleat and carry your bike across some obstacle or ford the river or climb a ridge (and that means climb, with bike in one hand, the other clawing on rock faces like a baboon).

Snapshot of the experience

It's up to Trans Lesotho guide Tumi to oversee making this route more rideable for future Trans Lesotho trailists and Spine of the Dragon adventurers. He has NGO funds, and while we were there he was already getting local shepherds to widen and fix the path in places.

The next obstacle is booking accommodation in a place that has little or no modern infrastructure. The plan is that trailists contact Tumi, who contacts the school to organise board and lodgings. We slept on mattresses on the school desks and washed in plastic basins on the floor (hot water provided). There was no food available, so we broke open our emergency rations – bread, bully beef, cheese wedges and crisps. If it's beer you need, you'll find it.

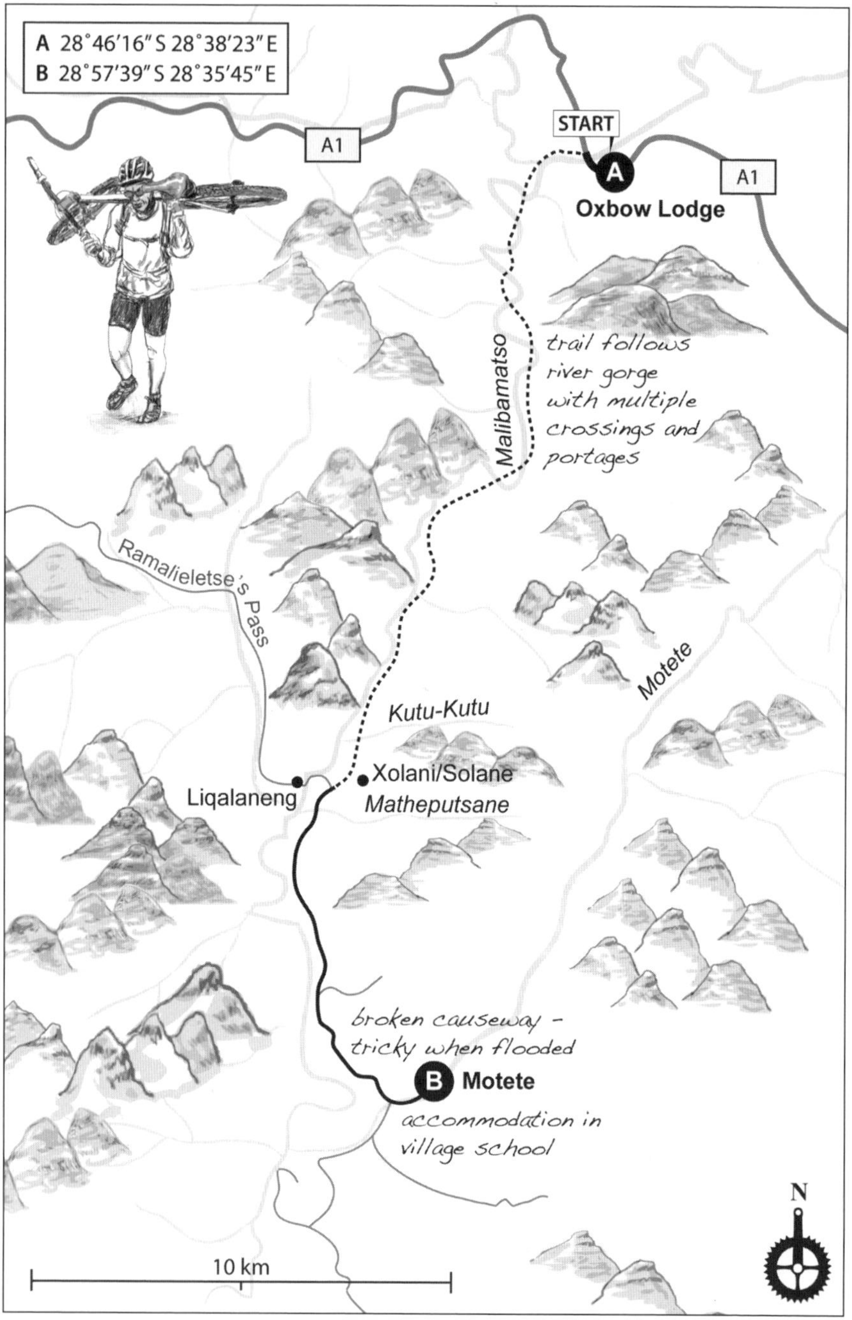

A 28°46'16"S 28°38'23"E
B 28°57'39"S 28°35'45"E

A1

START

A Oxbow Lodge

A1

Malibamatso

trail follows
river gorge
with multiple
crossings and
portages

Motete

Ramalieletse's Pass

Kutu-Kutu

Liqalaneng • Xolani/Solane
Matheputsane

broken causeway –
tricky when flooded

B Motete

accommodation in
village school

N

10 km

The route

Leave the lodge the way you came in, head to the supposed camping area, where you turn left down the right-hand bank of the Malibamatso on a jeep track. Just over 2km from the start is the first of several river crossings. A pony track runs along the left-hand bank, rising to crest spurs and descending close to the river in between, also bypassing where the river loops widely.

And so it continues for about 13km to the next crossing. At one point you ascend a side-stream gully to go around a hillock before regaining the main valley; scaling a rock band here requires concerted effort and much bike lugging and lifting. Any less-than-hardy members of the party might need help here. The river crossings, too, can be potentially dangerous in places if the river is in spate.

From the second crossing, another three follow in quick succession over a distance of about 1.7km (it's hard to be precise due to the nature of the path and all the dismounting, pushing and carrying). Make the fourth crossing at the gravel bank, but take care where the river runs narrowest and strongest (always keep the bike downstream of your body so it doesn't push you over).

Now you head down the right-hand bank. Where there is more than one path, opt for the higher one (even though it requires a 60m ascent) to avoid the dense riverine growth or coming up against steep cliffs lower down. Here you'll find amazing terraced cultivated fields – even on the steepest slopes.

You descend again to the river, pass through fields, ascend again, tracking left around a high spur as you head for the village of Xolani/Solane, lying between the Kutu-Kutu and Matheputsane streams. Cross the Kutu-Kutu, staying at that level, and wend your way to the right, just below the huts, until you pick up a gravel road – part rough jeep track, part half-decent gravel.

Fording the challenging Malibamatso south of Oxbow ... for about the 900th time that day.

Follow it for about 12.5km or so, as the road climbs and descends around high spurs – sometimes gently, sometimes steeply; sometimes above villages, sometimes below; sometimes zigzagging across streams and fields. The riding now is totally exhilarating. The Malibamatso is constantly below on your right, but if you take the wrong line around some of the very sharp bends it could be your carcass they have to retrieve from the slope.

Eventually you scoot down to the Motete, a large tributary of the Malibamatso, crossing via a damaged concrete causeway that will be underwater when in spate. At the T-junction on the opposite bank, turn left. Ride for about 1.2km to find the school on your left; you'll have been on the road for some nine hours. If you've made the necessary arrangements you will be welcomed there. Conditions and amenities are sparse, so just smile and play along.

STAGE 4
MOTETE TO HA LEJONE   40km

GRADE: Short, hard; severe to extreme riding
OVERNIGHT: Motebong Village Holiday Resort

IN A NUTSHELL
The accommodation might at times be sub-star, but you're in for a five-star mountain biking adventure. You have to surmount two quite hectic ridges, the first on a passable road-track (ride it as best you can but push-walk when you need to). The second involves some serious bundu-bashing, so here we again highly recommend a Basotho and his pony. But for two big hills, the day offers expansive views across the serpentine Malibamatso River, its many tributaries, and the high ridges and peaks that mark their headwaters.

Snapshot of the experience
Were the landscape to be all developed and the tracks well tended, the riding would seem so much easier. However, because we are moving through such dramatic, and in some ways aggressive, terrain we tend to think we are conquering much harder tasks than maybe we **are**. Then we **really** make hard work of it. Still, this trip 'ain't no disco, it ain't no foolin' around', as the Talking Heads song puts it.

A 28°57'39"S 28°35'45"E
B 29°06'18"S 28°30'03"E

START

A **Motete**

● Pulane

● Liteleng

road from Oxbow

Khutlo-Sea-Ja

Malibamatso

very long, steep
climb – consider
hiring a pony here

Senyenyane

cross
footbridge
here ...

● Vuka-Mosotho

Ligalaneng

A25

Ha Lejone **B**

...or here

tarred

Katse
Dam

Laitsoka
Pass

N

10 km

The route

From Motete, follow the road-track down the left-hand bank of the river, swinging around to south and keeping right where a path goes up a steepish valley to the left. The track contours and climbs above the river, rising steadily for about 300m to Liteleng village. It then begins to descend the crinkled, steep hillside below Pulane village towards the stream, where it doubles back to meet the road from Oxbow. Turn left here and follow the river upstream for 1km. Cross the river at a ford (it can get messy here), following the road for about 200m.

Where the road appears to cross a side-stream, double back but head up the hillside, west around the hill and towards the Khutlo-Sea-Ja stream (flowing north–south). Follow it uphill, crossing three times over roughly 1km before moving up the right-hand slope away from the stream. This is a particularly steep section where the path pretty much peters out for the most serious part (good idea to find yourself a sturdy pony to carry your bike up here). Eventually the track eases off and rounds a large spur at 2580m altitude. From here the track descends steeply alongside a stream that runs into the Malibamatso River, rounding a wide spur to the left; look down to the river and you can see the 'main' road on the other side.

If the track less travelled seems too daunting, another option is to simply follow the road out of Motete all the way to Ha Lejone. It's a good ride in itself, but you will miss out on the real adventure (the road has lots of smaller hills in place of a few really big ones).

The track – where there is one – meanders well above the river, heading south towards Katse. It's much easier as it generally contours slowly downhill, rising (and falling, of course), as you crest spurs and dip through stream courses. After veering sharply left (east) and back again to ford the Senyenyane tributary, the track reverts to a more southerly direction, following the general line of the main valley but above the steep hillsides flanking the river.

At Vuka-Mosotho village the path veers west to round a prominent spur that looms over the upper waters of the mighty Katse dam as they snake around the muscling mountainsides. You then wend your way east along the steep slope of a side-valley (the Ligalaneng) for about 1.3km, crossing and heading back west on the other side.

As you climb the slopes of the next spur, the Motebong Village Holiday Resort is on an isthmus of land jutting into the lake with Ha Lejone village spreading behind it. You still have to round two spurs, then a third, before descending to the lakeshore to cross via one of the 'Scandinavian' footbridges – common evidence of foreign aid in the country. Take the path to the right, parallel to the lakeshore, to go directly to the resort village. The floating circles you see hold salmon-trout hatchlings, which have come from Franschhoek to be fattened up here before being trucked on ice to your local deli.

STAGE 5
HA LEJONE TO KATSE   56km

GRADE: Medium, moderate
OVERNIGHT: Orion Katse Lodge

IN A NUTSHELL

By Lesotho mountain biking standards, today is a doddle. By most other
standards, you'd probably call it a really tough day's outing. But, when
you've been riding for more than a month on jeep tracks, footpaths and
donkey tracks, you tend to lose perspective. And, given the incredible
vistas here on the Roof of Africa, your perspective is so wide-reaching,
a day out in the hills feels nothing more than a happy caper.

Snapshot of the experience

For us, the sky finally shredded like
a spinnaker ripped apart by a sudden
hurricane blast. It's pretty much all basalt up
here, and when it gets sodden it turns into
the most depressing sort of goo – the kind
where, after a few kays of pedalling, your
bike is twice as heavy as its shop weigh-in.

*Ever wonder about the
'board' part of 'board
and lodgings'? Long ago in
greene olde England, when
you booked into the inne,
they gave you your own
wooden board to sup
on (the water in those
days was not potable
so you drank ale; we
recommend you continue
the custom).*

Now, Katse dam … if you could do the
Spiderman thing underneath the bridge
spanning the dam to get a better view of the
neat ferro-concrete post-and-lintel structure,
you might ask: wonder where those posts
go? The answer is, of course, to the lake
bed. Naturally, the bridge was built before the river basin filled – and then it
was a pretty impressive sight. Yes, dams drown many splendid things, but then
again Katse does provide water and power, without which ongoing large-scale
urbanisation (Gauteng) would not be possible. Good thing or bad?

The route

To get going, retrace your steps to the footbridge, then cross the Malibamatso
and take the footpath about 220m to the hilltop opposite. Follow this path
along the ridge, through planted fields, to meet a more substantial track that
connects the two villages.

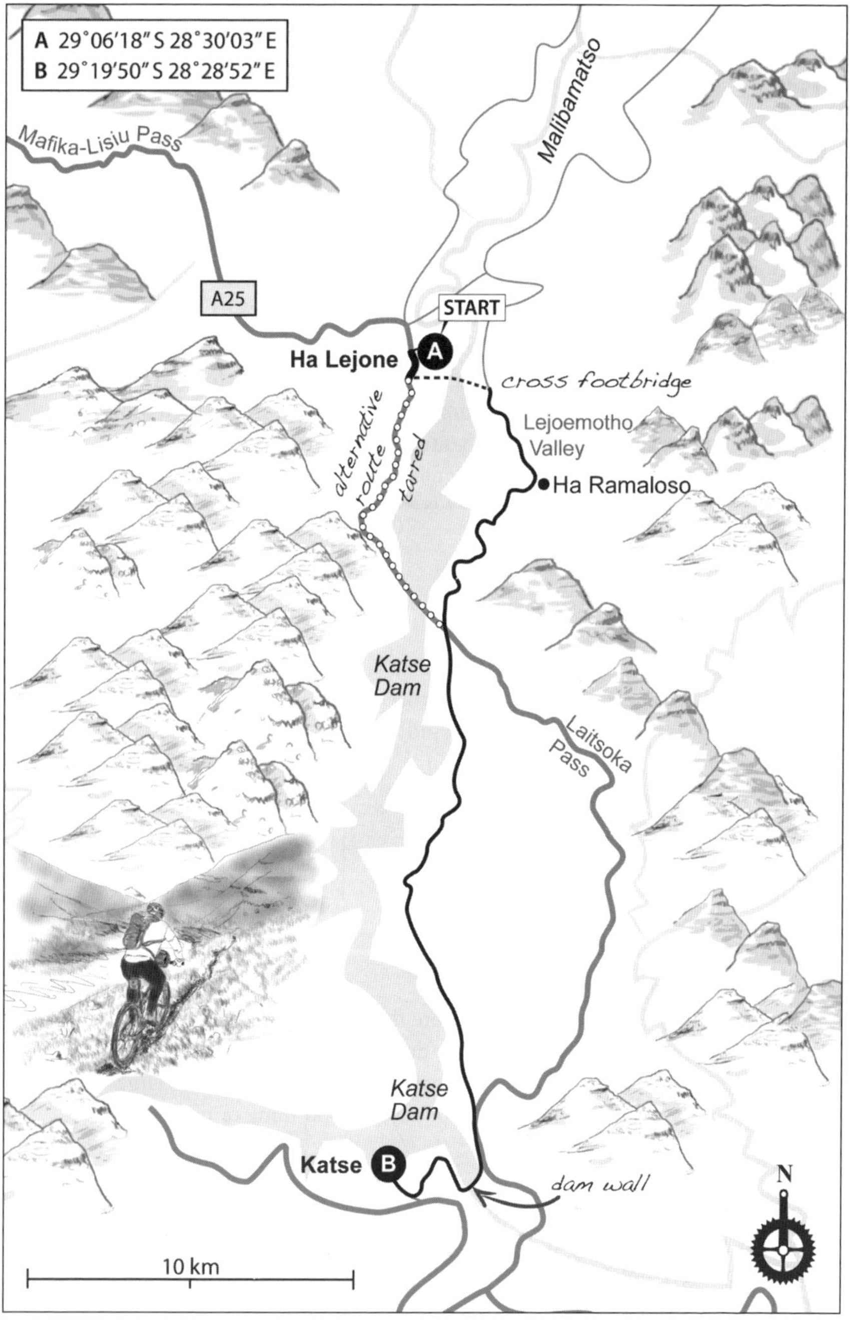

A 29°06'18"S 28°30'03"E
B 29°19'50"S 28°28'52"E

Mafika-Lisiu Pass

Malibamatso

A25

START

Ha Lejone A

cross footbridge

Lejoemotho
Valley

•Ha Ramaloso

alternative route

tarred

*Katse
Dam*

Laitsoka
Pass

*Katse
Dam*

Katse B

dam wall

N

10 km

Head right (south); thus begins one of the easiest, most pleasant runs through this daunting country. When we say it's pretty much all downhill, it is – other than the rises and falls in and out of side-valleys and over interconnecting spurs.

Even the long pull up the Lejoemotho valley is a delight, riding away from the dam, descending via contours to the stream, then riding upstream for 2km. Here the track veers south and uphill through scattered dwellings and fields to Ha Ramaloso village, perched atop a knoll. The next section is just over 7km and includes some really fun downhill streaks through an ever-changing diorama of mountains and flood-filled valley.

Alas, you do meet up with the tarred A25 from Ha Lejone, but only for about 700m. Turn left onto it, then duck right onto a gravel track, sticking close to the dam. The next 22km or so are pretty similar, the snaking lake always on your right. Then the track converges with the tarred road; the dam wall is ahead. If you're lucky the guard will let you through the boom so you can ride over the wall and wend up and around to the right into the village. If not, you'll have to take the long way – on the tarred road – crossing below the dam, then heading back up again towards Katse village. It's a good 6km and one stiff climb longer, so your bargaining skills will come in handy here.

If you wish to maintain the DIY level of board and lodgings you've grown accustomed to, the hotel also offers self-catering accommodation in the village as well as a backpackers' dorm.

STAGE 6
KATSE TO THABA-TSEKA   69km

GRADE: Medium, moderate
OVERNIGHT: The Buffalo's Hotel

IN A NUTSHELL

The route follows a quiet gravel road, carrying more pedestrian and horse traffic than motorised, all the way to Thaba-Tseka. From Katse it follows the general line of the Malibamatso River in a south–east–south course. And it's all downstream. Truly, there are no big climbs, the biggest (according to inexact memory) only 80m over a distance of about 4km – twice it does this. On the other hand, the road does go up-down, up-down, the entire way – as you would expect.

| A | 29°19'50" S 28°28'52" E |
| B | 29°31'17" S 28°36'18" E |

Katse Dam

START

Katse Ⓐ

Ha Mensel

Malibamatso

Linkaaneng

*a beautiful day's riding
through the central mountains
on 'easy' dirt roads – spectacular scenery*

Makhoabeng

Beresi

Kholo-Ntso

Ha Leoka

Ha Khomo
Li-Ileng

typical Lesotho spaza shop

Maboloka

Thaba-Tseka
Ⓑ

A3

Molikaliko

To The
Buffalo's Hotel

N

10 km

Snapshot of the experience

Thaba-Tseka is where, on the tarred road from Maseru to Sani Pass, the tar runs out. Actually, it runs out a few times between Maseru and here, with road works courtesy of the Chinese. It's strange to see workers alongside this road in Chinese straw hats; it kind of lets you know what the future will look like. The town is pretty much run by one Chinese family, none of whose members speaks any local Southern African dialect (there are quite a few to choose from).

You could summarise the day something like this: a lovely ride out in the African countryside, with more mountains to shake an energy bar at than you can count.

The route

The route-finding onto the Thaba-Tseka road is tricky, but here goes: head out of Katse village on the tarred road (watch out for the stop streets). At the T-junction turn left to ride past the dam wall and admin complex, and turn right with the road as it descends around the big hill. Just after it turns sharply to the left you come to Makhoabeng village, where our track heads uphill to the right (southwest). Follow this gravel road for 53km all the way to the T-junction on the outskirts of Thaba-Tseka, where you hit the road, tarred in places, from Maseru.

By now you know that following trails in Lesotho is all about dodging rivers and mountains, winding your way along the easiest path between points.

The track somewhere between Thaba-Tseka and somewhere else.

The first dodge is where the road circumvents the Kholo-Ntso valley and its many side-gullies, executing an 8km V-shaped southwest–northeast detour along the general contour. For the next 15km it meanders in an easterly direction, winding up-down, in-out of the gully-spurs and past villages above the Malibamatso, your constant, if distant, travel companion.

Where the river swings to the south (but not before offering you a foot-tingling drop-off to the river on the left), so too do you, rounding a conical hill on the left with co-joined villages strung out along the right-hand side of the road. From this point to Thaba-Tseka, still some 30km distant, it sticks pretty closely (with some weaving and winding) to the 2200m contour all the way.

After the first part, your average distance to the Malibamatso increases from some 2km (in sight most of the time) to about 6km (beyond the rise and fall of the heavily pleated landscape).

The Buffalo's Hotel is about 11km on the far side (Sani Pass) of town. Turn left and follow the road beyond where the tar runs out, continue south through a double zigzag, then a bend to the east and the red-roofed pleasure dome is ahead on your left. No card facility, cash only. We believe there is a 'local' hotel in town but didn't find it.

Note: Rohan 'The Rabbit' Surridge of Detour Trails has vowed to reroute this and the following stages off-road, so check the Spine of the Dragon and Dragon Trax websites for possible updates.

STAGE 7
THABA-TSEKA TO MANTSONYANE 59km

GRADE: Medium, hard; extreme riding
OVERNIGHT: St James Mission Hospital; Marakabei Lodge

IN A NUTSHELL
This stage is the least satisfying section of the Roof of Africa since it is presently being (badly) tarred. The contrast between green river valleys and heaven-high mountain-lands do make it something special, nonetheless. We just hope the wind gods are in your favour. In winter there is snow on the tops of the passes; summer brings just the opposite: heat and glare.

Snapshot of the experience
This road is part of the great Chinese neocolonisation of Africa (but, as one critic saw it, at least they're *our* chinas). The thing is, Chinese roads are, much like their clothes and videos, cheap knock-offs of the real thing. There's that old saying about Chinese roads: good for one year, bad for 1000 – and large sections of the road under construction between Jackals Pass and the Mantsonyane crossing are already the worse for wear from the past wet season. Around

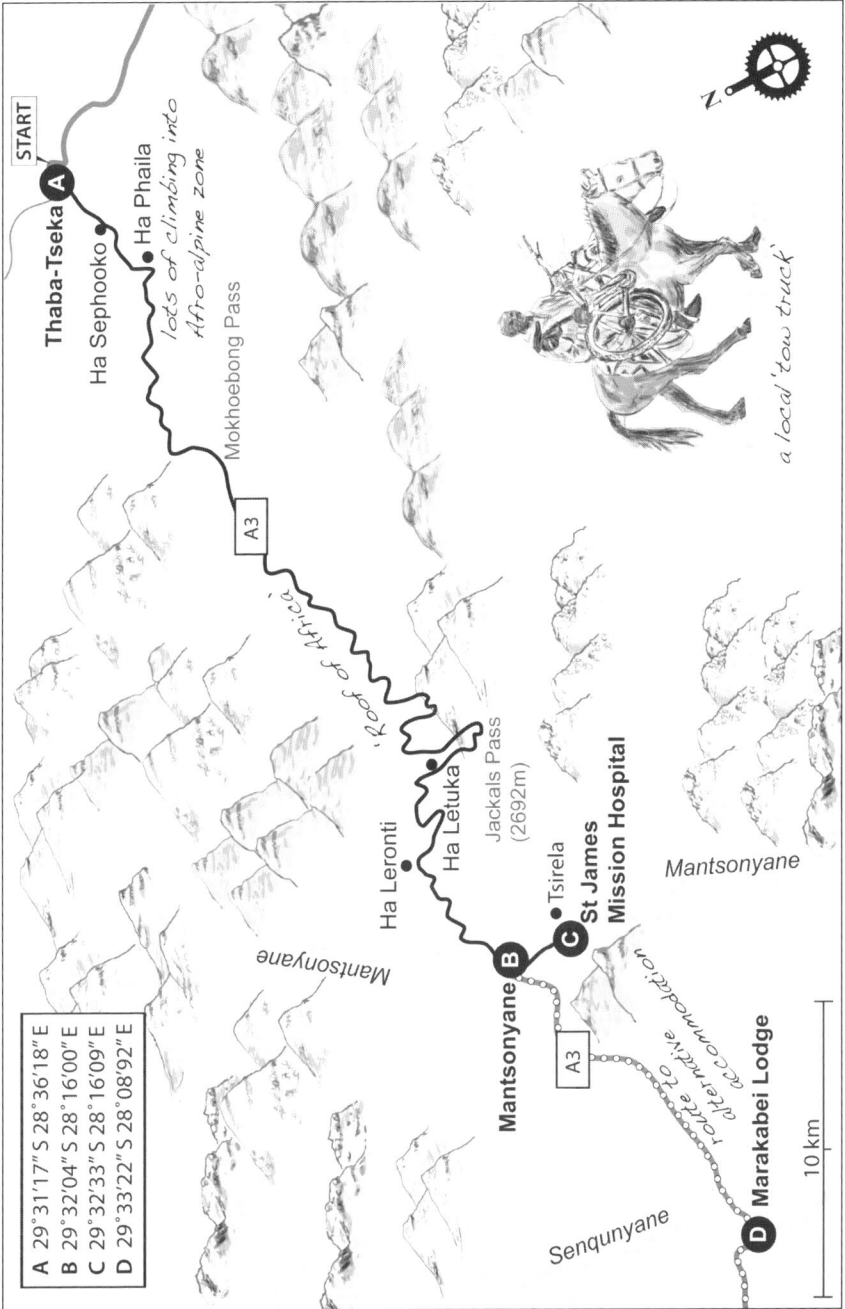

a local 'tow truck'

START

Thaba-Tseka Ⓐ

Ha Sephooko

Ha Phaila

lots of climbing into Afro-alpine zone

Mokhoebong Pass

A3

'roof of Africa'

Ha Leronti

Ha Letuka

Jackals Pass (2692m)

Tsirela

St James Mission Hospital

Mantsonyane

Mantsonyane

Mantsonyane Ⓑ Ⓒ

A3

alternative accommodation

Marakabei Lodge Ⓓ

Senqunyane

10 km

A 29°31'17"S 28°36'18"E
B 29°32'04"S 28°16'00"E
C 29°32'33"S 28°16'09"E
D 29°33'22"S 28°08'92"E

Oxbow you see clearly what this road will look like a few years hence – potholes increasing in size until you can barely find a patch that's driveable. Roads in this part of the planet need to be built to extra-high standards.

The route

If you stayed at The Buffalo's Hotel you have an 11km reverse ride back into Thaba-Tseka, the first part easy, the second slightly uphill. In town, continue left along the Maseru road, past the junction where you turned left yesterday and head out up the Molikaliko valley. Zigzag around Ha Sephooko settlement, then climb a steep windy-windy route to the head of the valley into crinkled (rather than high rolling) hills. You're now in the land of a thousand rivers, and each has cut its own little vale into the 120 million-year-old Drakensberg basalt plateau that is the volcanic crown of Lesotho.

The tarred road keeps climbing in steps, up and up from 2200m till nearly 2880m. There is almost always a cold wind blowing here, and the gravelly ground is clothed in only the sparsest Afro-alpine scrub and flowers. It's a pretty wild and desolate place, somewhat tamed by the presence of the tar.

This is the Mokhoebong Pass (the highest for the remainder of the Spine of the Dragon trail). Somewhere up here the tar ends abruptly – we say 'somewhere' because the road works have continued for several years and it remains a work in progress. From here you can only go down – and you do, up-down, river by river. About 12km on is the intimidating Jackals Pass (2692m). When we were there, road works were advancing eagerly, with lots of impressive machinery mashing up the countryside.

A steep descent to a tributary and hairpin-bend crossing is followed by a sharp climb up the valley, passing a strung-out settlement for the first time in many kilometres of barren mountainside. Cresting the ridge to your left, you find yourself above the river, in the Mantsonyane valley. Descending to the river, follow its winding westerly course for 3.5km. This newly tarred section was newly washed away, so we had to cross via the old steel-truss bridge.

The road rises and dips along the north riverbank through the fairly well-populated valley, winding above the more tightly snaking river, then veering to the south into Mantsonyane town, on a narrow table between mountainside and river. We could find no room at the inn (indeed no inn at all) in an extremely muddy town, so we bundled into the Amarok and drove up a long, steep, winding road for 2km, then down for 13km to Marakabei Lodge on the in-spate Senqunyane River.

To cycle this would be an arduous task as the next morning it's a return climb from 1900m to 2500m on tar, so organising a taxi would be by far the wisest option. We learned later there is accommodation available at the St James Mission Hospital so long as you book ahead.

STAGE 8
MANTSONYANE TO SEMONKONG   75km

GRADE: Long, hard; riding severe to extreme
OVERNIGHT: Semonkong Lodge

IN A NUTSHELL

This is one of the biggest adventure stages in Lesotho, a hectically long, tough stage so, if you want to make it in a day, get going early. It has two quite different halves: first, great riding following the Mantsonyane River course south; second, the strenuous descent, river crossing and climb out the far side of the Senqunyane valley – lots of sweat and maybe tears. Crossing the Senqunyane River by vehicle can be hazardous when it's in spate, and a plan that includes camping here is a wise one.

Snapshot of the experience

Semonkong means 'place of smoke', and the falls that make this spot so desirable a destination are on the Maletsunyane River, a short way south of the town. It's one of the natural wonders of Southern Africa and a must-see-before-you-die place. Consider making this a longer stopover as there's much to do, including what is reputedly the longest single-drop commercial abseil in the world, 204m down the cliff face next to the waterfall.

For some backup at Senqunyane, a vehicle could drive around via Roma – which it likely would have to do in any case – then drive towards the river and meet you at the top of the escarpment (using our GPS track to find the spot). Our omniscient driver organised a pony to come and meet us and ferry some bikes up the hill.

The route

Regardless of where you stayed, the route starts at St James Mission Hospital just outside Mantsonyane. From the hospital gate, take the gravel road to the left (south) – there's a rondavel koppie on the right and an airstrip on the left. The track heads up a ridge with fields on both sides, skirting above the river, turning sharp right around a side-valley and round Ha Nyane village. Then it climbs steeply up a ridge.

From there you keep mostly to the left side of a long mountain spur, with some sustained climbing along a pretty good road track that links villages, generally staying between the 2440m and 2240m contours for the next several

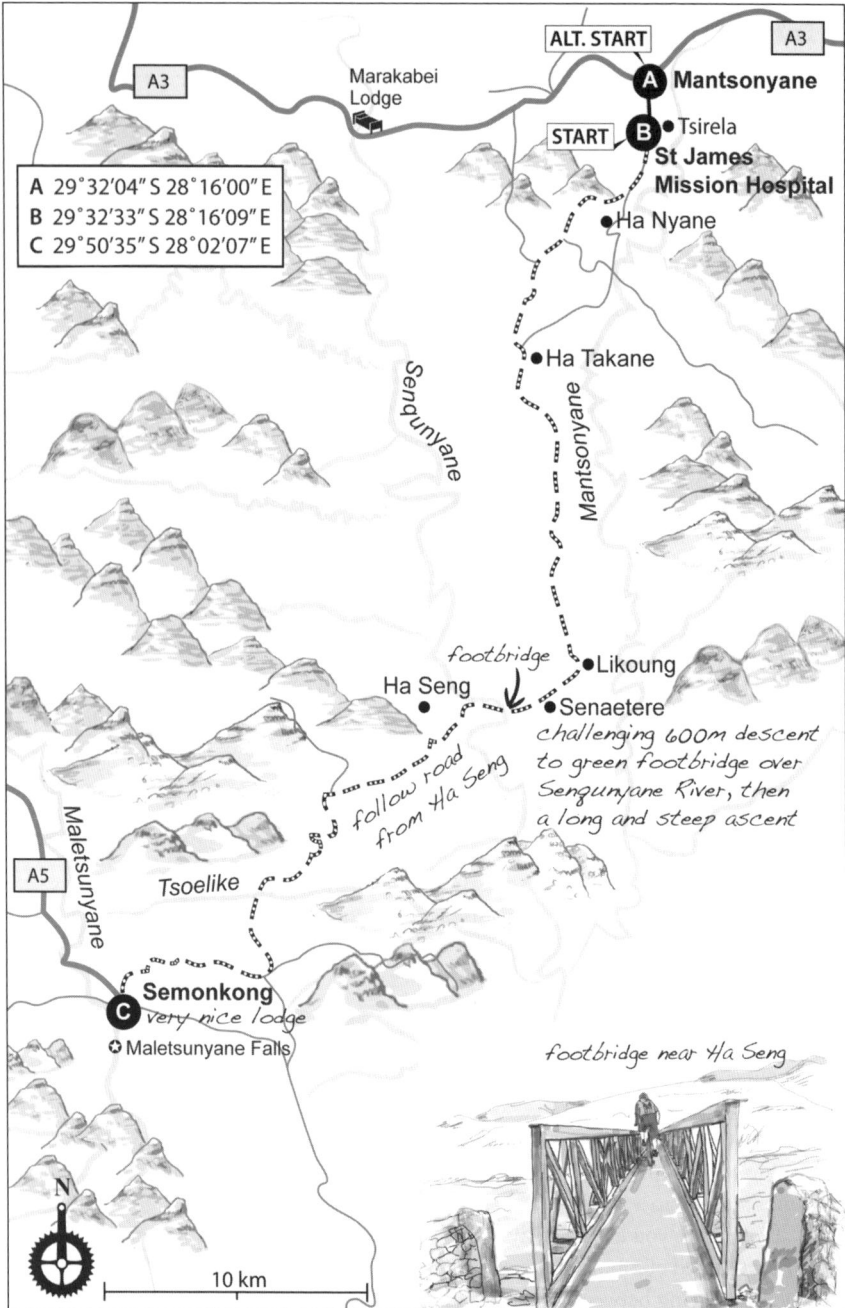

ALT. START

A3

Marakabei
Lodge

A Mantsonyane

START

B Tsirela
**St James
Mission Hospital**

• Ha Nyane

A 29°32'04" S 28°16'00" E
B 29°32'33" S 28°16'09" E
C 29°50'35" S 28°02'07" E

Senqunyane

• Ha Takane

Mantsonyane

footbridge
• Likoung

Ha Seng
•

• Senaetere

*challenging 600m descent
to green footbridge over
Senqunyane River, then
a long and steep ascent*

Maletsunyane

*follow road
from Ha Seng*

A5

Tsoelike

Semonkong
C *very nice lodge*

✿ Maletsunyane Falls

footbridge near Ha Seng

N

10 km

kilometres. A few kilometres past Ha Takane village, the road takes a spectacular leap down a tributary of the Mantsonyane, then roller coasters generally south past Likoung and Senaetere.

The previously good road (by Lesotho standards) devolves to a 4x4 track as you round a conical hill on your right, then head directly south along a spur on the 2220m contour for a few kilometres. When you come to a small unmarked village with a noticeably new school, this is where the big fun begins as you seem to fall off the edge of the known world into the Senqunyane valley. But fear not, because the local children will show you the way most willingly (admonishing you if you decide to take an alternative line to the 'official' track). Over the next 5km you descend an exhilarating 600m where your riding skills and braking power are tested to the max.

Finally you come to the Senqunyane River, crossing a Scandinavian footbridge to a rather nice camping spot. This is the only decent lunch stop on the route, and also a possible overnight campsite because the next half of the day is even tougher. We'd hoped to hire horses at the spaza shop 100m up the opposite hillside, but only managed to persuade some local social drinkers to push our bikes up the 600m rocky track. Some backup here would have been nice (we don't advise a backup vehicle in this valley as the climb out is extreme in the extreme, up a washed-away old wagon track). From the summit at 2220m, though, it's a pleasant 2.5km run down into the Tsoelike valley, where you cross the river and reach a real road.

Follow this road west-southwest for 18km to a crossroads, turn right and it's another up-and-down 7km into Semonkong, a large town in a wide fertile valley of the Maletsunyane River. The lodge is located across the river.

A general store about an hour's ride from the Maletsunyane falls had very little to entice us.

STAGE 9
SEMONKONG TO KETANE 57km

GRADE: Medium, hard; very steep downhill portage
OVERNIGHT: Nohana Lodge

IN A NUTSHELL

Semonkong is one of those places where roads that start off looking promising simply peter out: a road becomes a track becomes a footpath becomes nothing more then a vague rocky course. The route out of town takes you first to the famous Maletsunyane falls and, after looking pretty good, it then loses its way among the diced-up ridges, river valleys and gorges to Riverside on the Ketane River, and on to Ketane town.

Snapshot of the experience

The crux is an 840m descent of the escarpment to Ketane River (800m over 5.3km), involving much pushing and carrying of bicycles. As you stand on the edge of that escarpment, you'll see the land fall away, with the Ketane headwaters to your right and the deep chasm of the Maletsunyane to your left (east). The huge side-valley of the Ketane, into which you must descend, creates a giant V that could be 2km across its wide mouth. As you make your cautious way down, you'll see the path is boulder-strewn and washed away in places, so it's easier to carry than to push your bike. It will take at least an hour, maybe two, to do this.

The route

From the lodge, the road runs for 1.5km due west, then turns south and soon becomes a muddy track heading through a wide fertile valley. After 4.5km you see the Maletsunyane falls across the valley to your left. Do take time here to enjoy one of nature's marvels. Back on a surprisingly good road, you climb above and slowly away from the river, heading south-southwest past Ha Tsekana and Ha Mojalefa villages. The road then swings west, still going uphill, and passes a local mill and store (no Coke but avoid the oversweet grape-flavoured drink).

From here the valley narrows and the track steepens and deteriorates. It's a hard 200m pull for 2.8km up to the watershed, followed by a steep down-run to Ha Ramosothoana village. The next 9km past Ha Morumotso and Ha Khomo-a-Bokone villages is more rugged, wending through a tangle of river courses,

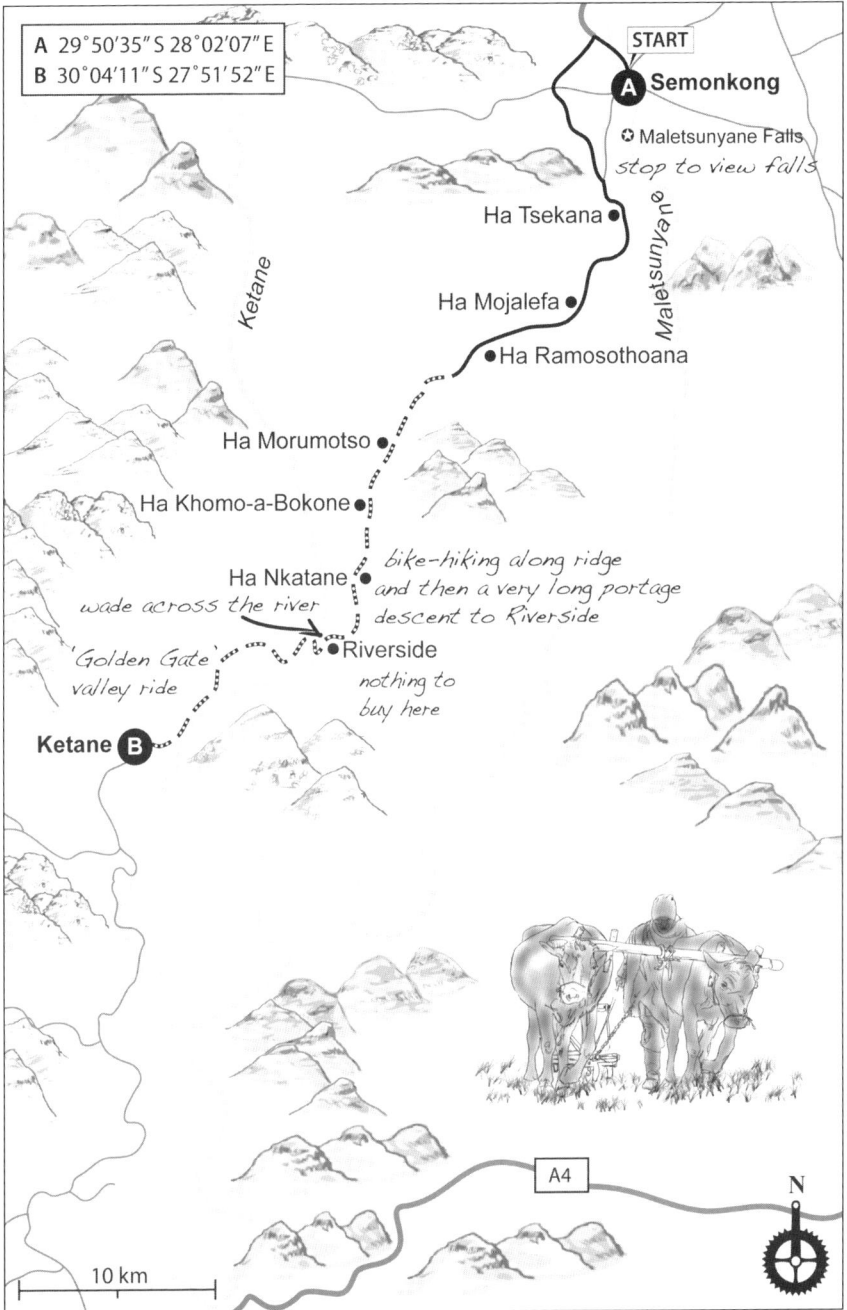

A 29°50'35" S 28°02'07" E
B 30°04'11" S 27°51'52" E

START

Ⓐ **Semonkong**

✿ Maletsunyane Falls
stop to view falls

Ha Tsekana ●

Ketane

Maletsunyane

Ha Mojalefa ●

● Ha Ramosothoana

Ha Morumotso ●

Ha Khomo-a-Bokone ●

*bike-hiking along ridge
and then a very long portage
descent to Riverside*

Ha Nkatane ●

wade across the river

● Riverside

*'Golden Gate'
valley ride*

*nothing to
buy here*

Ketane Ⓑ

A4

N

10 km

spurs and ridges with steep ups and downs. After sweeping very steeply around Ha Khomo-a-Bokone, it becomes a mere track after a while, skirting along a steep ridge for the next 3km. Looking down into the Ketane valley, you wonder how in blazes you're supposed to get there.

Parts of the contoured ridge section are rideable, some are not; it will test your technical riding skills. Then the track peters out and drops into a fearsome gorge. There is only one way down: a very rocky slope. You have to carry your bike for long sections as you descend the 800m. There is a track you can pick up at around 1820m (with two prominent rock bands up on the left) that takes you on a careening 250m ride to Riverside village. Just don't expect to find anything to eat or drink there. The entire descent from tiny Ha Nkatane village, perched on a small plateau above the main drop-off, to the Ketane River is about 5km of pretty heavy going.

Wade across the river where the old bridge has washed away and ride through the magnificent Ketane valley for 12km (up-down, up-down and far from straight) to the town. It's an absolutely gobsmacking sight and beats the pants off the Golden Gate Highlands for stupendous sandstone castles.

You can see the old flying-doctor airstrip dead ahead as you near Ketane. If you don't see it on your map, it's just short of Maponyane, a smaller settlement but more often marked. To find Nohana Lodge, turn left down the 'road' – more bedrock than paved – in the 'middle' of town, and it's on your left 600m down (look for the twin green doors of the long-drop loos). It ain't grand but you'll enjoy more comforts than you'd expect in such a remote place, seldom visited by *mlungus*. Note: unless you specify otherwise, they'll deep-fry the chicken for hours, and offer no gravy for the *pap*.

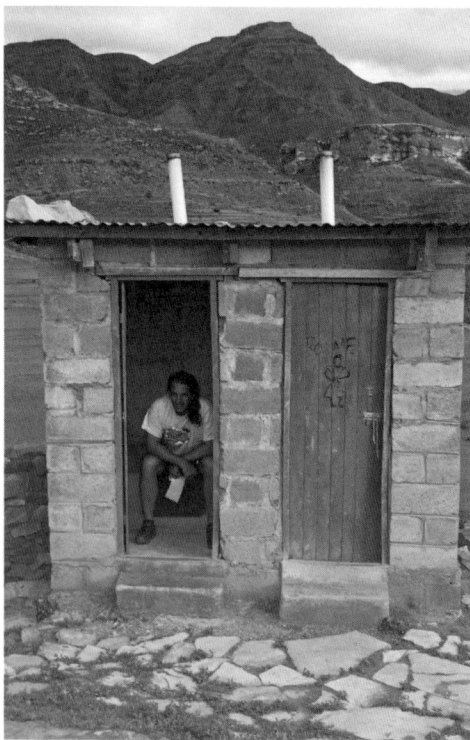

A loo with a view: Steve contemplates life at Ketane.

STAGE 10
KETANE TO HA QIQITA/BETHEL   42km

GRADE: Short, hard; severe riding
OVERNIGHT: Bethel Lodge

IN A NUTSHELL

The route to Ha Qiqita goes just about due south, but wends every which
way to get there. The first section out of Ketane and down the gorge is a
lovely track. Just as well, because after this section there is a mother of
an ascent – rideable, but it will test you, as it rises 520m over 7km. On all
sides are massive sandstone shields with footpaths etched into the rock
over time. We reckon they could yield the best slick-rock riding in Africa,
if not beyond. We didn't have time to linger and try out some routes in the
area, but we're equally sure that in time people will flock here. And then
remember who first told you so.

Snapshot of the experience

The previous day was one of Lesotho's and therefore, by default, the Spine trail's
biggest days. Today, after a fast run out of Ketane down the awesome Ketane River
gorge, our route swings away and up a very long hill, possibly the single longest
climb for those who ride it all the way.

From Bethel, Mount Moroosi – second only to Thaba Bosiu in historical
significance – is just a stone-skip away across the Senqu/Orange River. It is here
where, in 1879, Chief Moroosi's people endured a nine-month siege by combined
British and Boer forces, which ended in their gradual dispersal across the region
and the death of Moroosi.

The route

Leave the village going south. As you pass a big copse of trees, sho't right down
the slope to a stream. The road turns sharp left and descends tightly right round
the next stepped buttress, then the next, till you glide down to the steep side of
the Ketane River gorge. Near the bottom, the road executes a right-left-left U to
cross a side-stream via a concrete causeway. Follow the right-hand bank around
the base of a round hill for 2.3km till the road begins to climb away to the left,
through a broken area of exposed sandstone slopes.

From the river, at about 1500m, there is a not inconsiderable pull to 1820m
over about 5km. At a T-junction on the edge of a seriously steep hill, turn left

A 30°04'11" S 27°51'52" E
B 30°14'23" S 27°50'55" E

Qhoasing

START
Ketane **A**

Ha Mapoyane

slick-rock riding area

Ketane

concrete causeway

seriously long and steep hill

Ha Tlhabele

Ha Lempe
Ha Malephane

fast downhill keep left

Senqu

cultivated fields

Ha Qiqita/ Bethel **B**

Mount
Moroosi

N

10 km

along the escarpment edge and continue climbing past Ha Tlhabele village, wending your way around the big hill to the right. Go a short way down to cross a stream, then up the other side and around that ridge to the left. The road skirts the far side of the ridge and makes its way down to the head of the valley. Cross the stream, head over the next ridge, and repeat (ridge, valley, stream), but now through increasingly settled and cultivated land.

Wiggle west for 1.5km to cross the next stream, then waggle south-southwest for another 1.3km till you come to a junction among loosely scattered homes. You look down about 60m of scrubby, rocky hillside with a very eroded path and a road (your route) executing a tight bend in the valley below. So turn left here to go around and down to the bend in the crook of the valley.

Cross the stream and head east-southeast past Ha Lempe village on the right, then through HaMalephane (separated by fields). Continuing downstream and downhill, you reach an area of extensive fields where a road joins from the right. Here you look down the valley all the way to the Senqu: yes, it is downhill all the way. Continue southeast, then south, until you come to Ha Qiqita, larger than the previous villages, with a church and a clinic – and more important, unless you're in need of spiritual or physical healing, your inn for the night.

The village lies on raised land between two parallel streams flowing into the Senqu 1km further. The lodge is to the left, on the bank of the east-most stream. It's run by a fervent Canadian, 'solar missionary Ivan', who for the past 20 years has been trying to persuade the locals to turn to sun power and permaculture.

STAGE 11
HA QIQITA/BETHEL TO HOLY CROSS MISSION 49km

GRADE: Short, moderate
OVERNIGHT: Holy Cross Mission

IN A NUTSHELL
We called this the eye of the storm for two reasons: first, you are well out of the mountains here and more into the hills typical of southern Lesotho. Second, you're now on proper (dirt) roads all the way, with proper bridges across the rivers. Even in the worst weather, it might get muddy but you'll make it through – the predominantly sandstone soil is a whole lot less mousse-like than the black basalt soil of the higher mountains.

Snapshot of the experience

From Holy Cross, a 5km path cuts steeply up the mountain to a village perched right on top called Forosemethe. It's way up there because of the conflict between the Baphuti people and the colonials back in 1879. When their stronghold on Mount Moroosi finally yielded to siege, the Baphuti dispersed, congregating in seriously remote locations like this to avoid capture.

Look at the name of the village more closely: Foro-Semethe. In another guise it is Fauresmith, twin of the Free State town named after the missionary Rev. Phillip Faure and Cape governor Sir Harry Smith.

The route

Backtracking slightly uphill (north) out of Ha Qiqita for about 3.6km, veer left at a fork at Ha Malephane village to pass below a rock outcrop, then keep left to cut across three streams to Ha Rkarabele. From there keep heading roughly south, generally on the 1620m contour, for about 5km, passing through several small villages. Where the road swings around the ridge, beneath a hanging-rock outcrop, you look down on a loop in the chocolate-brown Senqu River 160m below.

For the next 3.4km you do a Lesotho traverse (that is, it's never flat) but here the landscape is kinder, along ridges high above the river. Keep high, skirting above Ha Mapolesa village, then take a descending line towards the next bend in the river ahead. Once close to the steep drop-off to the river, the road seems to take an illogical back-and-forth route downwards to a crossing of a side-river. Riding the circuitous 2.5km road route or a 500m scrambling short cut down the slope to your right are both options. In our experience, a road is always the shortest cut, and this one is mostly a steep downhill (take great care at the hairpin bend on the edge of the cliff-like drop-off).

From the bridge the road snakes up the (gentle) opposite side, continuing for 2.2km above the Senqu, then snakes down, crosses a stream, loops around the outside of a settlement (Ha Lesaoana/Shalane) and leads through the middle of the village. Make sure you ride due west out the other side. The road bends southwest, then due west again, going away from the river. For about 4km the road climbs into the hill country, crosses a stream above Anone village, then turns sharp right into an S-tending course in and out of valleys.

After 11km, at Pateng village the road swings west and snakes again – above a deep side-gorge, over a rise, looping in and out above and close to the river. Still tending mostly west, the road drops towards the river then flattens out till it reaches the old metal Seaka bridge.

Keep on for 2km to the new concrete bridge and turn right on the tarred road for 5km to the Holy Cross Mission, your overnight spot. It's an active place during term time, so try not to disrupt school proceedings too much.

A 30°14'23"S 27°50'55"E
B 30°20'32"S 27°32'41"E

Ha Malephane
Ha Rkarabele
START
Ha Qiqita/
Bethel
Phamong
Ha Mapolesa
Ha Lesaoana/
Shalane
Senqu
Anone
Pateng
A4
Forosemethe
Holy Cross
B Mission
Qomoqomong
Senqu
Quthing
A2
old metal
Seaka bridge
Alwynskop/
Mokanometsong
new concrete
Seaka bridge
A24
Orange
Tele Bridge
Border Post
Lesotho
South
Africa
10 km

RECOMMENDED
6 days

War Trail

Holy Cross Mission to Middelburg • 506km

STAGE 1
HOLY CROSS MISSION TO REEDSDELL FARM   75km

GRADE: Long, hard; severe in places
OVERNIGHT: Reedsdell Country Guest Farm

IN A NUTSHELL
The names of the area we ride through today seem to beckon like
way stations on a mythological quest – New England, Rhodes Village,
Tiffindell, Wartrail – not to mention the names of the local farms that
trip off the tongue like lines from a Wordsworthian epic. If it's mountain
biking you signed up for you'll get your money's worth today. To be sure,
there's not much off-road riding, but the scenic back-road nature of the
area makes up for that small detail.

Snapshot of the experience
From Tele Bridge, the road was a quagmire in places, a rubble bed in others,
washed away in parts, or potholed like the Somme back in 1916. In short, a great
road for cycling. It was around 45km to the top of Lundean's (Lundin's) Nek,
but only the final 11km were serious. In fact, of that, only 1 to 1.5km were
made for pushing.

Nearing the summit, the scenery got truly majestic – we were on top of the
southernmost extreme of the Drakensberg basalts. We could see the individual
bones along the spine of our dragon, etched across the jagged northerly horizon.

Then suddenly we were over the other side, through the farm-type gate at
the stock-theft police station, and into another world – one aptly called New
England with its verdant, rolling highlands and prosperous farms tucked in the
folds with names like Braeside and Glencoe. In May the poplars and willows
were golden, the fields green and the hillsides gold and charcoal.

The route
From Holy Cross, retrace your route back to the new Seaka bridge (about
5.5km), continue east on the A2 to Alwynskop/Mokanametsong for 5.6km and
turn right onto the gravel road. After leaving the river, the road climbs about
50m, then descends. Turn left (south) onto the gravel road and head for 10km to
the border at Tele Bridge.

Across the narrow bridge is Tele town, an untidy agglomeration of humanity
with nothing to recommend it and no reason to linger. After clearing customs,

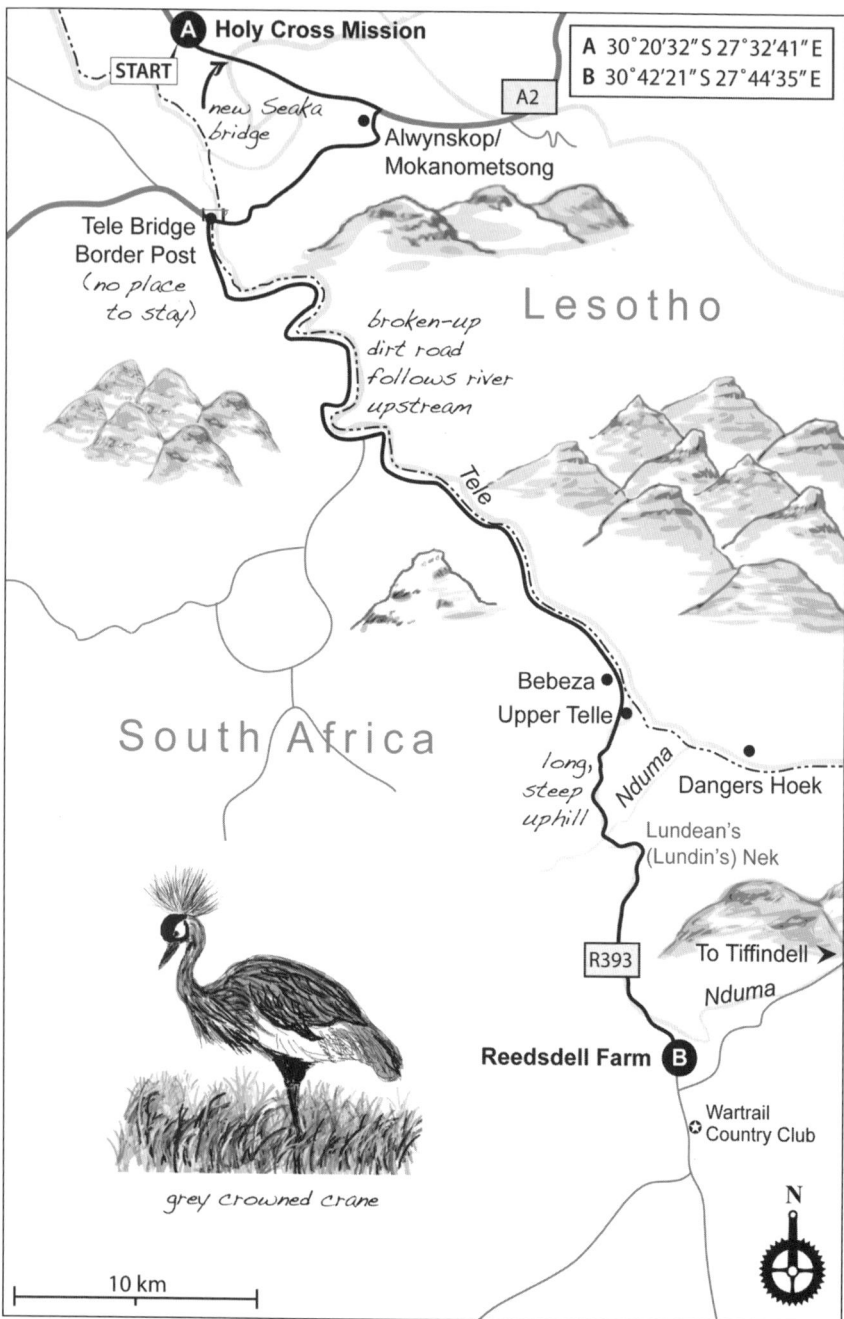

A Holy Cross Mission

START

| A | 30°20'32" S 27°32'41" E |
| B | 30°42'21" S 27°44'35" E |

A2

new Seaka
bridge

Alwynskop/
Mokanometsong

Tele Bridge
Border Post
(no place
to stay)

Lesotho

broken-up
dirt road
follows river
upstream

Tele

South Africa

Bebeza
Upper Telle

long,
steep
uphill

Nduma

Dangers Hoek

Lundean's
(Lundin's) Nek

R393

To Tiffindell ➤

Nduma

Reedsdell Farm **B**

Wartrail
Country Club

N

grey crowned crane

10 km

turn immediately left, continuing south to the edge of the half built-up area and, possibly, road works to follow the Tele River for the next 29km (don't take turn-offs to the right) – it's the worst road for driving but one of the best for riding!

At Bebeza (note the Russian-styled onion dome of its small church), the valley narrows as you approach Upper Telle and Dangers Hoek. The road rises about 500m

The emus at the dressed-stone Reedsdell Country Guest Farm, your night stopover, add an exotic touch. It's as romantically situated a farm as you're ever likely to see in this country. You'll love it.

along this stretch to Upper Telle, but it's a delightful ride; the only negative being that you leave the bucolic river valley, heading right and upwards – big time.

If Lundean's Nek is near the start of your ride, you'll need to *knyp* a bit when you turn right and up at the clinic. You first climb steadily but fairly painlessly for 3km, leaving the Upper Telle settlement and entering the mountain wilderness. And so it goes for another 3km, next to a stream (the Nduma), until the point where we can no longer fool you, because you now see the steep zigzags looming in your very near future.

The road crosses the stream at the first zig at 1940m. More zigzags later, you round the peak on your right, then level off but continue to climb till you reach 2160m some 4.5km from the Upper Telle turn-off. Now the fun starts, as you survey your elevated domain of sawtooth mountains. The vegetation up here is sparse Afro-alpine heath and montane grasslands, and the sheep are tough.

As you zoom down the left-hand side of the Lundean's valley, at around 2020m you might notice a police post blur past; this is one of many such outfits set up in the highlands to quell the rampant stock theft. At 1800m, about 9km

from the nek of the pass, the gracious Reedsdell farm is on the left, with either romantic stone-cottage living quarters or more communal bunkhouse-type lodgings for groups. The Isteds have been farming here for six generations and in autumn they host the extremely popular 4x4 Rally Raid. If you want to be sure there's room at the inn, call in advance to establish exactly when the event takes place.

The stone five-arch Loch Bridge over the Kraai River.

STAGE 2
REEDSDELL FARM TO BARKLY EAST   38km

GRADE: Short, moderate; hard riding in parts
OVERNIGHT: Siskin's B&B

IN A NUTSHELL

Where the previous day's route is dramatic, this section is all eye candy, more rolling riding than the previous stage's mountain bike warfare in Lesotho. The riding is still tough, though – but then it **is** mountainous here. Much like Alan Paton's KwaZulu-Natal Midlands, the place is lovely beyond the telling of it. The road rolls down into the Kraai River valley, towards Barkly East, past the famous old steam-train line and then over the stone-arched Loch Bridge, a church steeple peering over distant trees. It's more like Scotland, really, or Wales.

Snapshot of the experience

The man who surveyed the Wartrail area was an Irishman, Joseph Orpen, but it so reminded him of the Scottish Highlands he gave most of the places names such as Glengariff, Burnside and Bonny Doon. Many of the families have been here for several generations.

As for the district's name, Wartrail: when the early white settlers first arrived in the 1800s, the place was beset by strife between local Xhosa pastoralists who grazed their stock up here in summer and Basotho raiders who were busy creating their kingdom in the sky after the *Difaqane* wars. The tradition has not ceased, the only change being that now white-owned farms are mostly the target of the stock thieves.

The route

From Reedsdell turn left out of the gate and proceed about 2km, past the Wartrail country club (on your left), and bear right at the intersection. The road climbs gently for some 2km to another junction; bear right again, away from the valley.

A long downhill, past Burnside farm, is followed by a long uphill, the first of many such rollers, as the track wends south, then west, in and out of valleys and around hilltops, to a third junction at about 22km from the start. Lots of leg input is required on the ups.

Turn left (southwest) here to descend and cross the Diepspruit, ascend easily and then make the final serious descent into the Kraai River valley, taking a left

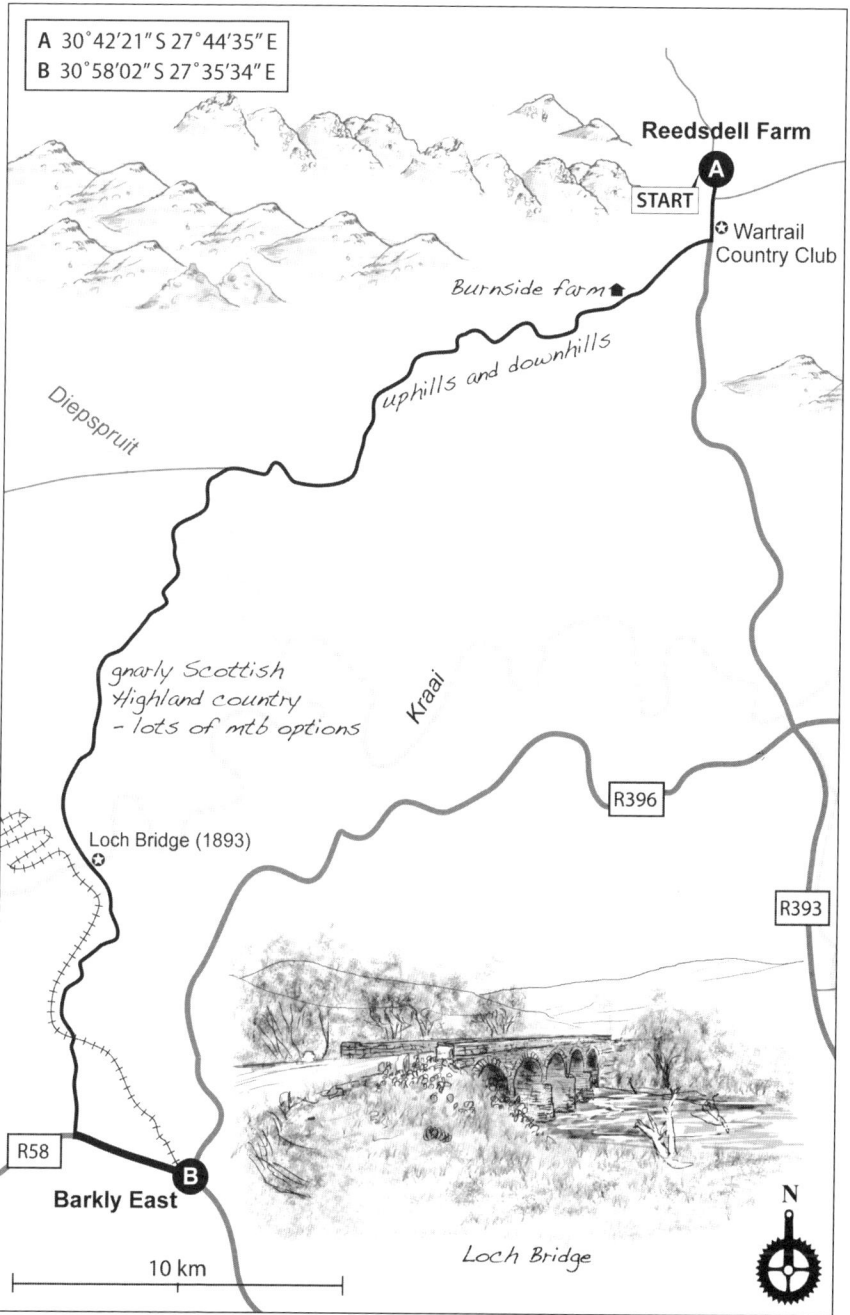

A 30°42'21"S 27°44'35"E
B 30°58'02"S 27°35'34"E

Reedsdell Farm
A
START
Wartrail Country Club

Burnside farm

uphills and downhills

Diepspruit

gnarly Scottish Highland country – lots of mtb options

Kraai

R396

R393

Loch Bridge (1893)

R58

B

Barkly East

10 km

N

Loch Bridge

turn to travel east along the left-hand riverbank. As you approach the Kraai River, just before the road makes a right-angled left turn, look back up the valley behind you to make out the triple-switchback railway line, necessitating reverse-tracks, and once a major drawcard to enthusiasts back in the age of steam.

About 2km down the valley, the road swings sharp right and crosses the Kraai by way of the lovely five-arch stone Loch Bridge, completed in 1893. For a while the road follows the railway towards town, crosses it, then takes a direct south route for about 4km to meet the tarred R58 where you turn left and head into town. Turn right into Graham Street, at the dressed-sandstone NGK church, and you'll find Siskin's (named after a small, canary-like mountain bird) on the corner of Copeland Street. (Note: the B&B might not still be running, so check with the people at Reedsdell farm.)

· ·

STAGE 3
BARKLY EAST TO DORDRECHT   99km

GRADE: Long, moderate
OVERNIGHT: Bradgate farm

IN A NUTSHELL
It's a long day's ride, never easy, with big climbs and big descents, but this is a picture-postcard corner of the country, so just try to cruise it.

If you look around you, so much happens along the way: squadrons of crested cranes, columns of storks in the thermals, mongooses, small antelope, meetings with locals.... Climbing and climbing and climbing up the Witteberg to Paardenek, you might come across (as we did) one of nature's seldom-noticed wonders – a migration of hairy caterpillars.

Snapshot of the experience
It was great to be back on the open road again, with weather suited to humans rather than the ice rats we'd become in the Drakensberg. Then the wind came up. It was a lazy wind, going straight through us instead of around. It followed us for the rest of the day, always seeming to change direction – into our faces – as our route turned this way and that.

Trivial Pursuit question of the day (we posed one daily): what is the significance of -21? It's the lowest temperature ever recorded in South Africa,

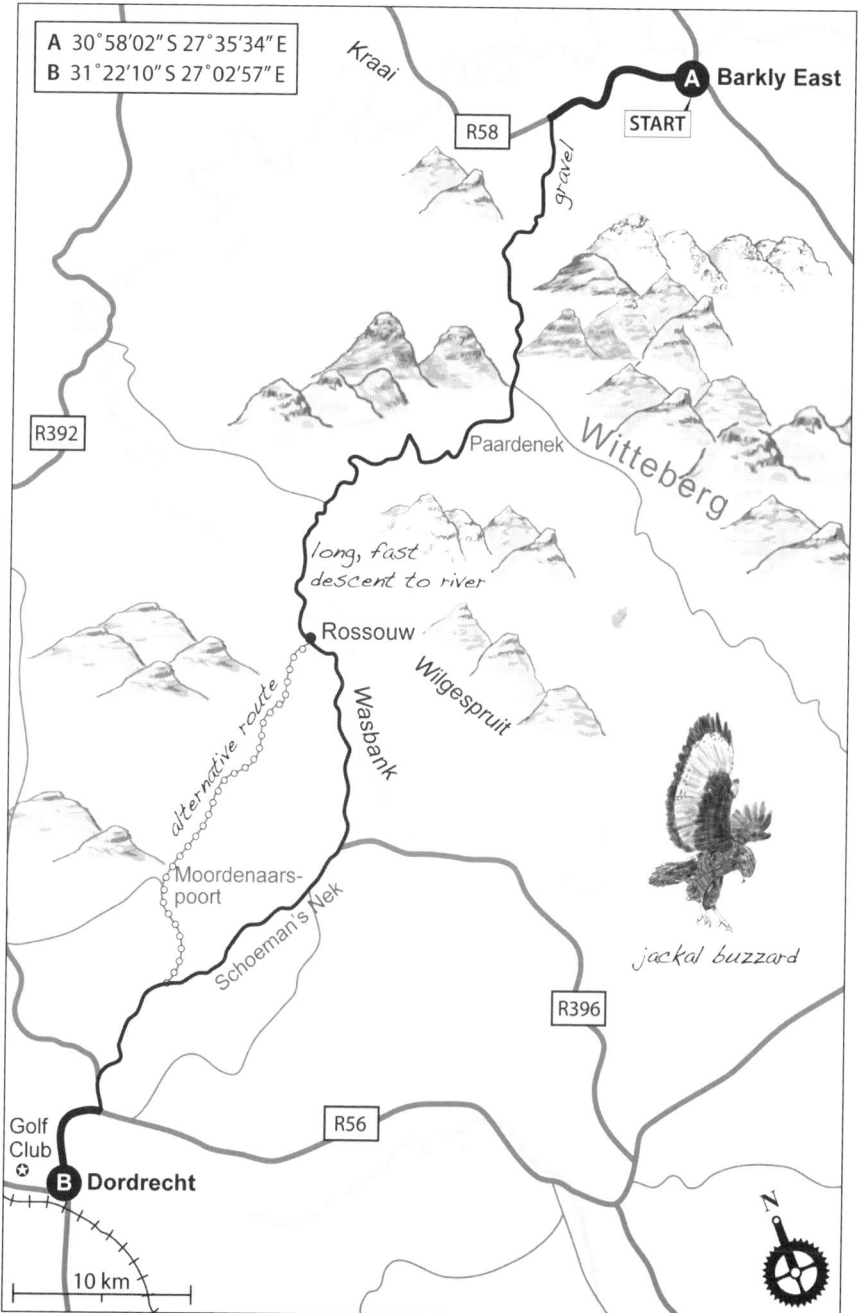

A 30°58'02"S 27°35'34"E
B 31°22'10"S 27°02'57"E

Kraai

R58

gravel

A Barkly East

START

R392

Paardenek

Witteberg

long, fast
descent to river

Rossouw

Wilgespruit

Wasbank

alternative route

Moordenaars-
poort

Schoeman's Nek

jackal buzzard

R396

Golf
Club

R56

B Dordrecht

N

10 km

I reckoned that if we rode over even one of the migrating hairy caterpillars we encountered, we could change the course of the planet. Steve reckoned it could be worse: they might gang up and overwhelm us, leaving only two piles of dust with huge itches.

and it was noted on a farm outside Dordrecht. I hope you've timed your ride well – because in summer it will soar into the 40s.

The route

Ride west of out town on the R58, through farmlands for 9.5km, then turn left onto a gravel road. After crossing the Saalbooms stream, take the right-hand fork (you cross two more tributaries) and for 20km ride south to southwest, slowly ascending the Witteberg from 1720m to 2000m to Paardenek. After a long climb there is always a down, in this case a winding 24km descent (mainly) through rugged mountains all the way down to the Wilgespruit-Wasbank confluence. This section is the nicest riding of a long day, so enjoy it.

Just beyond the river crossing you reach Rossouw, but don't rely on getting anything there. Even the church looks like it's been boarded up for years, so on the spiritual front you're pretty much on your own too. This is roughly the halfway mark for the day.

As an alternative to our track to Dordrecht, from the dead centre of Rossouw take the gravel road right (west) via Moordenaarspoort. The distance from here to Dordrecht is much the same for both routes. This is where Jan Smuts's recce party was ambushed and nearly wiped out in 1901 during the Anglo-Boer War, and before they did their life-saving 'death march' over the Stormberg to Elands River Poort through an icy night-time storm.

The Wartrail district was supposed to be dry in winter, but we got dumped on and dunked in more than once.

©Steve Thomas

For 8km past Rossouw our track follows the Wasbank stream, swings right up a tributary for 2km, then south for 4km, and meets the larger R396. Here, swing from south to west, ride through Schoeman's Nek and proceed for about 22km on this road. It's a long haul along dusty gravel, but all the way are hills and even mountains. And the occasional derelict farmhouse or windmill.

The road wends between some prominent hills, a road joins from the right, then you come to the tarred R56. Turn right, with Dordrecht peak dead ahead. The Dordrecht town outskirts are reached about 3km down the tarred road. The overnight place we used, Luluby B&B, is no more; try Bradgate farm, about 15km west out of town, which you'll pass on the next day's ride.

Dordrecht is no rose of the prairie, and the only place to get a decent meal is at the golf club, about 1km west out of town on the R56 (gate on the right, with a gravel driveway).

. . . .

STAGE 4
DORDRECHT TO MOLTENO   118km

GRADE: Long, moderate to hard
OVERNIGHT: Olive Cottage

IN A NUTSHELL
Whether you do this in one stage or two, what you'll be guaranteed is a spectacular route through the Stormberg mountains and across the high plateau, passing isolated farms – many deserted – and fields rich with wool-balls of sheep and fat cattle. In nice weather (September to October and March to April are best) the ride will be invigorating, extremely pleasant and easily within the capabilities of any healthy cyclist (it's the headwinds that take the wind out of your cycling sails).

Snapshot of the experience
Our plans for the night's stopover on a farm about midway were ambushed when we discovered it was no longer operating. Finding another guest farm along the way proved futile so we had to ride the hard miles all the way to Molteno. At times the wind was so strong we resorted to using our Amarok backup vehicle as a shield to make any progress.

Now, 110-plus kays might be okay for us nutters, but it could frighten off some touring riders. On the other hand, mountain bikers are a tough lot by nature. You could shorten the day by stopping at one of several farms short of Dordrecht, then overnighting at Bradgate farm or, 15km further, at Highlands (Boschoffskraal). From there all the major climbing is over and the road is a real back-country track all the way to Molteno.

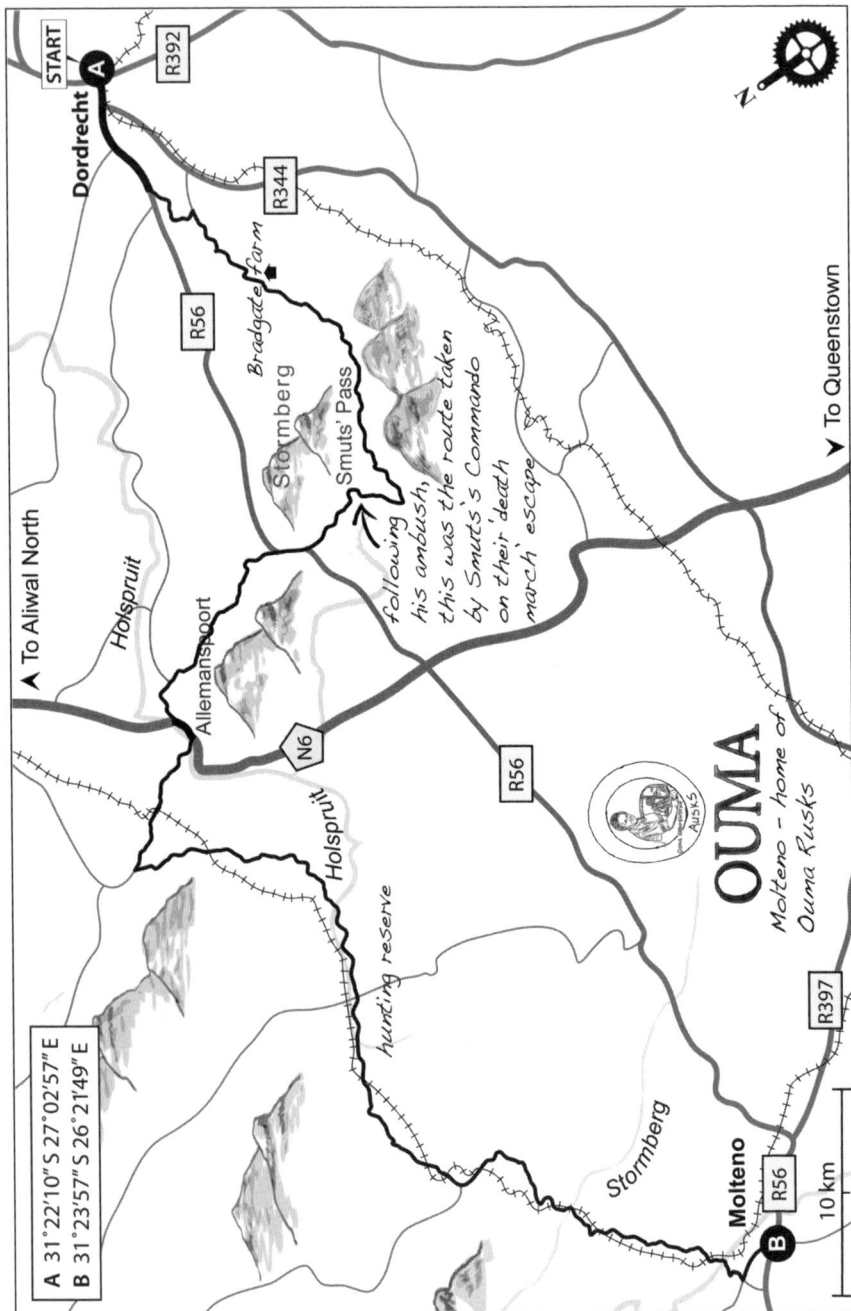

A 31°22'10"S 27°02'57"E
B 31°23'57"S 26°21'49"E

START
Dordrecht
R392
R344
R56
Bradgate farm
Stormberg
Smuts' Pass
To Aliwal North
Holspruit
Allemanspoort
N6
Holspruit
hunting reserve
R56

Following his ambush, this was the route taken by Smuts's Commando on their 'death march' escape

To Queenstown

OUMA
Molteno – home of
Ouma Rusks

Ouma Rusks

R56
R397
Stormberg
Molteno
R56
B
10 km

The route

From Dordrecht to Molteno on tar (R56) is only 70km, but we've gone to great lengths (about 48km) to avoid this. First we loop to the south; then back and to the north. You could avoid either of these loops by taking the tar.

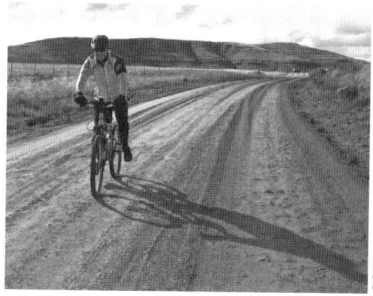

Riding from A to Z somewhere near Dordrecht.

You're forced to ride the tar out of town for 7km. Turn left onto a gravel road and then first right at Jakkalskop. You pass Bradgate farm 15km from town (an accommodation option); the road rises up from here into the Stormberg and 12km further it winds through Smuts' Pass, between substantial peaks. This is where Smuts's commando was shown a short cut through the hills by a shepherd, up to the left (marked by a cairn), to avoid a British blockade.

It's quite a pull up here, rising 260m from Bradgate to the pass, but it's 'big sky country'. There are always raptors in these parts, mainly rock kestrels and jackal buzzards. The gravel road descends gently to the tarred road; turn right for about 1.6km before turning left (north) onto another gravel road that will eventually reach the N6 (Queenstown–Aliwal North).

You're now on top of the world – this part of the world at any rate. The gravel road swings left. Keep going until you reach the N6; turn left onto the tar here (watch out for roaring trucks), pass through Allemanspoort, then after about 2km turn right onto a gravel road that wends through picturesque fields, an easy 100m climb in altitude till you reach a railway line.

There is no service road along the railway, but following the rail to the left for about 4km cuts off 4km from this section. Alternatively, carry on to the next junction, turn left, then head south across the railway again. From here the route follows the general line of the rail all the way to Molteno. It's a good 24.5km haul.

After going south, then bearing right (west) at a junction, the route picks up the Holspruit, following it and the railway uphill for about 10.5km, past two side-junctions. All the land on the left-hand side is a hunting reserve and you could see, as we did, different types of antelope. The route starts as a decent gravel road but steadily deteriorates, in places requiring a 4x4 or mountain bike to get through. In some spots the erosion of the stream banks and side-valleys is so bad it resembles the Dakota Badlands in miniature.

The road crosses the railway about five times, swinging from west to south, then southwest, still winding in and out, up and down, through the hills. Finally the railway branches off to the south into the back side of Molteno but you cross the Stormberg River and pass the factory for Ouma's (a real person apparently, Ouma Greyvensteyn) famous rusks, turn left, then enter town on the tarred R56.

STAGE 5
MOLTENO TO HOFMEYR

84km

GRADE: Long, moderate
OVERNIGHT: Karoobos Lodge

IN A NUTSHELL

For us this was a really fun day, starting off cold and wet but ending sunny and dry, if not exactly warm. The hills on this stage are kind – gentle climbs rather than slogs, while the downhills will give some real mountain biking thrills. To be sure, there is one big hill between 25km and 35km, climbing right to the edge of the escarpment at the top of the pass, but it somehow seems to go by like scenery past a car window.

And, for a happy change, you might get into town early enough to enjoy the awesome pies, ginger beer and coffee at the Karoobos Farmstall. They are definitely pies to ride at least 84km for.

Snapshot of the experience

All my scars and bruises from our tryst with Lesotho were healing nicely and for the first time in weeks I was able to ride out ahead instead of being tucked in tight behind 'Thomas the Tank Engine'. That is, except up the Kleindoringhoek Pass, when co-rider Rohan Surridge, code-named The Rabbit (he who always sets the pace way up ahead), stopped at the top to wait for Steve and me, before venting: '[Rude word]! I just can't ride as slowly as you two guys up the hills!' Slow but sure – that's us.

The route

The road out of Molteno, southwards past the school and cemetery, starts with a long uphill slog. It climbs slowly at first, then more steeply once you gain the Stormberg River valley. Keep heading upstream for about 15km; you will gain 100m in altitude.

At a fork where it levels off for a while, head right for 2km (17km from the start) and you pass the turn to Romansfontein, where the local farmers fed us and dried our clothes around an Aga stove after a storm.

From the farm, the road continues to climb steadily but never steeply for another 3.8km, then drops over and into the upper catchment of the Bamboesberg River. It runs over a ridge, goes down, up and over several small tributaries and leads past farm dams. From the concrete bridge a sharp-but-

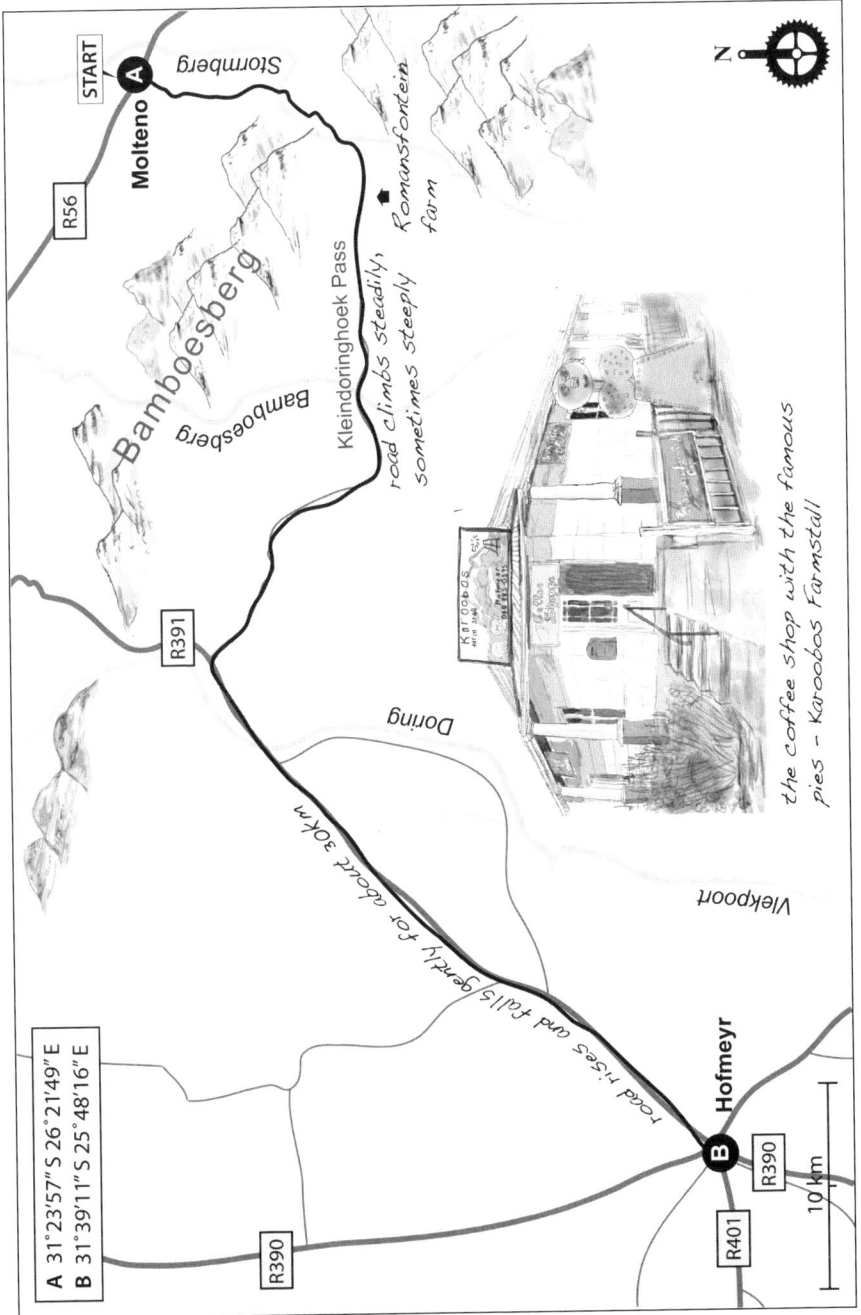

START

A

Molteno

Stormberg

R56

Bamboesberg

Bamboesberg

Kleindoringhoek Pass

road climbs steadily, sometimes steeply

Romansfontein farm

R391

Doring

the coffee shop with the famous pies – Karoobos Farmstall

Vlekpoort

road rises and falls gently for about 30km

Hofmeyr

B

R390

R401

R390

10 km

N

A 31°23'57"S 26°21'49"E
B 31°39'11"S 25°48'16"E

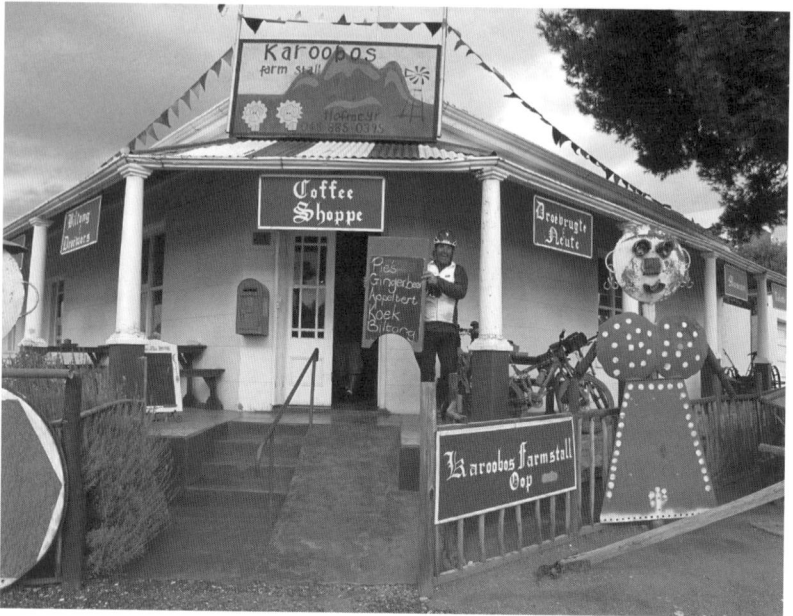

Distances in the Karoo are long: the pies at the Karoobos Farmstall couldn't come soon enough.

short haul up a winding track follows, rising from 1640m to 1720m (the 'rude word' spot). Here the land levels off again for about 1.5km.

The road veers from west to northwest and begins to climb again, slowly and steadily for 6.5km, till it reaches a gully on the edge of the plateau and takes a downhill plunge into the Kleindoringhoek Pass, dropping 300m over about 4.5km. The road here is broken and loose, so the riding is fast but a bit dicey. Take care, but enjoy it!

This brings you into the upper Doring catchment, with a bit of a climb through a low nek – the last bit is rather steep (out-the-saddle stuff) – then down to reach a larger gravel road. Veer left to join it. The road follows the Doring River downstream for about 5km, through a small poort. When the river heads south past irrigated fields, the trail veers away to the left (southwest).

Follow this road, virtually dead straight but for one minor and one longer dogleg in the middle, for just on 30km to Hofmeyr. The road rises and falls frequently, climbing to 1380m before the final down run to 1280m. It's not hard riding, but it's not easy either.

Hofmeyr is a small town, and, if one can talk of a centre, that's where you'll find the charming Karoobos Farmstall (really a tearoom), as well as the Karoobos Guesthouse. They are run by farmers' wives, and were taken over when the town was in a bit of a sorrier state several years back.

STAGE **6**
HOFMEYR TO MIDDELBURG 92km

GRADE: Long, easy
OVERNIGHT: Various options, see Useful contacts (p. 202)

IN A NUTSHELL
In Lesotho it took us seven hours to ride 25km; on our ride down to the
Great Brak River between Hofmeyr and Molteno we managed that distance
in just one hour. It is also the first time in a long time that your day won't
start with a huge climb out of some valley. The land rolls out towards the
Great Fish River and then to the Graaff-Reinet–Cradock road without
encountering a single ascent of significance over a distance of over
80km. When we looked at the profile of the route on our Garmins, Steve
commented it looked like the polygraph line in that silly film *Flatliners*
with Kiefer Sutherland and Julia Roberts.

Snapshot of the experience
The route to Middelburg circumvents the higher mountains, so this is a fairly
easy day in terms of energy output over distance. As for military history, this
flat cornerless tract of the country did not escape unscathed during the Anglo-
Boer War, as the graves of British soldiers in town imply. There is also the
Stoel monument on the Richmond road, commemorating where commandos
Johannes Lotter and Petrus Wolfaardt were executed in October 1901 by the
British during the second phase of the guerrilla war. Considered 'Cape Rebels' –
those who were born in the Cape Colony and fought with the Boers – they were
presumably tied to chairs and shot, as the stone-cairnlike monument features
the engraving of a chair.

The route
For a refreshing change, the day starts with a gentle decline for about 30km
down to the Great Brak River. It's pretty much typical Karoo: a dead-straight
road lined by barbed-wire fences, the landscape broken here and there by
dolerite-topped koppies and an occasional seasonal pan and windmill. The road
west out of town follows the railway line to the saltworks, the Zout Pan, on the
left, whereafter the railway swings away to the north.
    In the distance on the right are the twin peaks of Leeukop and Zoetfontein.
About 2km past Soetfontein farm (on your left), you cross an intersection and

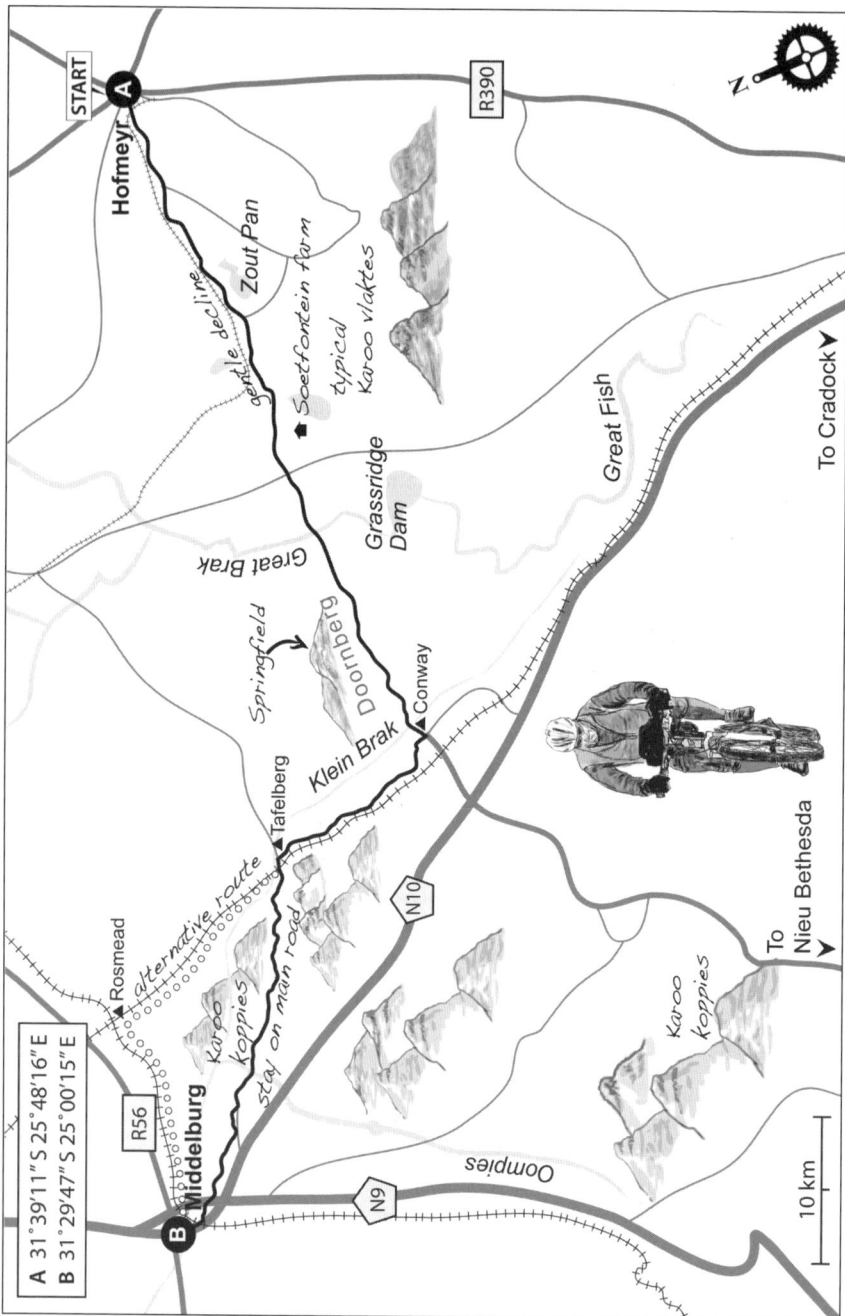

START

A 31°39'11"S 25°48'16"E
B 31°29'47"S 25°00'15"E

Hofmeyr

R390

To Cradock ▶

gentle decline

Zout Pan

Soetfontein farm

typical Karoo vlaktes

Great Fish

Grassridge Dam

Great Brak

Springfield

Doornberg

Conway

Klein Brak

Tafelberg

alternative route

Rosmead

N10

To Nieu Bethesda ▶

stay on main road

Karoo koppies

Karoo koppies

R56

Middelburg

N9

Oompies

B

10 km

3km later reach the river with irrigated fields on the east bank. A little further you cross a smaller stream, then the road rises towards the Doornberg ridge and passes over at a low point, with the main ridge to the right. The route heads down to the Klein Brak River, crosses via a narrow causeway, and hits a second junction with a railway line just beyond (the abandoned Conway station). The route to Nieu Bethesda goes straight here, but for Middelburg turn right.

The road generally follows the railway line, and rises again towards the Doornberg, reached 10km from the turn-off. The Klein Brak River is some way to the left. The first and highest peak of the area, on your right, is Springfield. The road keeps to the high ground; 15km from Conway it comes to Tafelberg siding. Tafelberg itself is the prominent flat-topped koppie (1655m) over to the left (west), about 7km distant.

A road joins from the right, the railway line goes straight north. Take the left-veering road, but don't turn left off the main gravel down a lesser farm road. For about the next 4km, the Klein Brak meanders along the right-hand side of the road, then it heads north and the route takes a more westerly heading.

The road takes a zig, then a zag, between a line of koppies, notably Rooikop on the right and Gryskop on the left, then passes a large saltpan on the right. A short way past that on the right looms Folminskop, then you cross the Oompies River, a tributary of the Klein Brak. Just short of 6km beyond the stream the route meets the N10, with Middelburg just 4km to the right (the N10 and N9 cross over just short of town).

With a small amount of creative route-finding, you can follow a series of tracks on the right-hand side of the N10, between the golf course and sewage works, into town. Alternatively, from Tafelberg station ride north on service roads, looping left around Wolweberg koppie. Just before Rosmead station take a track to the left to pick up another line running west into Middelburg. It runs parallel with the R56 for about 4km from Leeuwefontyn (just another loop in the line and a name on a map).

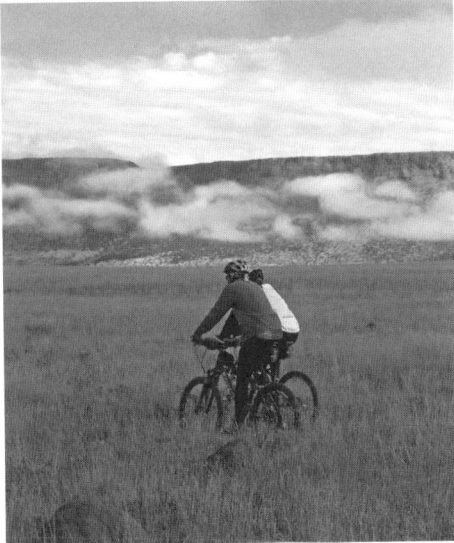

Near Middelburg, two figures going where, and why, you have to wonder.

Klaarstroom
Guest House

DB&B

RECOMMENDED
7
days

Great Karoo Trail

Middelburg to Prince Albert • 646km

©Steve Thomas

STAGE 1
MIDDELBURG TO NIEU BETHESDA   75km

GRADE: Long, hard
OVERNIGHT: Owlhouse Backpackers

IN A NUTSHELL

When you do this trail through the famously flat and arid Great Karoo, it might be somewhat disconcerting to discover that parts of it, like today's stage, are very far from flat. In fact, in places it's extremely mountainous, and in others also very fertile. The standout geological feature of the entire region, the fang-like Kompasberg, is your compass needle for the day's ride between Middelburg and Nieu Bethesda. You have to surmount two ranges today: the Rhenosterberg and the Sneeuberg, the latter which in wintertime more than lives up to its name 'snow mountain'. Even in summertime, when the area swelters in arid countenance, intensely green valleys bring relief along the way.

Snapshot of the experience

I consider Nieu Bethesda to be the spiritual heart of South Africa, so our route had to go through there. Lodestone of the area is a great dolerite peak, the Kompasberg, that rears up from Sneeuberg's jawbone axis like a dragon's canine. In winter when it's snow-covered, they call it the Matterhorn of the Karoo.

The village and surrounds have a magic that is hard to distil into words: as we arrived, the storm we'd cycled through finally abated and a triple rainbow arched over the Owl House (a fantastical place created by the troubled naïve artist Helen Martins), as we sipped coffee and red wine on the *stoep* of The Karoo Lamb restaurant across the road.

The route

Leave town on Richmond Way or the R398, between Smid and Coetzee streets, going west. From the edge of town the road climbs gently for a few hundred metres to crest the north shoulder of Middelburg koppie, which rises about 80m above the road. On the left you'll pass the Anglo-Boer War Stoel monument.

On the far side of the shoulder you keep pretty much to the 1280m contour; 3.6km from the monument, turn left onto a minor farm-feeder road (just after some fields and a seasonal stream bed at Coligny South farm). You follow this through the Sneeuberg until close to Nieu Bethesda. With a ridge on your right,

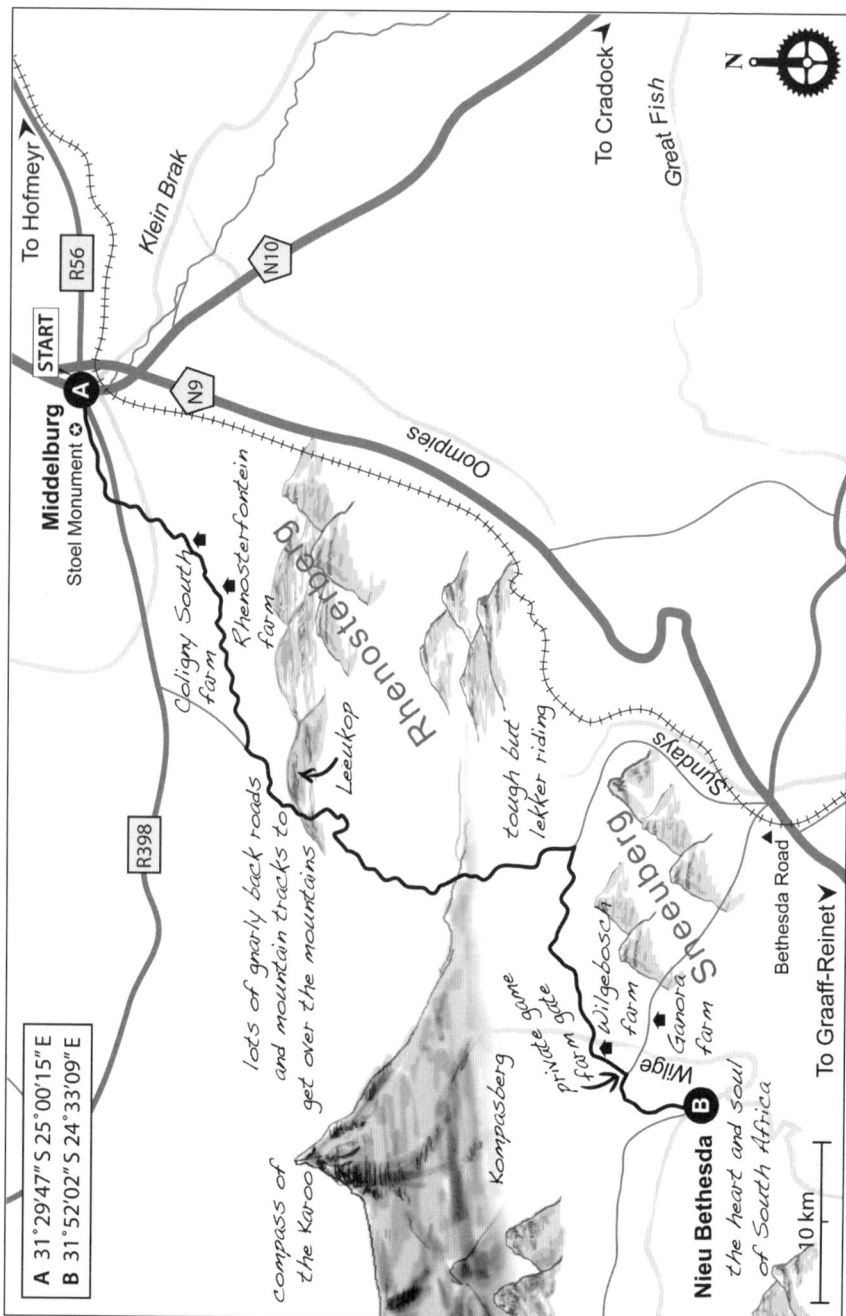

A 31°29'47"S 25°00'15"E
B 31°52'02"S 24°33'09"E

To Hofmeyr

R56

Klein Brak

START

R398

N10

N9

Oompies

To Cradock

Great Fish

N

Middelburg
Stoel Monument

Rhenosterfontein farm

Coligny South farm

Rhenosterberg

Leeukop

lots of gnarly back roads and mountain tracks to get over the mountains

compass of the Karoo

Kompasberg

tough but lekker riding

Sneeuberg

Sundays

Wilgebosch farm

private game farm gate

Wilge

Ganora farm

Bethesda Road

To Graaff-Reinet

Nieu Bethesda
the heart and soul of South Africa

10 km

follow the gravel road for 3km, through a farm *werf*, to cross the Klein Brak River.

Heading southwards, the road rises towards Rhenosterfontein farm, with Sneeuberg rising starkly up on your left. The highest point on the left is Rhenosterkop West. Now is not the time to falter in leg or spirit because, while the route does not do any real mountaineering, it does delve into and out of the mountains. It also offers spectacular views of the Sneeuberg, the Kompasberg, which looks like a gargantuan dinosaur fang as it plays hide-and-seek far off to the southwest, and surrounding

Who says the Karoo is dry and flat? The Amarok has some fun on the road to Nieu Bethesda.

valleys and farms as comely as the Great Karoo ever gets.

The track ascends with you feeling you're really deep in the mountains, stream-heads and hillsides rising all around you. Eventually you rise to about 1610m and round a high shoulder, where the track swings to the left in a wide arc, hugging the hill slope. A small farm lies in a tranquil nook below on your right.

The route swings right (south) to track along a spur and rises about 100m over 2.5km. Keeping high (1680m), it passes over a low nek, swinging west to make its way into a high valley with another idyllic farm nestling among the peaks. It gets very cold in these parts in winter, and very hot in summer. The track now climbs steadily, southwest, up towards the twin peaks ahead. The higher one (right) is Leeukop, the slightly lower one, nameless.

At 1830m the track hits a T-junction on a ridge coming down from Leeukop. Turn left here on a gravel road, going up for a short distance until the road loops to the right to descend the spur. It's tough riding to here, the highest point in the day. Then there are a few more loops as the road descends for 3.8km, going around the nameless peak to another junction.

The route turns sharp right here, continuing on a downward trajectory for a wonderful run towards the village. For 6km it takes an easy run west, dropping into another fertile farmed valley, then the road wiggles towards a nek in the ridge ahead. A steep but short stretch clears the ridge, heading downwards again on a southwest bearing.

Again, about 3.6km further, descend through a shallow bowl-like valley, take a low nek over a ridge and swoop down to cross the Wilge River, wending through Wilgebosch farm with its tree-lined lane. There's a 50m ascent up a ridge, a sharp right turn, a traverse on the contour, then a swing sharp left to cross a stream. The road ascends easily for 400m to a T-junction. If you just push the button at the very serious-looking game fence and electrified gate, it opens for you. Turn right for an enchanting 5km sweep around the Wilgenbosch hill as the view into the valley unfolds and the charms – in a uniquely Karoo kind of way – of Nieu Bethesda become apparent by metres and degrees.

• •

STAGE 2
NIEU BETHESDA TO GRAAFF-REINET   108km

GRADE: Long, moderate; hard in parts
OVERNIGHT: Betty's (self-catering)

IN A NUTSHELL
The sheer distance and the long climb up the escarpment will tax riders every which way. But there is a downhill run for 40km through a gorge all along the Sundays River. You could cross it up to 12 times – splish-splash! – particularly if the river is running high.

Then there's the 15km escarpment climb, but the countryside is lovely, all high green plateau and tall ridges with big vistas and lonely, mostly abandoned farms. If the climb up the Great Escarpment is a real character test, though, a reward follows: a 20km descent into a gorge cutting through the mountain edge.

Snapshot of the experience
This was a day that mostly whizzed by at great speed. It proved a point held firmly by both Steve and amaWriter: the Eastern Cape has maybe the best and least-explored cycle touring in South Africa. It's also got a pervading sense

Some days just roll over easy like a cowboy cigarette. This one was a real smoker.

of history and a frontier vibe that sets it quite apart. Its aura runs deeper than elsewhere, deep into those fossil-pocked rocks.

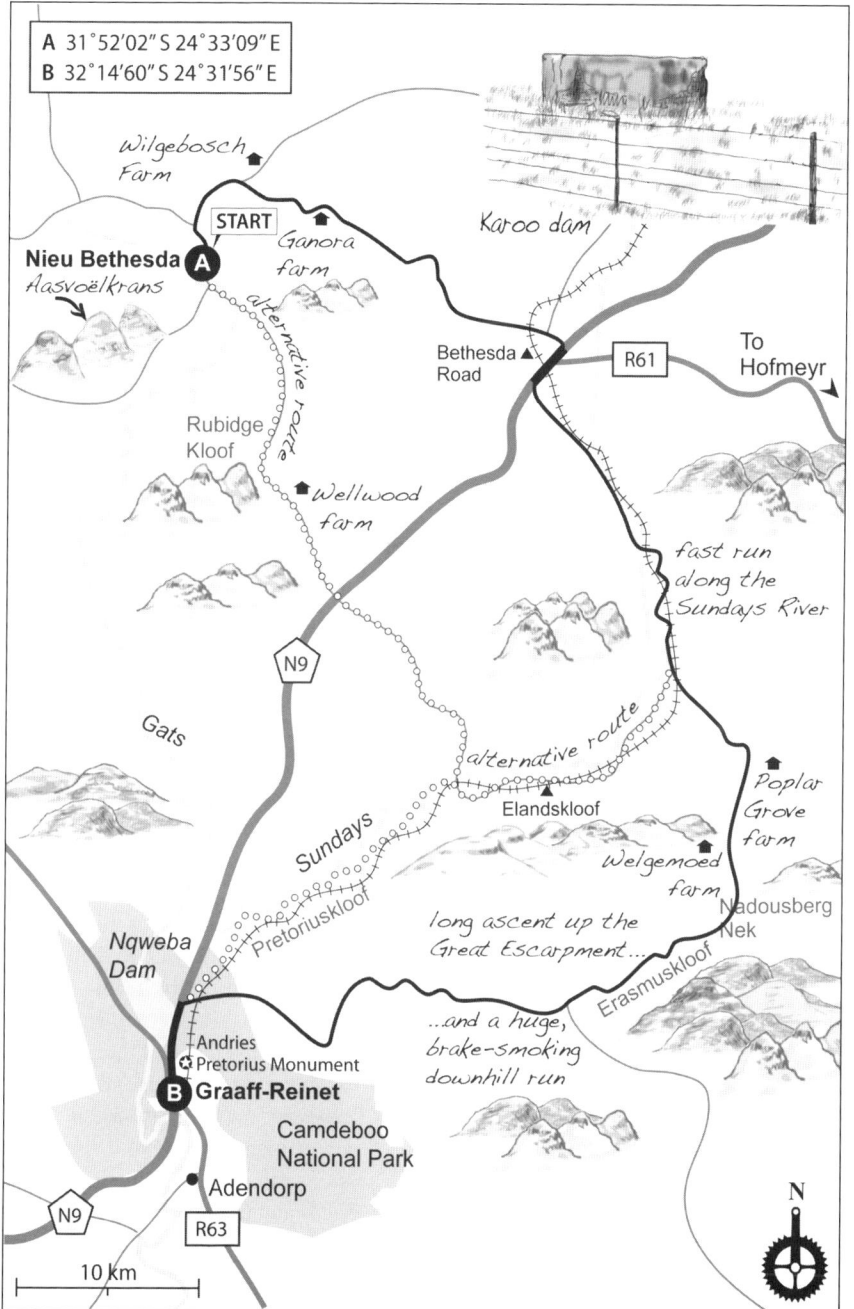

A 31°52′02″S 24°33′09″E
B 32°14′60″S 24°31′56″E

Wilgebosch Farm

Karoo dam

START

Nieu Bethesda
Aasvoëlkrans

Ganora farm

alternative route

Bethesda Road

R61

To Hofmeyr

Rubidge Kloof

Wellwood farm

fast run along the Sundays River

N9

Gats

alternative route

Elandskloof

Poplar Grove farm

Welgemoed farm

Nadousberg Nek

Sundays

Pretoriuskloof

long ascent up the Great Escarpment...

Erasmuskloof

Nqweba Dam

...and a huge, brake-smoking downhill run

Andries Pretorius Monument

B Graaff-Reinet

Camdeboo National Park

N9

Adendorp

R63

10 km

N

And for us it was the day we bid sad farewells to The Rabbit Rohan and amaDriver Denis, who had rolled with us since we'd entered Lesotho. We'd experienced together some hard days of riding, and even harder ones not riding. But joining us was Ray of Himeville, amaDriver number three.

The route

Either retrace your northerly way around Wilgenbosch hill, then head east for 29km to Bethesda Road station near the N9, or, for an alternative route, proceed to the T-junction at the south end of town, head left over the new bridge and ride via De Toren, Aasvoëlkrans, Rubidge Kloof, then past Wellwood farm. This one starts off easier, but the first is shorter.

Following our route, turn right onto the N9; after several hundred metres pass the road left to Hofmeyr, and after a further 2.5km turn left onto a gravel road, into the Sundays River valley. After about 1.5km the road meets the railway; after another 3km it begins to run parallel to the river on your left. The ride alongside the river is verdant and exciting – about 13km downhill. You will ride through a large private game reserve where you pass an old farmhouse where Voortrekker leader and hero of Blood River, Andries Pretorius, was born.

When you get to an obvious side-junction, with a sign to Elandskloof, keep left. (A route we don't know but looks worth a shot is to follow the road right to Elandskloof for about 19km. When the road veers north, back towards Nieu Bethesda, bear southwest by following the old railway line to Graaff-Reinet.)

Our road climbs steadily up for the next 17km, starting at 1160m. First it passes through a steep and rocky gorge with evocative rock formations, all aloe-fringed, then finds its way into a montane valley with fields and pasturage. The farm Poplar Grove, perched halfway up towards the edge of the escarpment, is the only one

Crossing the Sundays River for the umpteenth time, that black *bakkie* still close on our tails.

around that seems like it might still be occupied – but we had no time to dally. Nearing the escarpment edge, Welgemoed, in grand old Victorian style, alas was boarded up and deserted.

You reach a high at 1620m, followed by the mother of all descents as you pass through a nek in the Nadousberg. The first 3.5km are super-steep and windy, then it flattens out a bit and a road comes in from the left. That's the top of Erasmuskloof, and the road descends again with purpose. The riding is exhilarating in a more controlled way – but it's a 22.5km run, so your arms could get pumped to the max and your brakes start smokin' as you descend onto the Plains of Camdeboo.

Where it flattens out and proceeds straight for 5km to the N9, you're riding through a section of the Camdeboo National Park. Cross the railway line (unless you've followed it all the way from Elandskloof) and turn left onto the N9. Directly ahead is the Nqweba (formerly Vanryneveld Pass) dam, where you turn left and ride the shoulder for a final 3km to the centre of town.

Just before you enter the town is a small monument to Andries Pretorius on the far side of the road (his top hat is distinctive). Where the main street kinks left, turn right into Caledon Street. Pass the church and three blocks further is the cottage on the left-hand side (sleeps eight without a squeeze).

. . . .

STAGE 3
GRAAFF-REINET TO JANSENVILLE   114km

GRADE: Long, moderate
OVERNIGHT: Oak Villa Guest House

IN A NUTSHELL

This is a bad news, good news, kind of day. The bad news is the long distance; the good news is that you're following the general course of the Sundays River valley. The only hardship you might endure is the fact that there are no hard parts – it's pretty much flat, and even slightly downhill. But you will fly, like eagles.

Jansenville – on the map a long, boring line – in our memories was a very boring stop on the route between Grahamstown and Johannesburg, but it has proved to be 'just right' for some city escapees who have set up shop here as artists or guest house owners.

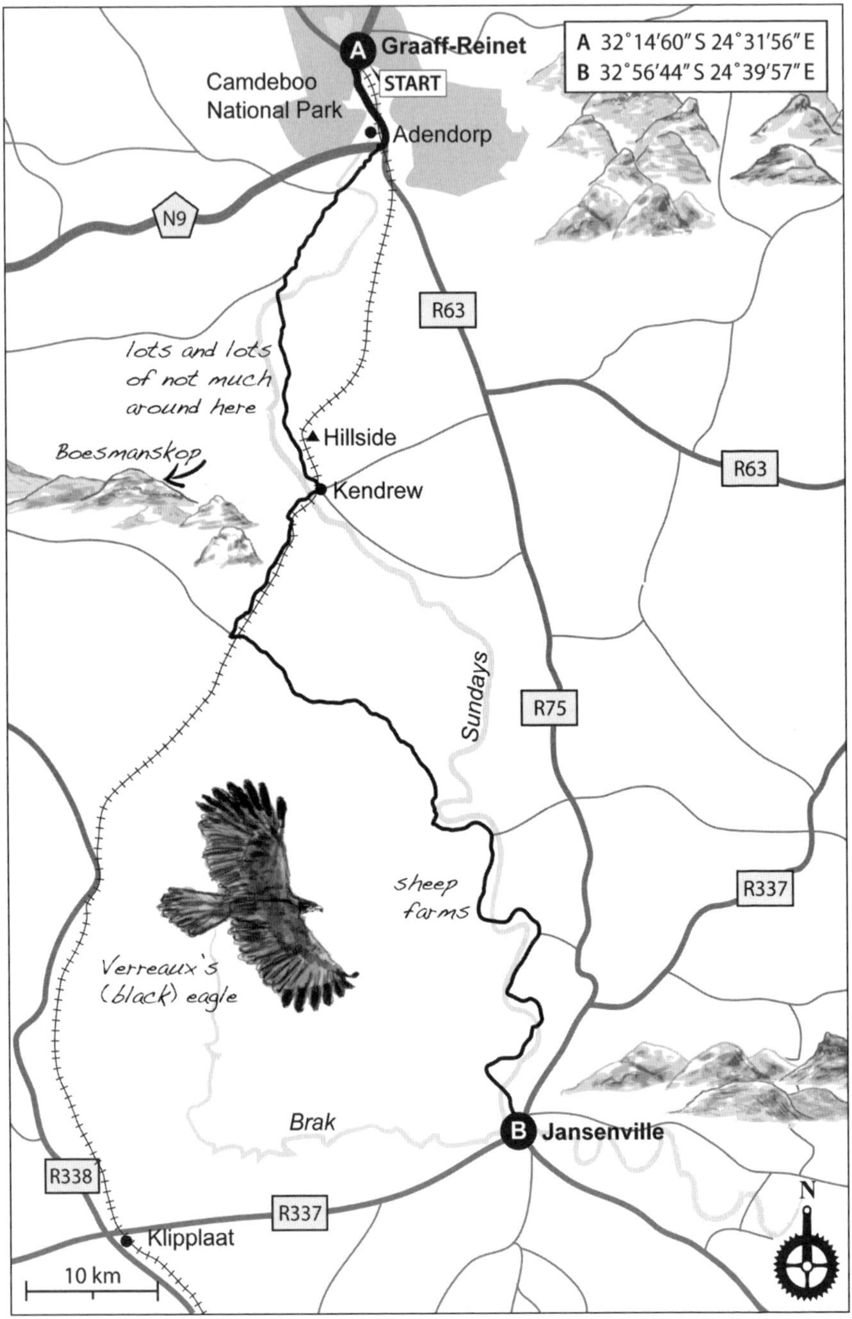

A Graaff-Reinet
START

A 32°14'60"S 24°31'56"E
B 32°56'44"S 24°39'57"E

Camdeboo
National Park

Adendorp

N9

R63

*lots and lots
of not much
around here*

Hillside

Boesmanskop

Kendrew

R63

Sundays

R75

*sheep
farms*

R337

*Verreaux's
(black) eagle*

Brak

B Jansenville

R338

R337

Klipplaat

10 km

N

Snapshot of the experience

We were cruising somewhere between Adendorp and Kendrew, where it is so flat you can – as an old English teacher once told me – see tomorrow coming down the road. Steve rode up to me with an uncharacteristically concerned look on his face. He said he was worried that he had thought all the thoughts he had to think, because he'd been trying to think of something new for the past hour – and nothing new was forthcoming. I told him to go off and try again. Later, nearing Jansenville, he rode back up and confessed he had still not been able to have a new thought. I told him to try again the next day.

Yup, this trail is about the people. One farmer in a bakkie helped us with directions, shot off, his truck loaded to the gunwales with timber, then returned some time later at great speed just to clarify a point, zipped around and disappeared in a dust cloud. There is a generosity of spirit out here that matches the great big eagle-winged sky.

The route

Leave town on the R63 south (don't take the N9 to the west) and ride a few kilometres to Adendorp, where you turn right. Just beyond the *dorp*, cross the Sundays River for the first of six times, as well as several tributaries.

The Sundays feeds the fence-to-fence farms in the valley, although the river doesn't always flow and the farms are not always occupied. Just short of 14km after the second river crossing, the route converges with the south-bound railway line at Hillside (no hill though). About 1km later turn right (west) at a

The sad remains of an old Karoo farmhouse in the Sundays River valley.

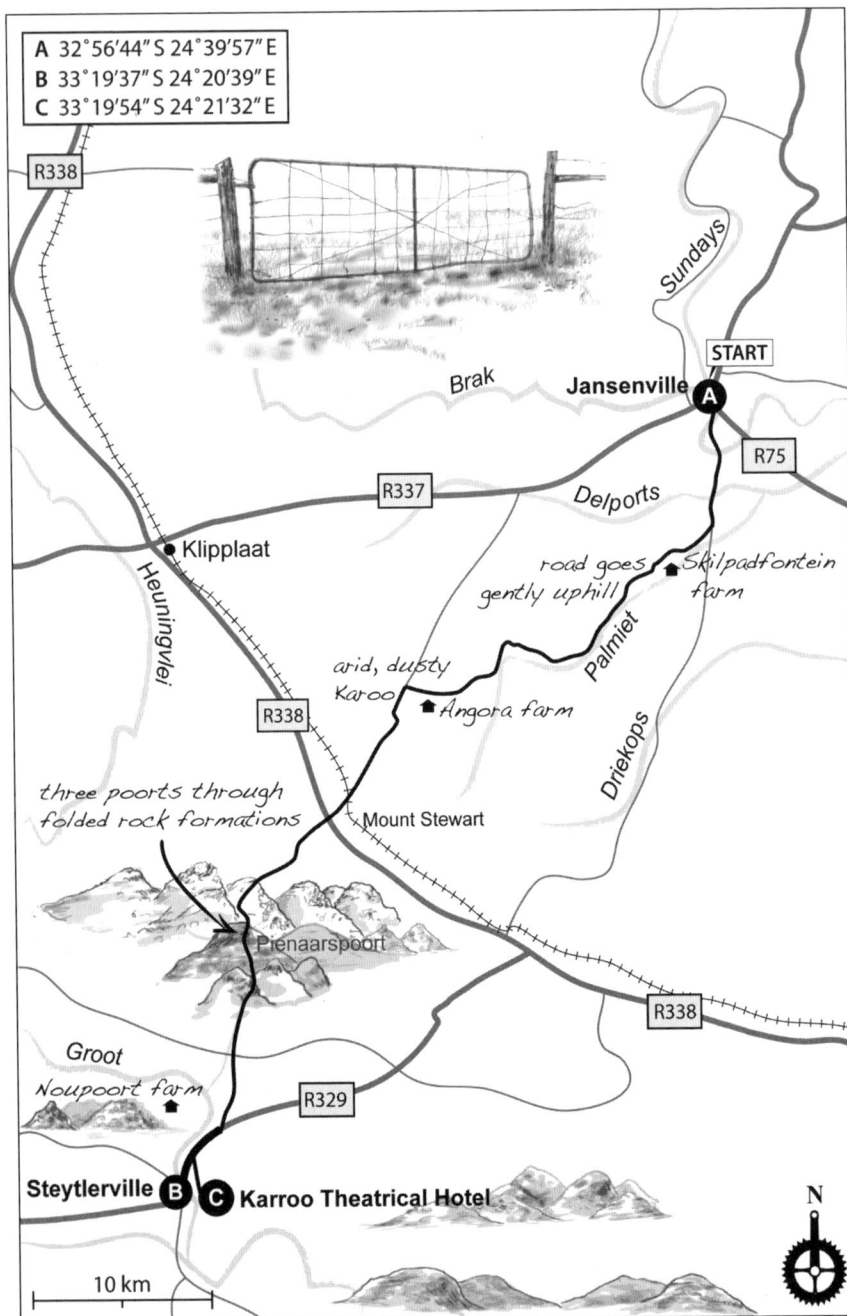

A 32°56'44" S 24°39'57" E
B 33°19'37" S 24°20'39" E
C 33°19'54" S 24°21'32" E

R338

Sundays

START
Jansenville A

R75

Brak

R337

Delports

Klipplaat

road goes
gently uphill

Skilpadfontein
farm

Heuningvlei

Palmiet

arid, dusty
Karoo

Angora farm

R338

Drietkops

three poorts through
folded rock formations

Mount Stewart

Pienaarspoort

R338

Groot

Noupoort farm

R329

Steytlerville B C Karroo Theatrical Hotel

N

10 km

Ivan, the Canadian – solar champion of Ha Qiqita/Bethel – gives a sneak preview of the cabbage rolls cooking in his solar oven. (*Roof of Africa Trail*)

Near Holy Cross Mission we watched this guy working on his Hi-Ace, wondering how long it would take to get it back on the road again. (*Roof of Africa Trail*)

As we rode towards the Tele border post, this 'last chance' stop was, as so often proved to be the case in Lesotho, closed. (*Roof of Africa Trail*)

The Kraai River wends its bucolic way through the hills of New England, also known as the Wartrail district. (*War Trail*)

Dr Rohan (The Rabbit) diagnoses a brake piston snafu – or something like that. You've got to be able to 'fix and ride'. (*War Trail*)

From Barkly East to Dordrecht the roads rolled nice 'n' easy, but a cold wind did its best to give us a hard time. (*War Trail*)

Halfway between here and nowhere clearly was also what the people of many Karoo farms thought of the place. (*War Trail*)

Taking a break out of the wind on top of the Stormberg, pretty much where Smuts's commando came unstuck during the Anglo-Boer War. (*War Trail*)

Sometimes, like here between Molteno and Hofmeyr, you just get so bored with riding that you get off your bike and walk. (*War Trail*)

Approaching Hofmeyr and the many culinary delights of the Karoobos Farmstall (really a tearoom run by farmers' wives). (*War Trail*)

Great, I've got these clowns to rely on to get to Middelburg... (Things will tend to get silly around day 40.) (*War Trail*)

We were glad to have the Amarok while biking through the Karoo on days when the wind was so strong, we used the vehicle as a wind shield. (*Great Karoo Trail*)

Karoo means something like 'big dry place' – and so it is, so much so that even the windmills *lus* for a drink. (*Great Karoo Trail*)

'Sho't Left Steve' decides on a whim that we have to take a short cut over the Sneeuberg – and he is usually right in matters navigational. (*Great Karoo Trail*)

Riding down the Sundays River between Graaff-Reinet and Jansenville was one of the most boring days ... and dusty. (*Great Karoo Trail*)

The third Pienaarspoort, where the road climbs from Mount Stewart towards Steytlerville on the Groot River. (*Great Karoo Trail*)

No-one comes here ... but the person who tends the open-air wheel museum in Steytlerville doesn't seem to mind. (*Great Karoo Trail*)

The Groot River valley between Steytlerville and Willowmore reminded us of the Baviaanskloof, only less visited. (*Great Karoo Trail*)

The first fangs of the Cape Folded Mountains chew their way up through Karoo sediments as they start their procession to Klaarstroom. (*Great Karoo Trail*)

Where's Steve? The Eardstapper has to try to find the Daytripper hiding among the mountain biking fraternity of Klaarstroom. (*Great Karoo Trail*)

This is where you start to *knyp* ... the Great Swartberg looms up ahead and there's that big pass to come.... (*Folded Mountains Trail*)

Thomas Bain had convicts cut this road up, over and down the Swartberg – and we moaned just riding it. (*Folded Mountains Trail*)

The significance of a poort: the Swartberg mountains crowd around you, but the road goes easily and a river runs through it. (*Folded Mountains Trail*)

Deep in the Gamkaskloof valley, you can expect the weather to be always extreme: icy in winter and fiery hot in summer. (*Folded Mountains Trail*)

You've been through Die Hel and the worst of Die Leer (The Ladder) is now behind you ... but the road to Rouxpos is still a long one. (*Folded Mountains Trail*)

The miracle of morning light can make even the most dire of places, like Touws River, seem like a pretty picture. (*Folded Mountains Trail*)

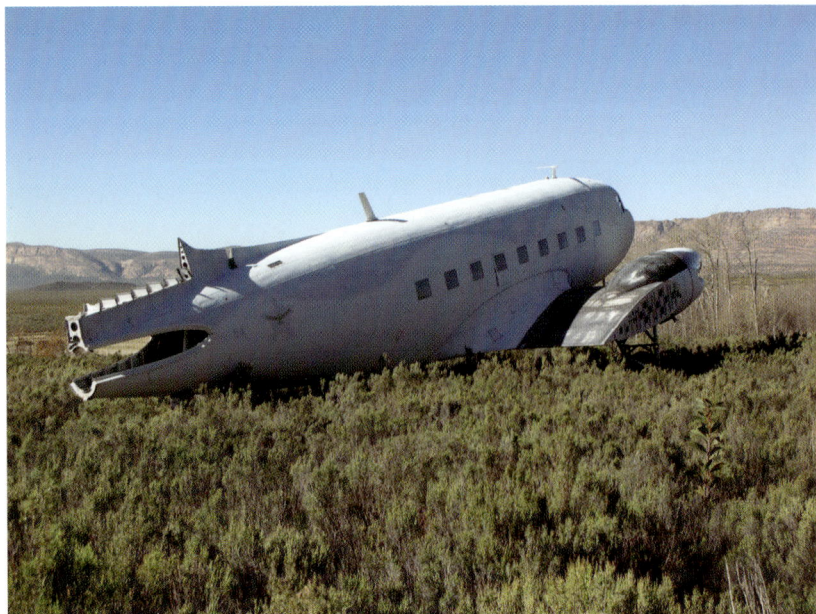

Mayday! Mayday! The pilot of this Dakota seems to have made as heavy weather of the Hex River mountains as we did. (*Folded Mountains Trail*)

Looking down the Nagmaal track across Tulbagh, you can almost smell dinner cooking at home. (*Folded Mountains Trail*)

Doing a bit of home maintenance alongside the Little Berg River where it cuts through the mountains not far from Tulbagh. (*Fairest Cape Trail*)

The route into and through the Swartland wends this way and that, trying to avoid tar – with varying luck here. (*Fairest Cape Trail*)

At Blue Peter in Bloubergstrand, where Cape Town is visible across Table Bay. With one more day to go, the Spine of the Dragon ride is almost over. (*Fairest Cape Trail*)

How long was the trail? The Eardstapper earns his Dragon Master shirt ... and all the saddle sores and head winds are forgotten. (*Fairest Cape Trail*)

junction, cross the river, then swing south again. The land rises steeply on your right; the high point opposite is Boesmanskop (1104m).

Pick up the railway line again near Kendrew. Follow it southwest for 9km, then turn left near a junction of routes and head southeast for 23km of mundane cycling, broken only by two stream crossings towards either end of this stretch.

Shortly thereafter you meet the river again, following the west bank through a sweeping S-formation, next head south for about 6km, then go around another sweeping S-formation in the meandering river. Who knew there was a diamond mine here? This section is by far the most interesting of the day, with more closely packed farms (abandoned, mostly), irrigated fields and pastures with fat Karoo sheep (you can almost smell the chops braaiing).

Rocky ridges flank the river, and sometimes you have to power over a spur or ride a tight course between ridge and river as you cross from one side to another. The river here is what geographers call mature, flowing in wide loops through the rugged (but not hilly) topography, except in those places where the river has eroded its winding course hard up against a ridge. Hills can rise as much as 300m on the bank opposite the road.

In all you drop from 740m altitude at Graaff-Reinet to 400m at Jansenville – just 340m. So you could say it's pretty much braai-grid flat again. In terms of route-finding, just follow the river for the final 42km to Jansenville.

. . . .

STAGE 4
JANSENVILLE TO STEYTLERVILLE   63km

GRADE: Medium, moderate
OVERNIGHT: Karroo Theatrical Hotel

IN A NUTSHELL

This stage is mostly uphill in a series of big steps – altogether 850m up. But roads have this tendency to find the most unexpected ways through hills: poorts. (The English word 'pass' just doesn't seem to match it; 'canyon' comes closer). Poorts and passes, that's what riding in the Karoo is all about. You crest the pass, then shoot for kilometre after kilometre down a river gorge, twisting and weaving and bucking through the slots and playing the momentum game over each hump. You beat some, some beat you. And with each push you get a big lactic-acid leg burn.

Snapshot of the experience

As you turn onto the tarred road for your approach to Steytlerville, the rocks on the side are decorated with painted flags showing the little town's various family origins – mostly old colonial ones – the last one a huge new South African flag brightly painted onto the frayed rock face. It's great fun. So is the Theatrical Hotel's Karoo fantasia. It's all glitter-ball, laughter and fine food.

The route

Leave from the south end of town on tar for a very short distance as you cross the Sundays River for the last time. The tarred road splits into the R75 (left) and R337 (right). First head left, then right (south) onto a gravel road 1km from town.

The road crosses the Delports River, then picks up the Palmiet River which you follow gently uphill until, 8km from town, you turn right at Skilpadfontein farm, going west then swinging southwest. There are no noticeable downhills as you rise evenly towards the far mountains, and there is only one significant climb on this stage. It's all pretty much flat Karoo here, broken by the occasional farm and a turn in the road (at Angora farm, for instance, you swing from south to west for about 12km).

The next 8.5km to Mount Stewart is one big hump – from 620m to 710m at Middelpunt (indeed) – and then easily down to 660m where you cross a railway line, past the pretty little Victorian-style church that serves the little not-so-pretty community of Mount Stewart (Cawoods general store looks like it hasn't had much custom since its doors opened in 1937). Cross the gravel R338 and pass through a barely noticeable poort 1.5km further. If you're looking for seriously dead-straight, boring, arid, dusty Karoo, you'll find it here.

A single-lane steel-girder bridge leads over the Groot River into Steytlerville.

However, another 5km on you reach a more apparent poort with a climb up to 720m, swinging left through Pienaarspoort, where the rock strata have been pushed from horizontal to jagged vertical bands, and into the Pienaarspoort valley. Get your camera ready, because you pass one of the best folds of sandstone strata (Cape Folded Mountains) this side of the Swartberg Pass. Ahead is the second part of Pienaarspoort, but this time it's a general – not steep – downhill affair, swooping through the defile, from 620m all the way down to 480m where you cross a small gravel road. And dead ahead is Pienaarspoort number three. You're still following the Pienaars River (stream, usually dry) so again it's downhill.

It's also rather pretty; once you pass through poort number three, you're into the very appealing Groot River valley where Noupoort guest farm creates a linear green oasis along the river line. There's a not too arduous climb out of the Pienaarspoort valley to the tarred R329. Turn right and ride gently up through yet another poort, along and above the Groot River, then down to the town.

Just before you would cross the river and enter the town, turn left onto a gravel road for the last 2km or so to the watered gardens and welcoming façade of the Karroo Theatrical Hotel. You won't be disappointed.

STAGE 5
STEYTLERVILLE TO WILLOWMORE   112km

GRADE: Long, moderate
OVERNIGHT: Willow Historical Guest House

IN A NUTSHELL
This stage is a steady climb just about all day, with only one big spike showing on the Garmin profile – 769m of ascent over roughly 110km in total. Not too bad, really. There are some farms (some guest, some game) along the way, but all on the Willowmore side of the valley, so only of partial use as stay-overs. This is one day, maybe, that's best to do in one go. Just be sure to start early.

Snapshot of the experience
We stayed in an unexpectedly gracious Victorian house in a town that, from the main road, looks unassuming in the extreme. Coffee and apple cake with cream

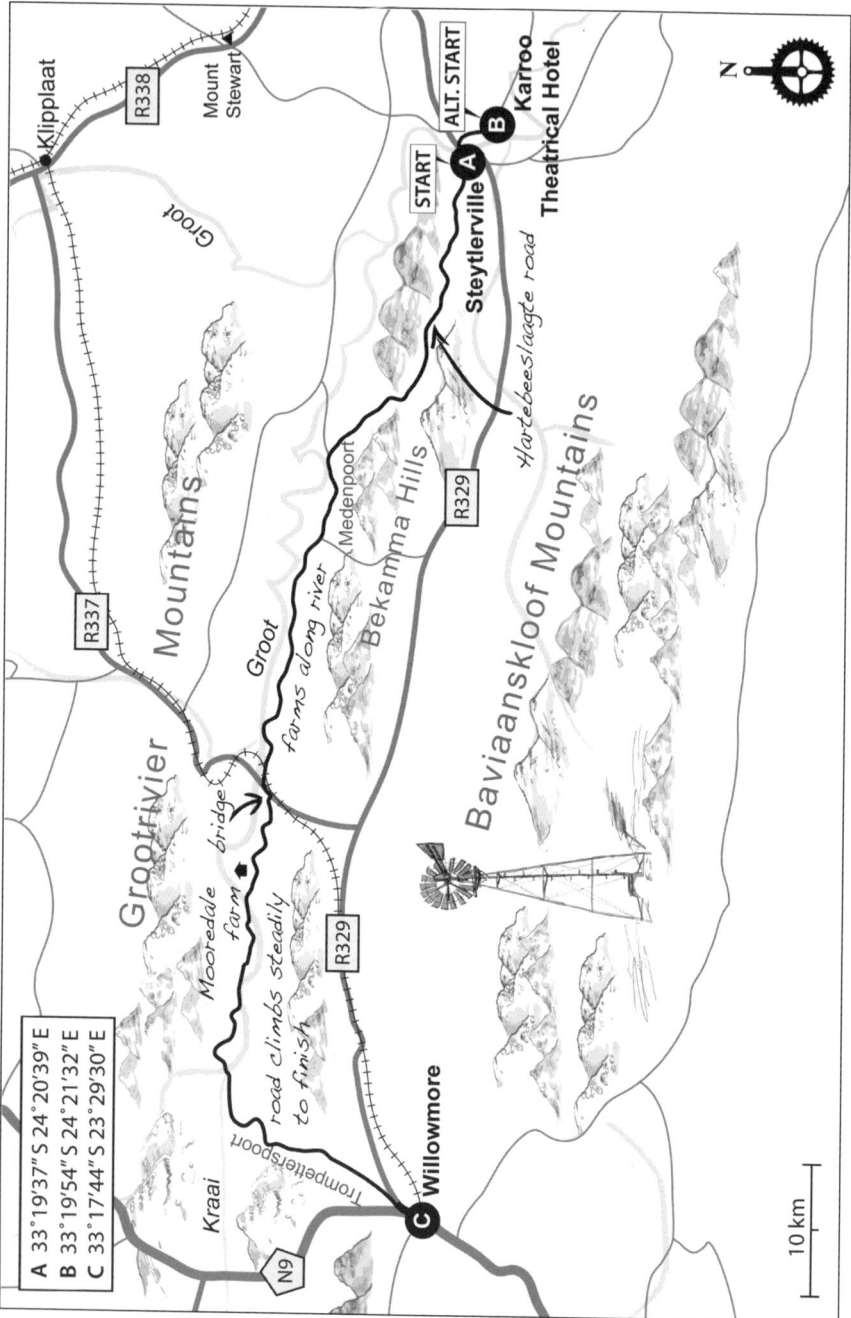

N

A 33°19'37"S 24°20'39"E
B 33°19'54"S 24°21'32"E
C 33°17'44"S 23°29'30"E

Klipplaat

R338

Mount Stewart

Groot

R337

Groot

Grootrivier Mountains

Mooredale farm

Kraai

Trompetterspoort

Willowmore

N9

ALT. START

Karroo Theatrical Hotel

B

START

A

Steytlerville

Hartebeeslaagte road

Medenpoort

Bekamma Hills

R329

farms along river

Grootrivier bridge

road climbs steadily to finish

R329

Baviaanskloof Mountains

C Willowmore

10 km

at Sophie's Choice is as good as any you'll find anywhere to carbo-load at the end of a long day's riding.

The next day started off misty and flat, then it got really interesting – the mountains kind of jumped up on each side once we got into the Groot River valley, very much like the more famous Baviaanskloof.

The route

If Steytlerville can be said to have a centre, it will be at the Middleton Street intersection: to get there, cross the narrow cast-iron bridge over the Groot River, stop to check out the unassuming but charming open-air wheel museum, then head into town and turn right up Middleton. Tar soon becomes gravel, then it's a long, slow slog west along the gravel Hartebeeslaagte road for 20km before anything happens – other than kori bustards eagerly making like feathered B52s taking off from the veld.

Then, hills on either side of the road converge up ahead as the road swings north towards the Bekamma hills, and you reach 590m, with peaks about 300m above you to the left and right. Ride down into the Groot River valley and turn left, upstream, at Medenpoort. You can't follow the river for long before you have to take a squiggly line left, up around the back of a conical hill that forms a cliff face along the river's edge.

The river makes wide loops across its valley so this is actually a short-cut route and one that offers some of the best mountain biking of the day. After 8.5km you look down on the river again. The first substantial farm you encounter is Beerpoort (but no succour for riders there). Further on is Bhejane – half farm, half game reserve, we wondered? A little further Timbila seemed kind of the same.

Continue through farmlands till you reach the railway and the R337, the Groot River bridge off to the right. Turn left, proceeding for 3km to another junction. The district road and railway head south through a poort, but turn right to stay in the main valley. Cross the river about 6km further, near Mooredale farm.

After an assurance of accommodation at Glenmore farm about 7km further, we

Lovely Willow Historical Guest House.

found it to be defunct so on we rode, past a place with high electrified fences, which hinted that it might offer accommodation but was so intimidating and uninviting, we decided it would not suit the spirit of our tour. And, so, on we rode. After 11km you cross the river again, then leave the Groot to its own course.

The road continues to rise steadily, as it has for most of the day, this time up the Kraai River valley for 5km, when it swings left and climbs through Trompetterspoort (the peak on your left is Trompettersberg). Alas, this is one poort that has no downhill, so that slog continues, if ever so slightly, for another 10km before you reach the outskirts of town (the less affluent side, but we enjoyed the cheering kids). Find your way to the guest house in Wehmeyer Street.

. . . .

STAGE 6
WILLOWMORE TO KLAARSTROOM   97km

GRADE: Long, moderate
OVERNIGHT: Klaarstroom Guest House

IN A NUTSHELL
Once again the Karoo – or the Little Karoo, in this instance – delivers on the riding side. Back roads, roads beyond those back roads, roads that become tracks with a dozen farm gates and a dozen 'dry' river crossings which, in our case, we found far from dry. It seems odd to say that a 100km ride could be easy, but for us it was – and for once, we did it without a headwind.

Snapshot of the experience
It never ceases to amaze us: throw a dart at any little *dorp* in the *platteland* – or the hills – and you'll hit a guest house or farm with an inspiring patron or couple who have created a little sophisticated oasis. And thank goodness for them, for not only do they make this trail possible, but also they have all helped – in their individual and collective ways – to reinvigorate tiny places like Willowmore and Klaarstroom.

Every time we saw merino rams – with the largest horns we've ever encountered – my game was to shout 'wolf!', but Steve always looked a bit embarrassed to be riding with me.

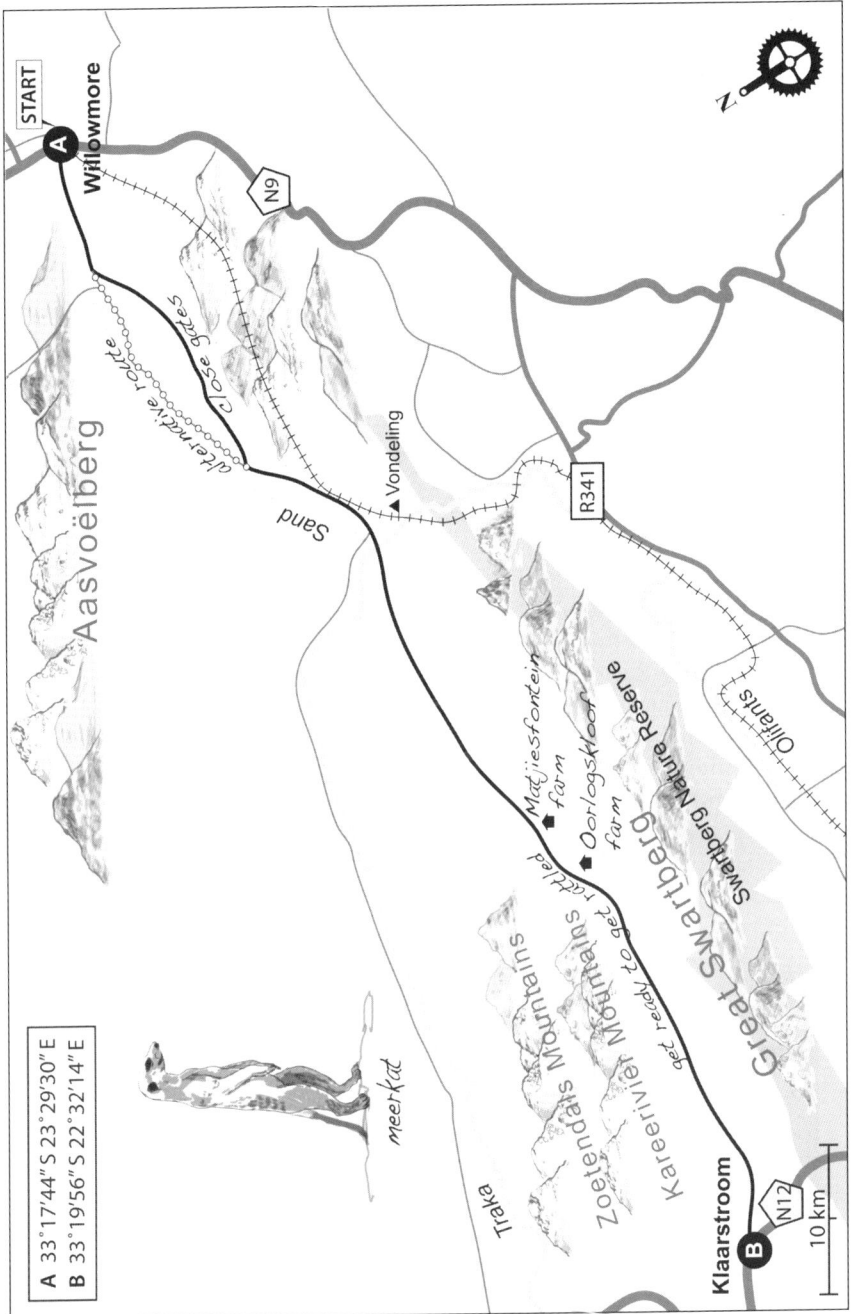

A 33°17'44" S 23°29'30" E
B 33°19'56" S 22°32'14" E

START

A Willowmore

N9

Aasvoëlberg

alternative route

close gates

Sand

▲ Vondeling

R341

meerkat

Matjiesfontein farm

Oorlogskloof farm

get ready to get track

Traka

Zoetendals Mountains

Kareerivier Mountains

Great Swartberg

Swartberg Nature Reserve

Oliflans

Klaarstroom

B

N12

10 km

The route

Leave town on the same road as the guest house, heading west under the N9 bridge. The gravel road is pretty flat here, a formation of low hills ahead equating to an easy climb over a watershed, 10km from town, followed by an easy descent. Around 3km further is a fork; we chose the lesser track to the left around Klipspringerskraal hill (they meet up again around 13km on, so the choice is yours). The left track was stupendous: a few short stiff climbs, some stream crossings, short sharp downhills, little farms with rickety gates to open and close, and those merino rams with the largest horns ever.

The next 7km, though surrounded by rugged hills, are as flat as, well, the Karoo. On the right, tributaries converge and form the Sand River, while on the left the railway merges with the track. They run together for 4.5km to Vondeling station, now abandoned, near the (dry) Traka River.

Cross the river; where the road forks, go left. From there it's 57km to Klaarstroom on a constant, rolling track – which means pedalling pretty much hard all the way (the road is seriously sandy and corrugated in places, sporadically needing extra effort).

On the left-hand side the land rises up in steps of ridges, each one representing an ancient fold in the landscape caused when Africa tore itself free from the rest of Gondwana. On the right-hand side is the lesser but not insignificant Kareerivier range, and beyond them the somewhat higher Zoetendals mountains. Highest of course, and in great contrast, are the Great Swartberg, on the left-hand side, where Meiringspoort peak rises to 2131m.

Over this stretch the road first rises from 800m to about 920m before dropping by the same amount as you approach Klaarstroom – once you reach the watershed a little way beyond the halfway mark, the farms around Klaarstroom lie dead ahead. At Matjiesfontein the monotony is broken momentarily by a farm and fields, and soon thereafter you cross from the

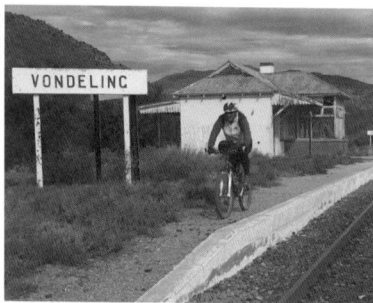

Halfway to Klaarstroom – but nothing to stop for here.

Eastern to the Western Cape province on the Oorlogskloof farm boundary.

The mountains then begin to crowd the valley floor as the road starts its long, easy descent to the Meiringspoort road. With about 7km to go, the stream peels away and the road veers from west to northwest, crossing the N12, a busy trucking road, so take care. Then you enter the haven of Klaarstroom, pretty as a picture with its Victorian cottages and mountain backdrop.

STAGE 7
KLAARSTROOM TO PRINCE ALBERT   77km

GRADE: Long, moderate
OVERNIGHT: Dennehof Guest House

IN A NUTSHELL

It's an easy ride (long, straight, gravel roads), so long as you're happy
navigating donga-sized corrugations or deep sand for long stretches at
a time. Anyone with dentures be warned – it will shake your bones and
teeth all about (it reminded us of an old road sign in the Baviaanskloof:
'remove dentures' and a hand-painted picture of a car being shaken up
by bumps in the road). That notwithstanding, it should seem like an easy
ride out in the country; it took us only about four hours of actual riding.

Snapshot of the experience

Prince Albert has to be the most attractive small town in South Africa, backed
up against the muscular Swartberg, all Cape cottagey and historical. Like most
small towns, it probably has its foibles, but it will still charm the cycling shoes
off you. And, in this land of comely cottages, Dennehof is a princess, while
milkshakes at the Lazy Lizard went down like well water in a Saharan wadi.

The route

Again, trying to avoid tar for dirt tracks,
we rode 77km instead of 54km (and
still we had to ride 20km on tar, north
through the Droëkloof – very pretty,
though). The truth is, try as we might, to
date we just haven't found an alternative;
no local knowledge has come to the
rescue, either. There just might be a
rideable track over the Witberg, which
joins the N12 near the head of Droëkloof,
but, if there is, it will be for hardcore
mountain bikers only.

   So … leave Klaarstroom on the N12
(direction Beaufort West), with the Groot
River on your left. Where the R407 goes

*There was a minor gold
rush around Sleutelfontein
in the late 1800s, but
only after the local
burghers had seen to the
extermination of the local
San inhabitants in one
of the country's most
heinous cases of genocide.
(Pesky Bushmen, stealing
sheep after the colonists
had fenced off the area
and shot out the game!)*

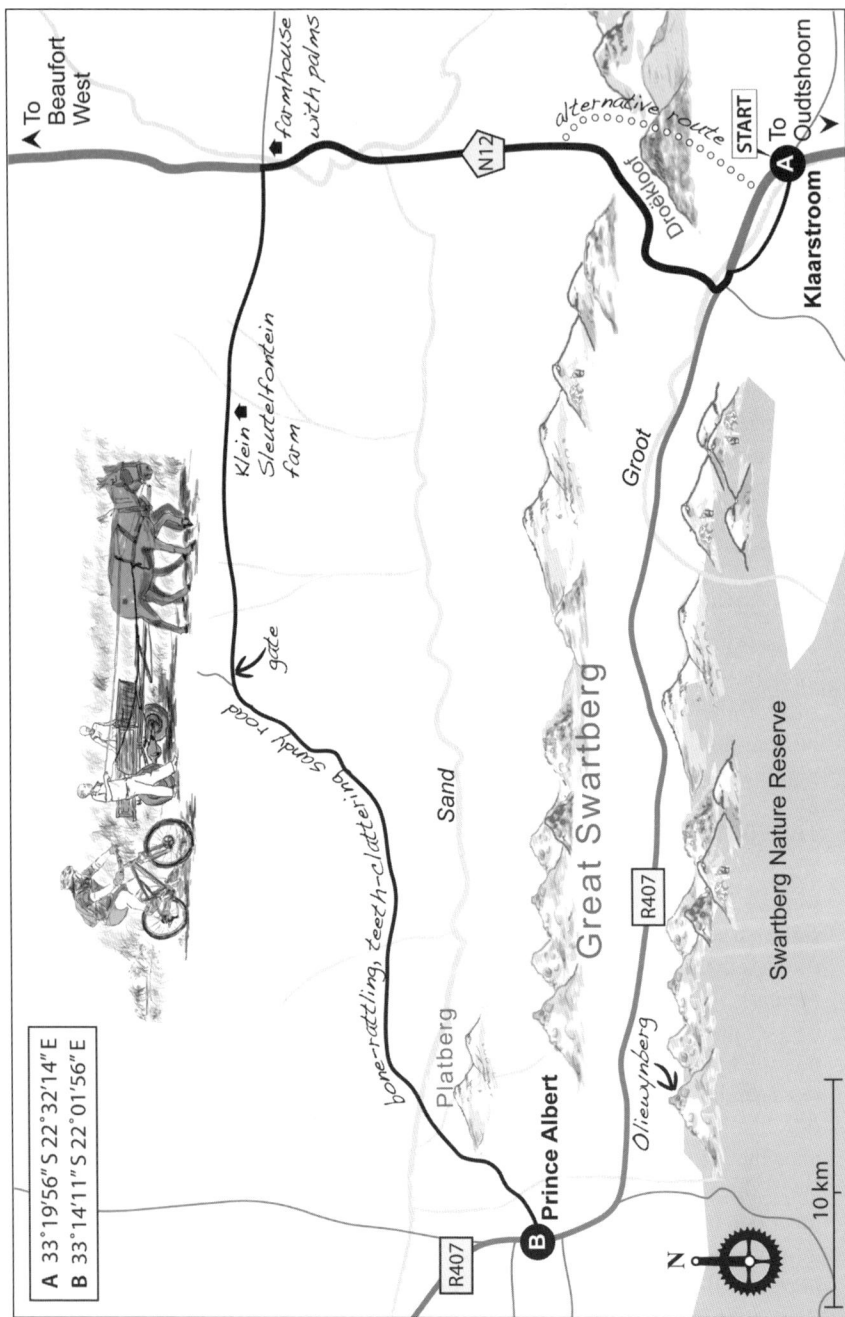

A 33°19'56"S 22°32'14"E
B 33°14'11"S 22°01'56"E

To Beaufort West

farmhouse with palms

alternative route

N12

START

A To Oudtshoorn

Klaarstroom

Droëkloof

Klein Sleutelfontein farm

gate

bone-rattling, teeth-clattering, buttock-bruising sandy road

Groot

Great Swartberg

Sand

Platberg

R407

Olienynberg

Swartberg Nature Reserve

B Prince Albert

R407

N

10 km

straight up the valley towards Prince Albert, turn right (north) with the N12, winding through Droëkloof for about 15km – crossing four bridges. You climb about 100m to where you emerge from the kloof and another 70m to the high point (Remhoogte at 930m).

A short distance past a farmhouse and palm trees on the right, turn left onto a gravel road to Klein Sleutelfontein farm. Cross the Sand stream after several kilometres; 9km further, wend through Klein Sleutelfontein farm. Nothing much seems to happen here but the place does have an interesting windmill. Just on 20km past the farm, the narrow track merges with a wider district road at a skew junction. Now it gets seriously rutted *and* sandy – but that's all. There aren't even sheep hereabouts.

The road crosses, via concrete causeways, two dry river courses with thorn-tree fringes but precious little shade. Where the road takes a sharp left-turn towards Prince Albert, the Platberg lies just across the Sand River on your left. Beyond and above that, Oliewynberg, at 1857m, is the high point on the Great Swartberg range.

Ride into town (as you approach the stream bed on the outskirts of Prince Albert, take the left fork if you're unsure) and turn left into the main street. Drop in at the Lazy Lizard for sustenance if you need it (the guest house is only a B&B), then proceed to the end of the road, going straight on a gravel driveway kind of road where the tar bends right. And do close the gate – a big but friendly dog lives there. You can call him Wagter, because all dogs like him should be. He'll understand.

Riding through the Bekamma hills, heading for the Groot River valley and Willowmore.

RECOMMENDED
6 days

Folded Mountains Trail

Prince Albert to Tulbagh • 381km

STAGE 1
PRINCE ALBERT TO GAMKASKLOOF 60km

GRADE: Medium, hard; riding extreme
OVERNIGHT: Fonteinplaas; CapeNature cottages

IN A NUTSHELL

The 15km climb up the Swartberg Pass to the Gamkaskloof turn-off takes about two hours. It's an invigorating, tortuous ride through wrenched, violent rock layers, where even 4×4 drivers inch their way up or down in awe. From there it's another 40-plus kilometres to the cottages, on some really rough track; this section is much harder than the first 20km. Apart from the many lesser ones, there is one major descent followed by a mighty ascent **before** you reach the famous switchback descent to the Gamkaskloof valley floor. The entire route will take the average cyclist no less than seven to eight hours of riding – and that doesn't include gasp breaks, or technical or emotional breakdowns.

Snapshot of the experience

We did Die Hel in deteriorating weather and on occasion had to take shelter from the wind. Wet? We looked like dunked monkeys. As we approached the last big climb – about 5km with nowhere to slink away and hide – all hell broke loose: angry clouds, lightning, thunder and hail. For a short while the valley floor was white with frozen rain-balls.

Down in the valley things were a tad chaotic. The cottages were all booked so we ended up in leaky caravans, drip, drip, drip all night. We were wet, muddy and cold in one of the best off-the-beaten-track destinations in the country, and so kind of happy in a way only fools like mountain bikers know.

The route

Prince Albert lies on the Dorps River which flows out of the Swartberg Pass, so follow it back into the pass, first heading south down Church Street (R407) for 4km, past the old mill. Where the tar swings left (east) to Klaarstroom, turn right onto the gravel road that goes directly towards those imposing mountains. The road goes reasonably straight and gently uphill for 3km, then begins to twist and turn through the Dorps River gorge.

The first few kilometres into the gorge are mercifully level, as you stare up in awe at the muscular, contorted rock strata of the Table Mountain Sandstone

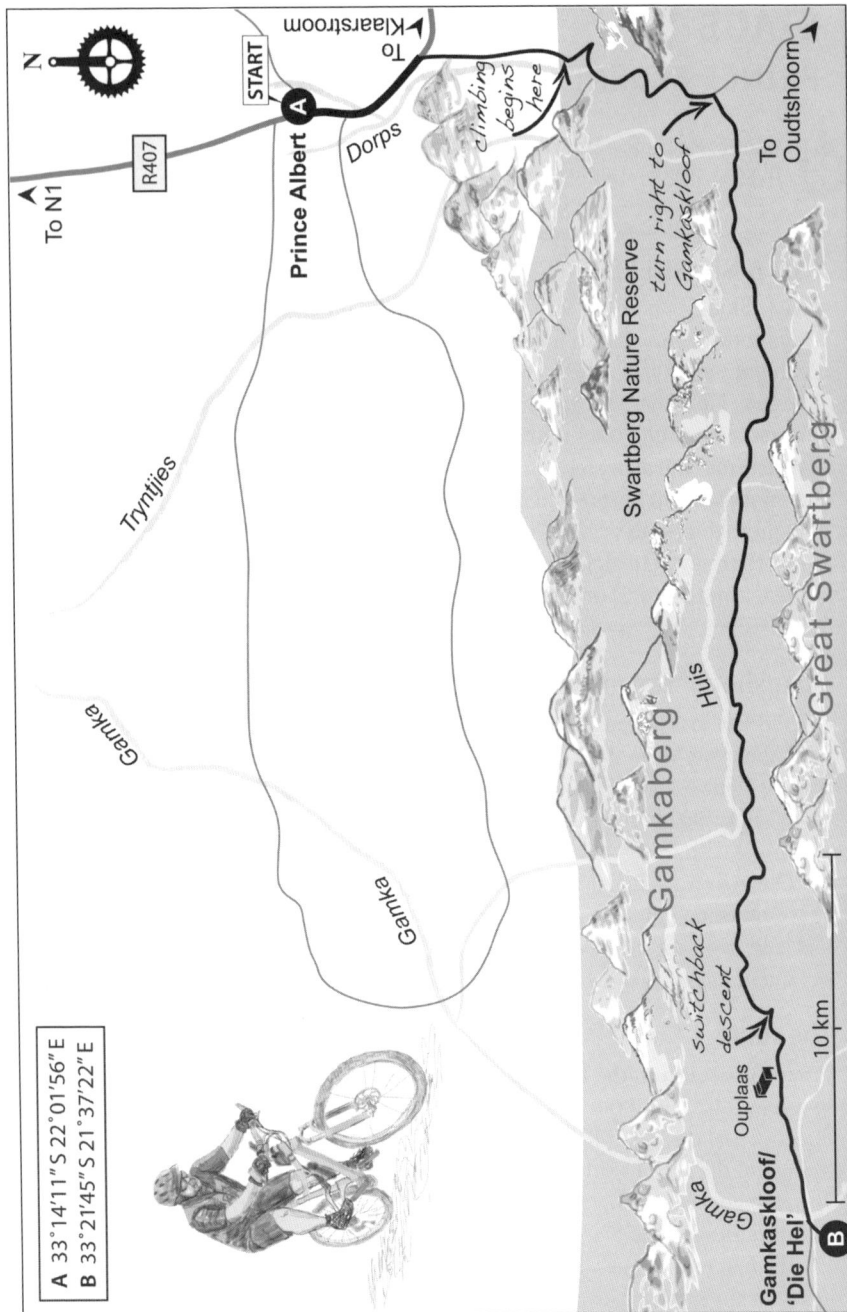

A 33°14'11"S 22°01'56"E
B 33°21'45"S 21°37'22"E

N

R407

To N1

START

Prince Albert

To Klaarstroom

Dorps

climbing begins here

Tryntjies

Gamka

Gamka

Swartberg Nature Reserve

turn right to Gamkaskloof

To Oudtshoorn

Gamkaberg

Huis

Great Swartberg

switchback descent

Ouplaas

10 km

Gamka

Gamkaskloof/ 'Die Hel'

B

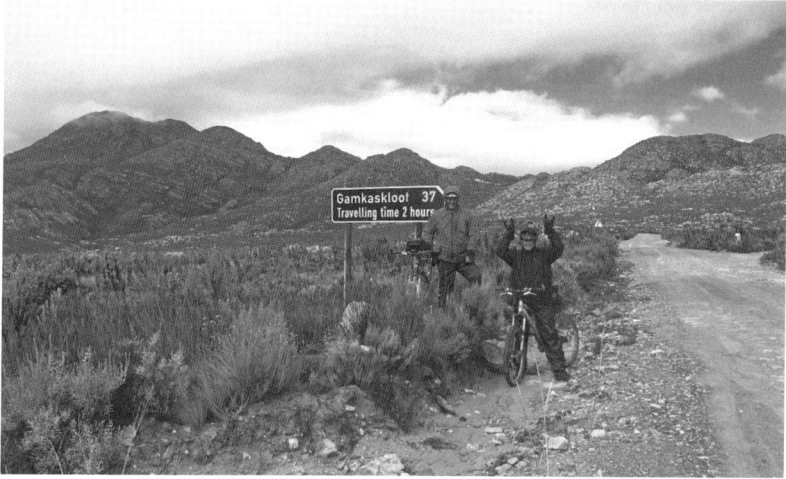

The road to hell, aka Gamkaskloof, is not so much paved as a mud puddle in the winter rains.

sequence. They almost 'shout' at you, seeming to crowd you out, given the enormity of the mountain drama being played out all around.

The real climbing begins as you cross the imaginary line into the Swartberg Nature Reserve at around 800m altitude. From that point you have to *knyp* for the 3km steep climb up towards the much-photographed zigzags. Then you climb and climb some more (with luck, in the dry and not in rain and sucking mud, like us). Once you pass the tight twists, retained by dry-packed stone walls laid by convict hands nearly 130 years ago, you are still some 3km and one tight corner from the actual summit.

Turn right at the sign to Gamkaskloof – still 37km to go. You're now at 1370m, but going west you rise to 1440m, then descend to 700m. A long, hard pull for 5km back up to 1060m follows – made all the worse because you can see the entire route snaking towards a distant nek – before you begin the final descent into Die Hel, bottoming out at 320m. (And these are only the main inclines and declines. In between are some quite extreme lesser ones, requiring care and leg-burning bursts.)

There is a public campsite at the base of the drop-off on the valley floor. 'Civilisation' in the form of a CapeNature office at Ouplaas, and a few private cottages, is still several kilometres distant along the Oshoekshang River. There is also a small shop and rustic restaurant. The main reserve office at Ouplaas, including a display of the valley's amazing history, is reached shortly after you cross the Gamka River, 12.5km from the Elandspad campsite.

If you insist on avoiding Die Hel and Die Leer, you **can** find a way north on the north side of Gamkaskloof dam, or south via Calitzdorp. But why would you?

STAGE 2
GAMKASKLOOF TO ROUXPOS 58km

GRADE: Medium, hard; riding extreme in places
OVERNIGHT: Rouxpos farm; Seweweekspoort Guest Farm

IN A NUTSHELL

Be warned and be prepared: Die Leer (The Ladder) is only an early stage on a long day. In fact, once you reach the top of Die Leer (which is also further than you'd think), you are still nowhere near the top of the mountains. The 'other side' is a long way up and way off. It's pretty hard work getting over the Swartberg in the best of weather; when it's bad it's horrible (as we discovered). And it does involve more than one simple ridge. The section to Rouxpos, between the Swartberg and Laingsberg ranges, winds through fearsome-looking terrain, crumpled jagged rock bands taking bites out of the sky. And yet that part of the ride is really quite easy – weather permitting.

Snapshot of the experience

As we started down the mountain track after reaching the real end of the climbing, the cracks in the sky widened and we were ceremoniously dumped on – sound effects courtesy of surround-sound thunder. Then towards Seweweekspoort we hit a wind tunnel. In a perverse way, it was fun to pedal into the wind as hard as we could, and stand still. You have to keep your humour at times like these, or you might start to question what you are doing there.

Our noses, hands and toes were chilled to icy pain so we ducked into the Hunlun's guest farm at Seweweekspoort (halfway), where we were given coffee and blankets; our hostess even tumble-dried our muddy threads. Depending on the weather conditions (midsummer or winter), you might need to break your ride here. The farm is a good poort in a storm.

The route

Wherever you spent the night, the starting point is the Ouplaas CapeNature office. The valley is well wooded and the ride to Boskloof gate an easy trundle. At about 5km the climb up Kleinberg starts – pushing may be required, in places, but not for long. The views from the top in both directions are stupendous.

One Google Earth photographer reckons Die Hel is the most beautiful valley in the world.

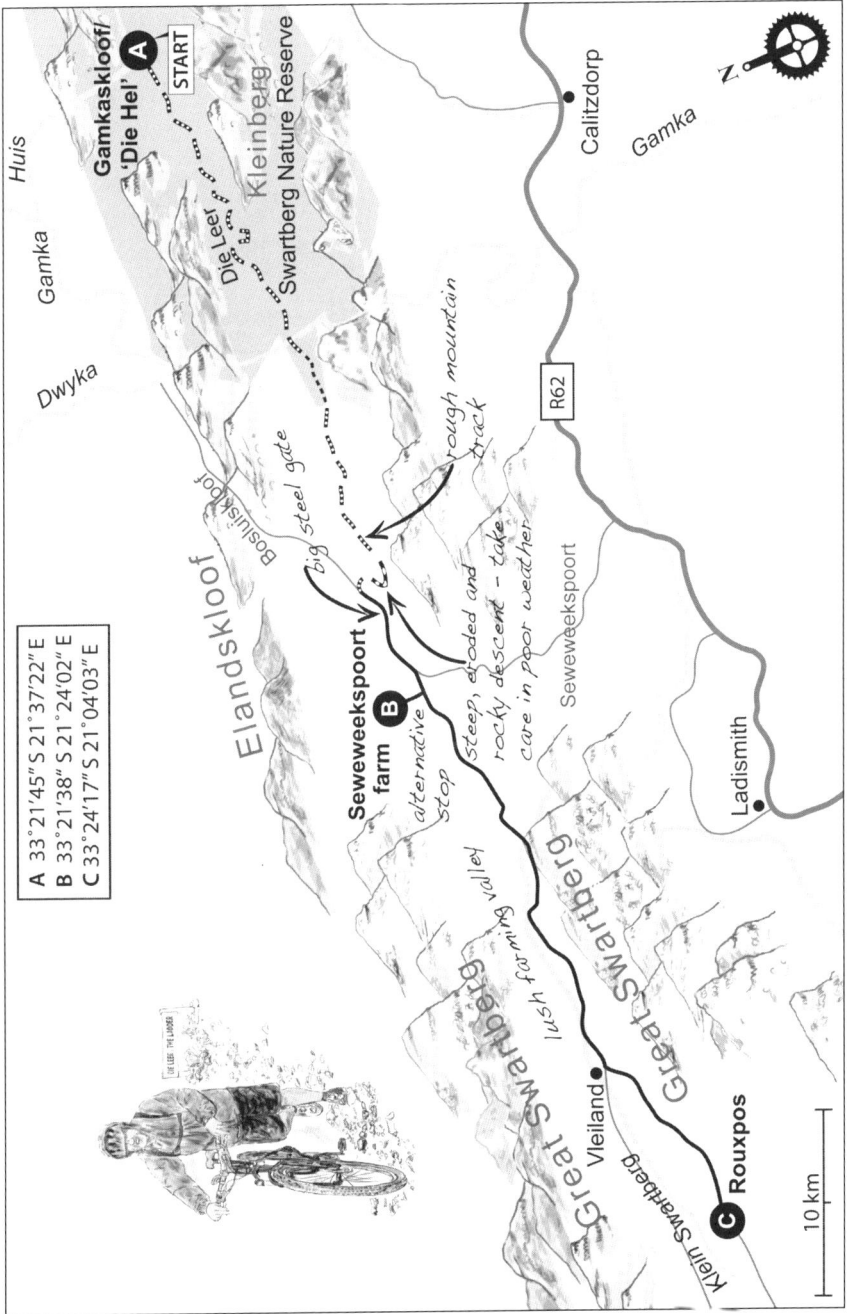

A 33°21'45"S 21°37'22"E
B 33°21'38"S 21°24'02"E
C 33°24'17"S 21°04'03"E

Gamkaskloof
'Die Hel' **A**
START

Kleinberg
Swartberg Nature Reserve

Die Leer

Huis

Gamka

Dwyka

Gamka

Calitzdorp

N

rough mountain track

Bosluiskloof

big steel gate

Elandskloof

R62

Seweekspoort

Steep, eroded and rocky descent – take care in poor weather

Seweekspoort farm **B**

alternative stop

Ladismith

lush farming valley

Great Swartberg

Great Swartberg

Vleiland

Rouxpos **C**

Klein Swartberg

10 km

Swoop down the other side and turn right up the gorge, then head for the clump of willow trees that guards the way to Oshoekshang. It's a bit of a Narnia wardrobe kind of entrance: across the stream and then up, vertically, along the start of Die Leer. In places you use your bike as a kind of two-wheel walking stick, in others as an anchor or a ladder. The very steep part starts at 500m and eases off at 740m but continues up a rocky spur full of prickly stuff to 860m, where there's a barely useful rock shelter and table. And still there's another 100m before you reach the real summit ... of **this** ridge. There's a lot of heaving and hauling, pushing and shoving, sweating and cursing.

From the top of Die Leer you ride upstream between the two main ridgelines of the Great Swartberg, rising to 1230m over a distance of 9km. Sometimes you can ride, sometimes not. It's a heck of a slog, with little chance of finding drinking water (there is a stock trough and water tank en route, but not useable). The short (1.5km) but sharp descent down to the Bosluiskloof (Gamkapoort dam) road is really treacherous in places, so take extra care. Don't be too proud (that's stupid) to walk if you feel unsafe.

Turn left (west) and just 2km down the road you come to a large security gate that you can push open (and closed). About 4km on is the Seweweekspoort turn-off, with the eponymous guest farm 1km further on the right.

From Seweweekspoort farm to Rouxpos is 32km of mixed riding through rolling foothills (more like rumples). The riding is defined by a succession of

We stopped to feed the local wildlife en route to Rouxpos, although we knew we really shouldn't.

streams and humps – up a spur, down to the river, up again. Starting with a 9km rise of about 170m to the Klein Swartberg River, you then enjoy a 13km run along the fertile, narrow farming valley, dropping 500m to the Vleiland agricultural settlement area.

One climb of 200m over 6km remains, crossing two successive ridges that take you away from the river before dropping 200m over 3km. Rouxpos is really just one historic farm that has given its name to the valley it occupies. Most of the others are abandoned or not doing so well. **Note:** Rouxpos farm is Freedom Challenge friendly but not really a guest farm, so do contact them beforehand to check if they're willing to extend their hospitality.

STAGE 3
ROUXPOS TO ANYSBERG NATURE RESERVE   64km

GRADE: Medium, moderate
OVERNIGHT: CapeNature cottages

IN A NUTSHELL

At Anysberg it looks like the landscape is going to beat the stuffing out of you. It's all tectonically violent geology and moonscape barrenness. There's a feeling of foreboding. And yet the road just goes and goes, easily, all the way. Even when you have to pass through the monolithic gates of Witnekke, the gravel track turns inexplicably to tar for 10km until the turn-off to Anysberg Nature Reserve. From Witnekke it's pretty much flat or downhill to the Touws River, at the far end of the park.

Snapshot of the experience

Om Mane Padme Hum: this is the prayer Buddhist pilgrims chant as they negotiate the mountain passages of the Himalayas. There's no literal translation, but in essence it's said to embody the jewel in the heart of the lotus flower: some call it perfection – or the sound of one hand clapping. In other words, the unconditional middle of absolutely nowhere. And that is the ride into and out of Anysberg.

It was Steve who commented: 'I don't know much about finding yourself, but if you wanted to lose yourself out riding, Anysberg would be as good a place as I can think of to do it.'

A 33°24'17"S 21°04'03"E
B 33°27'49"S 20°35'19"E

START

Rouxpos

Klein Swartberg

Swartberg

Buffels

To Laingsburg

Witnekke Pass

Groot

alternative route to be explored

Joubertskop

Anysberg

Leegte

alternative route through Klein Spreeufontein

north gate into reserve

Prins

Anys

Anysberg Nature Reserve

B

10 km

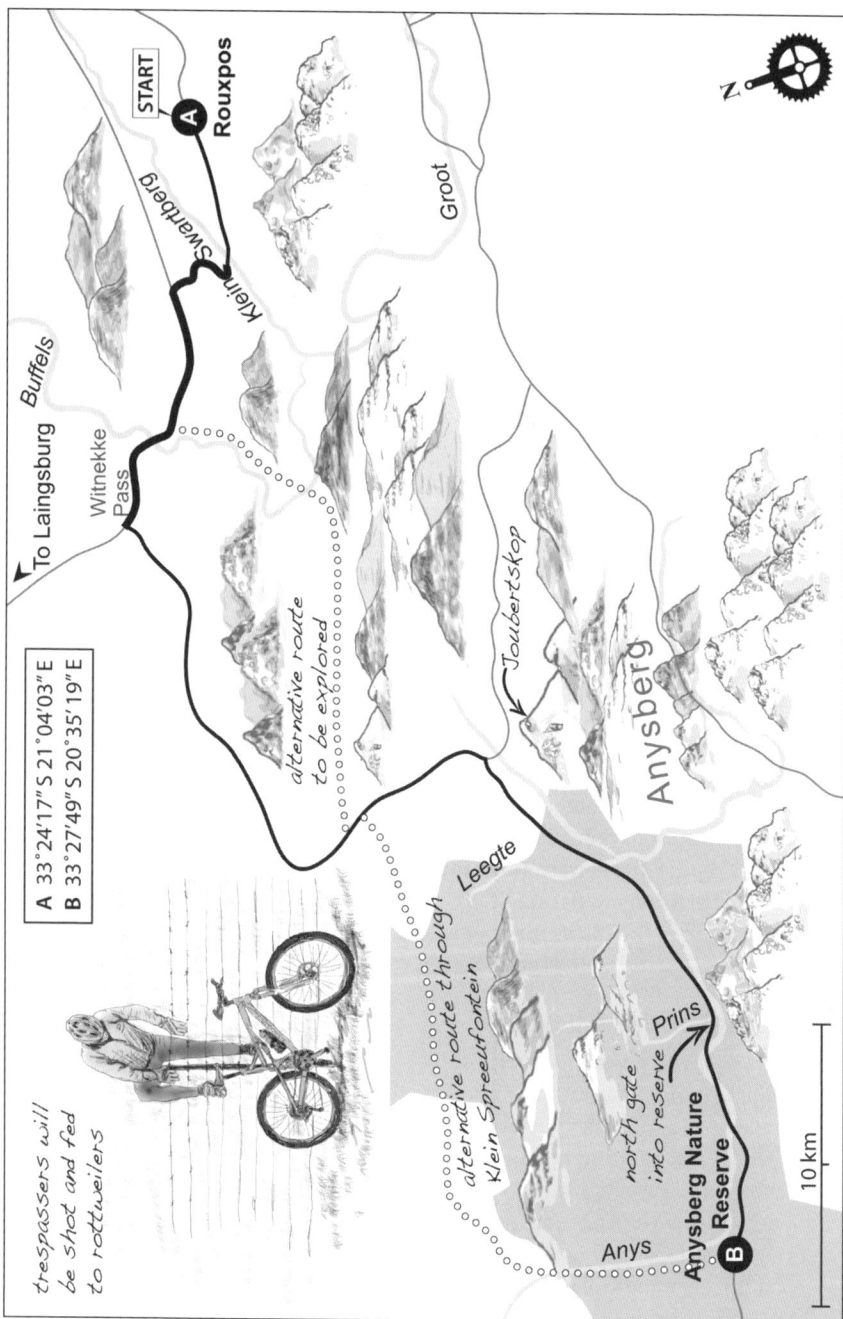

trespassers will be shot and fed to rottweilers

The route

If we could find a way through, rather than around, the Buffels River gorge we could lop about 20km off the distance of this stage, and increase the riding fun exponentially. The long way around is on gravel and tar, while the short cut would be on farm tracks and footpaths (we just have to negotiate permission). It's on the cards, so watch the website.

Head right (west) out of Rouxpos farm for 6km to reach the Klein Swartberg River, where the road swings east, then north, for 3.2km to reach the Laingsburg–Seweweekspoort road. Turn left (the short cut we hope to open goes up the Klein Swartberg valley). The gravel road becomes tar, rises 100m, loops to the north and then descends to cross the Buffels River.

From the river crossing the tarred road ascends the Witnekke Pass for about 4.5km. Take the turn-off left onto a gravel road and follow a stream course through a defile. Continue up the stream course to another defile, or nek, where you wiggle through. A short climb to a watershed follows, before descending to the Leegte River (about 13km from the tarred road).

About 1km later the road swings south and continues across a gently rolling wide valley before cresting the low shoulder of Joubertskop. From here it's downhill for the next 7km as you follow a tributary down to the Prins River, where you come to the Anysberg reserve gate. Then the track veers up (west) to the Anysberg River valley. It looks like it's flat but it's not. And yet, surrounded by fearsome-looking sawtooth ridges, it rises only 100m over 15km to the main reserve office at Vrede – and the cottages.

There is a monster 4x4 trail in the park and you can go on a horse trail if that is your pleasure... Then again, maybe next time. You will promise yourself there'll be a next time.

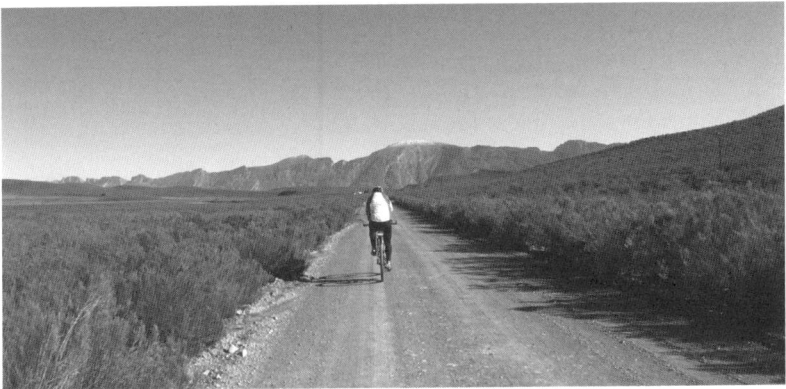

The Anysberg is behind us, the Hex River mountains lie ahead – with a dab of snow on the top of Matroosberg.

STAGE 4
ANYSBERG NATURE RESERVE TO TOUWS RIVER

76km

GRADE: Long, easy
OVERNIGHT: Loganda Karoo Lodge

IN A NUTSHELL

The ride from Anysberg starts off well enough, as you work your way into the valley of the Touws River, following the stream, when there is one. For most of the way it's uphill, not so steeply that it hurts, but just enough to let you know it's uphill all the way. But the path to limbo (see below) goes in stages: first the wonderful downhill turns to a long sustained uphill; then the rough wilderness track becomes a farm road, then a divisional road – straight and boring as a *Christmas Hits* CD. It just goes on and on.

Snapshot of the experience

Catholic dogma aside, 'limbo' in its more common usage is a state of indecision or uncertainty. Having spent some time in the hell that was the Gamkaskloof, followed by our icy escape via Die Leer, and, after that, real mountain biking heaven in Anysberg, we feel well qualified to describe Touws River and the ride there as limbo. Not the fires of Hell, nor even the freeze of Purgatory. Just limbo.

The route

For the first 5.5km, the track west from the Anysberg reserve office is pretty much dead straight and dead flat. Then, another 11.5km from camp, it dips down a little side-valley to the Touws River. Once you reach the river it's much prettier, even if it means you now have to move your mass against gravity because you're in fact going upstream. This is often hard to discern because the landscape is much more featureless than dramatic, and, if there is no water in the river, you can't see which way it might flow.

The prettiest spot is where the road crosses the river bed via a narrow causeway at the confluence of the Kruis River. You can make out an embankment up on the right – the remains of an old steam railway line dating back to who knows when. Road, river and railway run together from here on.

At one point the track turns a sharp left-right-left around a vlei and farm dam. Outside the reserve, the track meets a more substantial gravel road at the

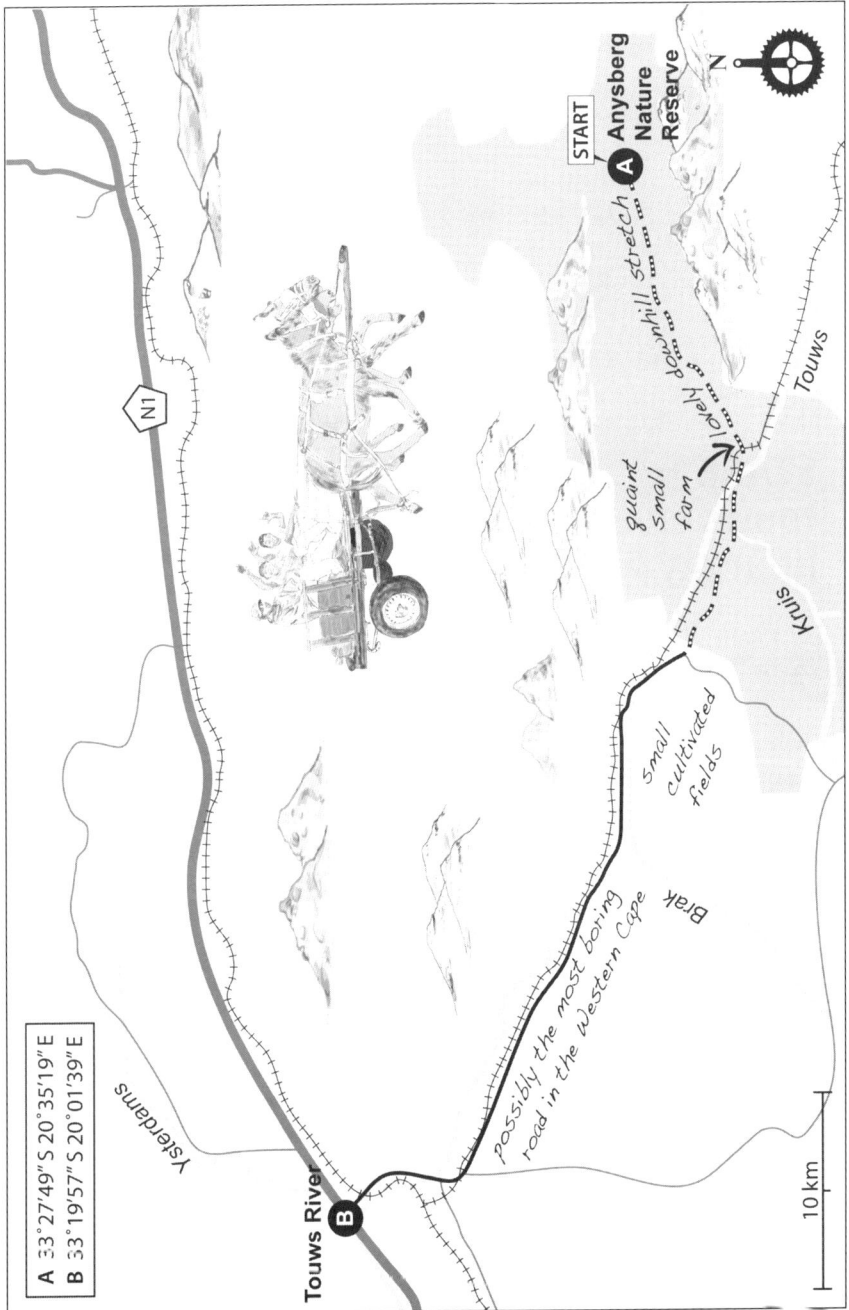

A 33°27'49"S 20°35'19"E
B 33°19'57"S 20°01'39"E

Ysterdams

N1

Touws River

START

A Anysberg Nature Reserve

N

lovely downhill stretch

guaint small farm

Touws

Kruis

small cultivated fields

Brak

possibly the most boring road in the Western Cape

B

10 km

valley's first prosperous farms. About 8km from the river crossing there is a skew junction; turn right to follow the valley where it cuts a pass through a line of hills, crossing the river and old railway within the poort.

The next 12km are rendered pleasant by the details of the landscape: river, hills, small cultivated fields, windmills. In contrast, the 20km thereafter are among the most mind-numbing kilometres between the Limpopo River and the Atlantic Ocean. The only relief offered: the distant Langeberg profile to the left and the Hex River mountains ahead.

It does seem to take a year to reach the dreary outskirts of dreary Touws River, but you will find cloistered relief at the Loganda Karoo Lodge, a decent and actually pleasant place to stay; the pub throbs till the early hours.

· ·

STAGE 5
TOUWS RIVER TO FORGOTTEN HIGHWAY MANOR
70km

GRADE: Medium to long, hard; riding severe
OVERNIGHT: Forgotten Highway Manor; Village Guest House and Restaurant (Ceres)

IN A NUTSHELL
This is a big day. Trying to keep any riding on tar (the N1) to a minimum led us on a wild-goose chase. The easier route is to ride west along the N1 for 8.5km, then take the tarred R46 right (north) into the Koue Bokkeveld to meet our route behind the Matroosberg. (You could avoid most of the N1 by following the railway out of town to Hartebeeskraal – where one line splits into three – then take the dirt track right (north) to the N1, doing a 2km right-left dogleg onto the R46.) We suspect there are tracks all the way along between the N1 and the railway lines; we plan to check it out.

Snapshot of the experience
Steve had a David Waddilove map (a duplicitous thing) for a scenic route over the Hex River mountains. It started well enough, but a road became a wagon trail became a track became a path became a vague line … and then we lost it. In every sense. We spent the next four hours, which should have been no more than one, grovelling over rocky ridges, thick fynbos and even thicker swamp

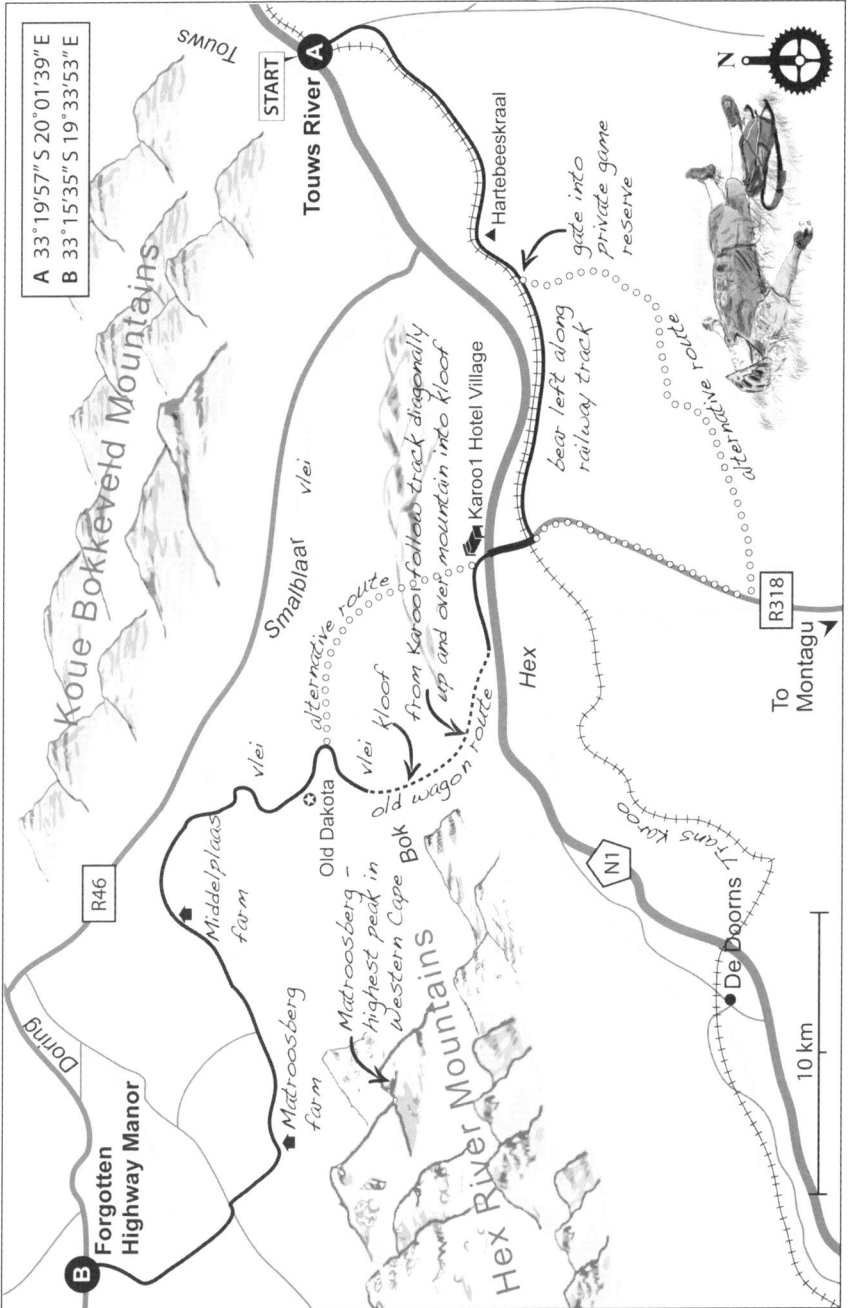

A 33°19'57"S 20°01'39"E
B 33°15'35"S 19°33'53"E

Touws

START

Touws River

Koue Bokkeveld Mountains

Hartebeeskraal

gate into private game reserve

bear left along railway track

alternative route

Smalblaar vlei

vlei

Karoo1 Hotel Village

follow track diagonally up and over mountain into kloof

from Karoo

Hex

R318

To Montagu

alternative route

vlei kloof

old wagon route

vlei

Old Dakota

Bok

Middelplaas farm

R46

Matroosberg – highest peak in Western Cape

N1

Trans Karoo

Doring

Matroosberg farm

De Doorns

Hex River Mountains

Forgotten Highway Manor

B

10 km

sedge that all but did us in. In the meanwhile, we've given you a more direct line over the ridge – we've been assured it 'goes'.

The route

On our route, leave town following the railway south, then west, for 13.6km to the Hartebeeskraal rail divergence. We turned left here, through a gate into a private game reserve. This alternative route follows an 18km-wide arc around and through the hills south of the N1 and the Trans Karoo line to meet the tarred R318 from Montagu to Karoo1 Hotel Village resort. A better route is to keep going alongside the railway line, following the left-hand track. (The right-hand track disappears into a very long tunnel.) Keep going all the way to where the track meets the R318. Turn right here to reach the Karoo1 resort on the other side of the N1.

From just inside the resort entrance, take the gravel road to the west, past a fire outpost and around a quarry, to reach the old wagon route into the mountains. Soon it becomes a footpath and then just a vague track. A new 2m-plus-high fence has been placed across the path, without the courtesy of a stile, so that's something to work on with the landowner. Using your bike as a leg-up (it's on a slope, so quite tricky), climb over the fence and stay on a diagonal left-bearing course to make your way over and into the big gorge to the west. It's about 14km from the resort to where you pick up the path at the apex of the gorge (the Bok River starts its flow to the northeast here); you more or less follow the contours to the saddle of the gorge.

Turn right down the gorge, soon picking up an old road – rather rocky where it has been built up to cross the large vlei area (in which we got trapped) – and follow it to some old farm and military buildings. Veer left at the first side-junction and follow this road/path/track parallel to the mountains for 3.5km, then follow it right where you see the old Dakota standing in the veld. Turn left to Middelplaas fruit farm, where you follow farm roads through orchards and past the homestead area (they seemed friendly to us but do be polite and ask). The second left turn along the Bok River goes through a vlei, which is impassable in wet conditions, but is easier otherwise. It's pretty rough in places and we had to sense our way through.

From the farmstead a great road winds steeply up the Smalblaar valley and past some large irrigation dams as you round the northeast base of Matroosberg and the massive Matroosberg fruit farm for 9km. The road arcs around and levels off past the orchards and farm buildings. Cross a stream and turn right to the edge of the farm property. Turn left here onto a gravel road, then right after a few hundred metres (go over or around a gate). Follow this narrow farm road for 7km to reach the tarred R46 and the Forgotten Highway Manor entrance on your right (you can take a short cut to the farmstead before you reach the tarred road).

STAGE 6
FORGOTTEN HIGHWAY MANOR
TO TULBAGH

53km

GRADE: Medium, easy; one very technical descent
OVERNIGHT: Various options, see Useful contacts (p. 202)

IN A NUTSHELL

You get an inkling of the kind of landscape you ride through from some of the names – Witzenberg (white mountain) and Koue Bokkeveld (cold goat field). In summer, of course, the opposite is true: the place bakes in a dry, dusty, natural oven. Luckily, we skipped in just ahead of the first winter snow.

The old wagon trail must be one of the best technical downhill rides (about 7km in all) in the country. That it was even passable by horse carts is simply amazing.

Snapshot of the experience

An impending snow storm aside, our main problem was the farmer who guards the way onto the old Nagmaal wagon pass. We were putting on our rain gear at the gate as he drove out. A short conversation revealed that he would let us ride up the mountain to have a look, but he didn't want us to ride over and into the Tulbagh valley. By the time we got to the crest of the range, we were all but enveloped in rain cloud, so we reckoned what he could not see would do him no harm. We raced down just ahead of the weather – and a possible hail of birdshot. (We hear this route is now open, as long as you give the mysterious 'chocolate lady' and her dogs on the far side a wide berth.)

The route

Set off from Forgotten Highway Manor, immediately crossing over the tarred road, taking the gravel farm road in a northerly

The Tulbagh valley was first settled around 1699 and named Het Land Van Waveren (from the wife's family name – they were rich) by the incumbent governor, kleptocrat Willem Adriaan van der Stel. He was eventually dismissed by the Dutch East India Company for corruption and sent back to the Netherlands in disgrace.

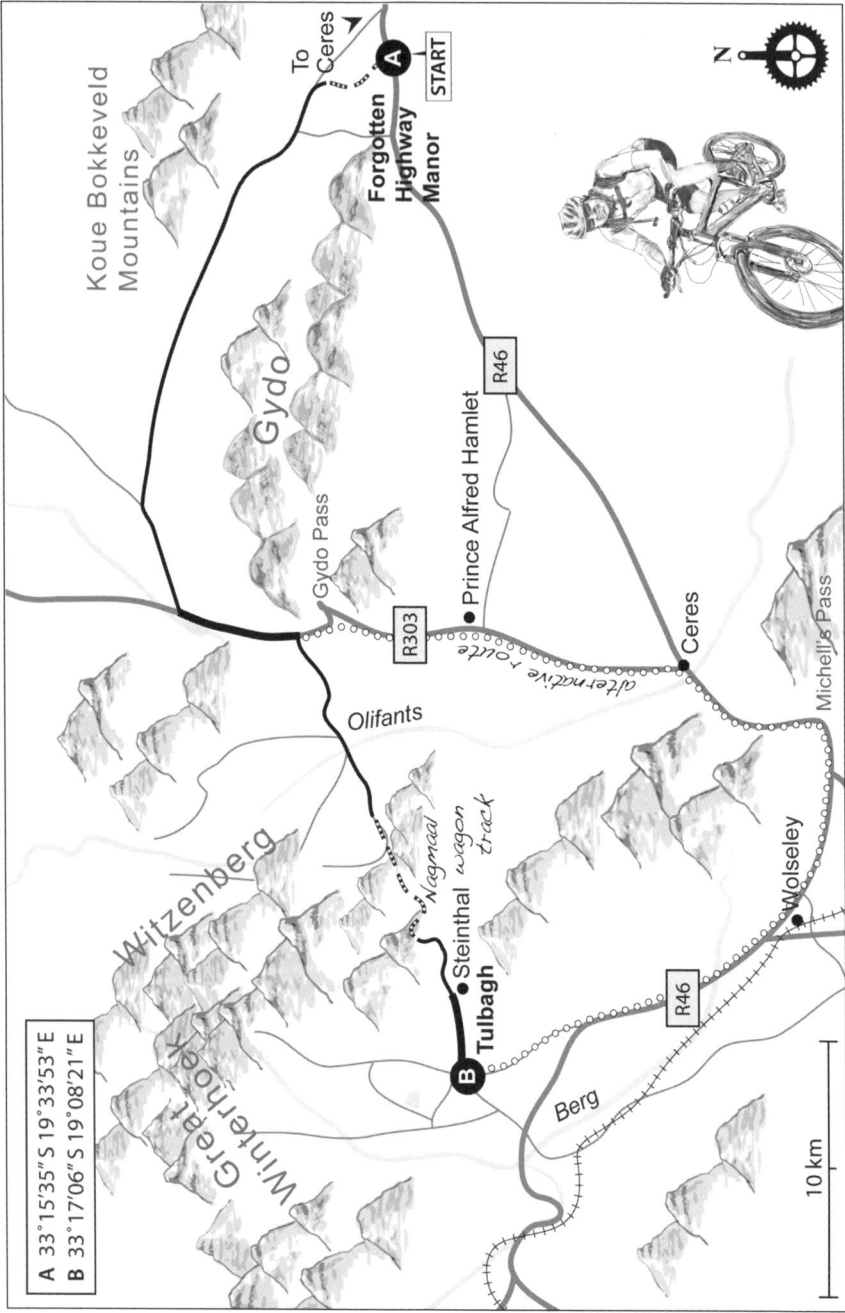

Koue Bokkeveld Mountains

To Ceres

A START

Forgotten Highway Manor

N

Gydo

R46

Prince Alfred Hamlet

Gydo Pass

R303

alternative route

Ceres

Michell's Pass

Olifants

Witzenberg

Nagmaal

Steinthal wagon track

Wolseley

Steinthal

B Tulbagh

R46

Great Winterhoek

Berg

10 km

A 33°15'35"S 19°33'53"E
B 33°17'06"S 19°08'21"E

direction for about 3km. This is a winter wheat and deciduous fruit farming area (the Ceres area is named after the Roman goddess of the harvest). At a back road, turn left and wend your way along the base of the Koue Bokkeveld mountains.

In summertime this is a sweltering, arid, sandy waste, while in winter it is green – or white depending on frost and snowfalls. Continue in a northwesterly direction for 20km to a triangular intersection where the gravel miraculously turns to tar and swings left (southwest), with the Gydo range rearing up on your left. After 4.8km you come to the Gydo Pass road (R303), where you have to turn left (south) along the main tarred road.

The farms around here are much more prosperous than further east, locked between sandstone ridges. After 4.5km, just above where the main road plunges down the Gydo Pass, duck right through a concealed corridor in the mountains, dropping into the Arcadian Witzenberg valley, then scooting southwest across the southern floor of this dead-end dale for 10km.

The old wagon road is on a private fruit farm and the farmer is wary cyclists might offend his over-the-mountain neighbour, so assure him you won't. The alternative, long way around is Gydo Pass, Ceres, Michell's Pass, Wolseley and on to the Kluitjieskraal-waterfall gravel road to meet the railway line outside Tulbagh – hardly an awful prospect but more a road ride than mountain biking.

If you're on the wagon route, ride steeply up around the farm dam; at the top of the ridge the track swings left (south), then turns sharp right – this turn can easily be missed when the vegetation is rank. From here you cannot lose the path, as it bends and bucks, weaves and wobbles down the mountain ridge – extremely steep and rocky in places. Where it is rideable – and this will vary greatly, depending on your riding skills – it is spectacular. It's one of those runs where you fear your hands and forearms might give in before your nerves.

At the bottom of the wagon track keep to the right to avoid the chocolate lady and her big dogs, then bomb down through Steinthal village, and on to Tulbagh. It's about 5.5km from the crest of the Witzenberg to where you reach private land, so make sure your brakes are in good working order. From there it's a fast 7km to Van der Stel Street in the historic town – just take care at all the stop streets.

On top of the Witzenberg, psyching up for the big Nagmaal track descent.

RECOMMENDED
4 days

Fairest Cape Trail

Tulbagh to Cape Point • 179km

STAGE 1
TULBAGH TO RIEBEEK KASTEEL   54km

GRADE: Medium, easy
OVERNIGHT: Royal Hotel; Môreson Manor; Various options (Malmesbury),
see Useful contacts (p. 202)

IN A NUTSHELL

On this route you clamber onto the old Nuweberg Pass track, then
ride through the Nuwekloof Pass, bidding farewell to the Cape Folded
Mountains and saying hello to the Cape coastal plain. In the last stretch,
you wend through wheat fields to Kasteelberg. The truth is, the experience
will be quite different for Spine of the Dragon riders who are nearing
the end of a long trail and those trying out only a small trail section. The
former will want to get home while the latter will want to linger longer, so
we've given you some options here.

Snapshot of the experience

We had historic reasons for choosing Kasteel
but, when we arrived to take our booked
rooms at the Royal Hotel, were greatly
surprised to find we'd arrived a day earlier than
planned. As this was a Saturday night, this and
just about every other inn in town was chock-
a-block with wedding guests. After having
the stuffing knocked out of us by the prices
of most other places in 'the valley', we were
relieved to find Môreson Manor, at the south
end of the village, at a third of the price.

*We awoke to see the
ever-present cold front –
an ocean of cloud spilling
over the band-saw blade
of the Witzenberg. These
cold fronts started to
really annoy us, like the
unrelenting Pinkerton
bounty hunters tracking
Butch and Sundance
across America.*

The route

Ride down Van der Stel Street to the south end of Tulbagh, then take Meiring
Street to the right, heading southwest for about 5km (crossing the R46) to the
railway line. It's very much in use by the Trans Karoo service so don't tarry on
the lines. Ride along the railway to where the old bridge was knocked through
to accommodate newer electric lines (of course, all trains are now diesel). You
have to clamber here onto the old line and follow the Little Berg River as it cuts
a gorge between the mountains.

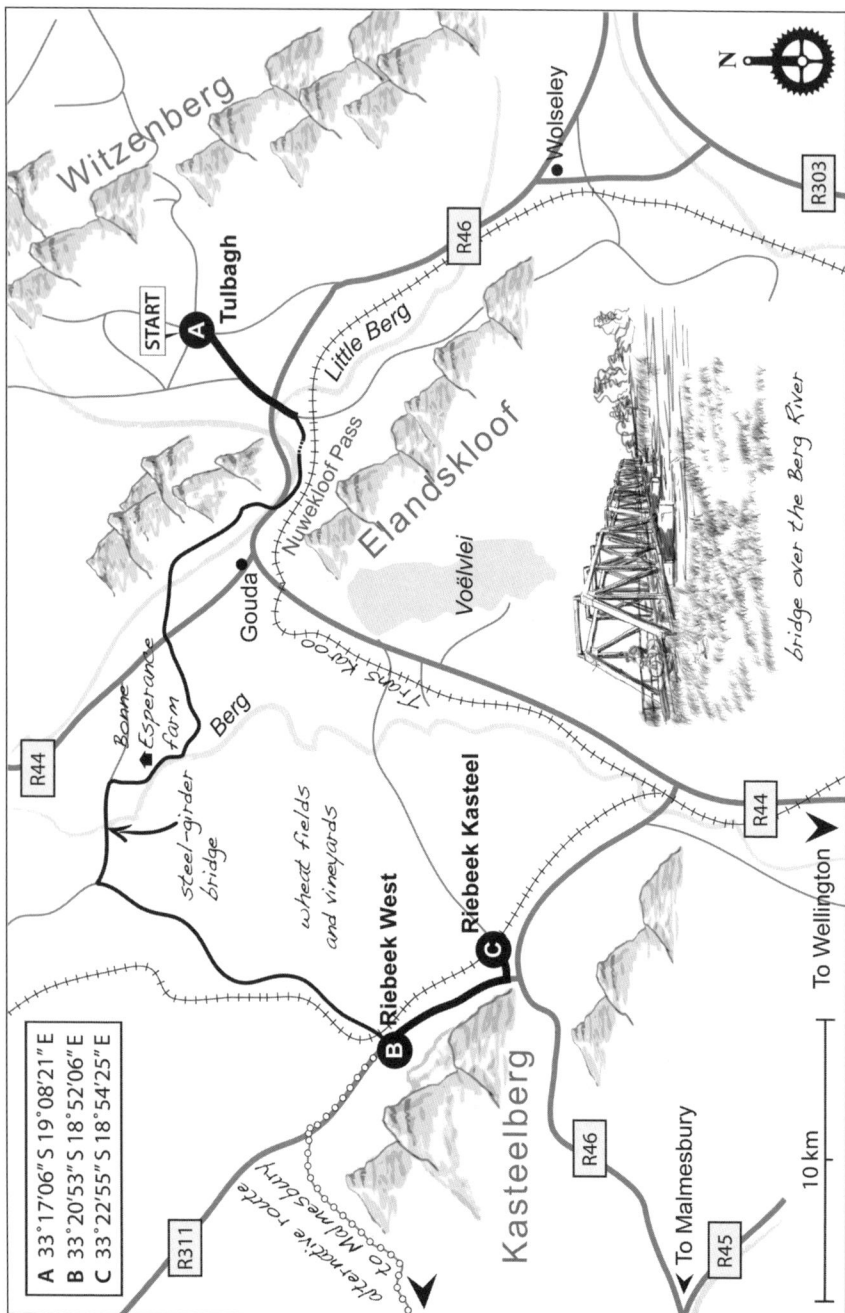

bridge over the Berg River

A 33°17'06"S 19°08'21"E
B 33°20'53"S 18°52'06"E
C 33°22'55"S 18°54'25"E

Witzenberg

Wolseley

R46

R303

N

START

A Tulbagh

Little Berg

Nuwekloof Pass

Elandskloof

Voëlvlei

Gouda

Trans Karoo

R44

Bonne Esperance farm

Berg

steel-girder bridge

wheat fields and vineyards

Riebeek Kasteel

Riebeek West

B

C

R44

To Wellington

Kasteelberg

R311

alternative route to Malmesbury

R46

To Malmesbury

R45

10 km

At the north end of the Nuwekloof Pass, cross the road and go through/over the gate to ride along the right-hand side of an irrigation channel for some 5km, then turn left to cross the river via a low concrete bridge (don't take the earlier track across the river if you want to avoid tar).

Ignore the sharp-left turn of the gravel track; instead follow lesser tracks to the right along a stream, towards the entrance of Bonne Esperance estate. Cross the R44, heading west along a gravel road. After 5.5km, cross the (main) Berg River via a narrow steel-girder bridge; 2.4km further, turn left. Follow this road in a general southwest direction for 14km. First it's flattish, then, on reaching the railway line, it ascends gently through wheat fields, then vineyards, towards the looming Kasteelberg.

As a place to overnight, Riebeek West is much the same as Riebeek Kasteel, except if you choose to take a westward route to Malmesbury rather than our southeast route to avoid Malmesbury, which might influence your choice.

If you're headed for Malmesbury, ride to the R311 at the north end of Riebeek West and turn right. Ride uphill (north) on tar for 4km, then turn left onto a gravel road. The road crests the north shoulder of Kasteelberg, then descends to the Sandspruit, where it crosses another shoulder. It descends across the upper Riebeek River (Krom River) and then to a bigger road; turn left here.

This road keeps to high ground until you begin to drop into the Malmesbury bowl and can see the town in the valley below. You enter what seems to be the back end of town, past what looks like a failed, or dormant, pipe-dream estate housing development.

Pardon, sir, is that the Trans Karoo choo-choo? Looking for an easy ride from Tulbagh to Cape Town.

STAGE 2
RIEBEEK KASTEEL TO BLOUBERGSTRAND 30km

GRADE: Short, moderate
OVERNIGHT: The Blue Peter Hotel

IN A NUTSHELL

From either of the Riebeek villages, the non-tar way onto the Swartland plain hugs the west side of Kasteelberg. It then merges with the Malmesbury route on the tarred R46 before heading south on gravel. The rest of the day is a case of playing with farm roads and tracks, trying to avoid the many tarred roads that dissect the region. We worked extremely hard to figure out a route to Cape Town befitting the grand finale of the country's premier mountain bike touring trail. It's a fabulous ride through an area that most people know only from the highways.

Snapshot of the experience

Since we were so close to Cape Town, exploring the back roads of the area seemed hardly worthy of the effort. How wrong we were. A big bonus proved to be the farmers of the Swartland, who not only have that wonderful *bry* accent but also hearts as wide open as the green and gold wheat- and canola-covered plains in spring.

The route

To bypass Malmesbury: once you leave Riebeek Kasteel or Riebeek West and have ascended the north shoulder of Kasteelberg, and you're just starting the descent, turn left onto a lesser dirt road, heading south for 9km; the peak rears up to your left. The first third is uphill, but then it's a lovely down run. Turn right onto the tarred road (R46) – this is where you rejoin the trail if you decided to go via Malmesbury – and ride the almost flat section for 3.5km, then turn left onto a farm track. In springtime the golden canola and green wheat fields form a stunning foreground to the often still snow-coated mountains.

Head south through farmlands, do a right-left manoeuvre across a tarred road (R45 to Wellington) and cross the Diep River. Continue south along a gravel public road. You reach the next tarred road in 22km. The first half of this section winds through farmlands; the second half does six distinct right angles, skirting farm boundaries. Round about halfway on this section, don't miss the

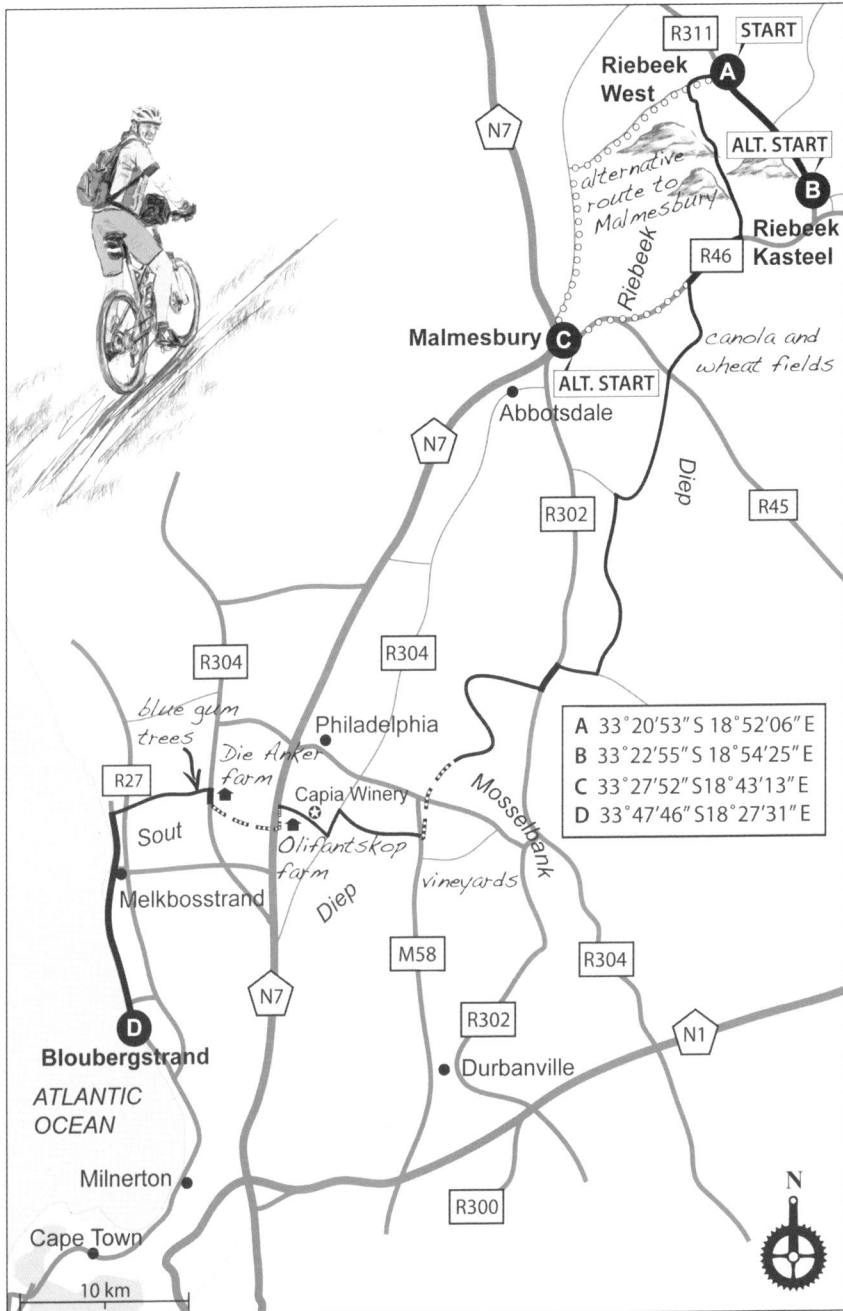

START
R311
Riebeek West
ALT. START
Riebeek Kasteel
R46
A
B
alternative route to Malmesbury
Riebeek
canola and wheat fields
N7
Malmesbury C
ALT. START
Abbotsdale
Diep
R302
R45
R304
R304
blue gum trees
Philadelphia
Die Anker farm
R27
Capia Winery
Sout
Olifantskop farm
Diep
Mosselbank
vineyards
Melkbosstrand

A 33°20'53" S 18°52'06" E
B 33°22'55" S 18°54'25" E
C 33°27'52" S 18°43'13" E
D 33°47'46" S 18°27'31" E

M58
R302
R304
N7
Durbanville
N1
D
Bloubergstrand
ATLANTIC OCEAN
Milnerton
R300
Cape Town
N
10 km

sharp left turn onto a lesser gravel road (after a long uphill haul, the road bends right and descends for about 1km, turns hard right, and 750m on is the turn-off). It's a feel-good ride this, as you wend through fields and around farmsteads, feeling that you're getting a glimpse into this close-knit farming community.

When you meet tar, turn right, past vineyards, then a chicken battery farm and, some 2km on, the R302. There's no alternative but to take this tarred road left (for 1.4km). Turn right onto a farm road, past a dam. You ride through the farm barnyard and west past another 'chicken factory'.

Continue to the railway line and turn left to follow it south for about 4.5km, then turn right onto a gravel road, doing a quick right-left around a farmstead. About 2.8km on, the track crosses the Mosselbank River drift, does a few twists, then hits the tarred R304. Turn right for several hundred metres, then right onto a dirt track that wends through a wheat field till you cross the tarred M58. Ride past a farm on your right and turn left onto the Frederickskraal gravel road. Follow the farm tracks to a crossing of the Diep River. Shortly after, the road turns right (north) and reaches the old Kalbaskraal–Malmesbury tarred road.

Turn left here for about 1.4km, then right onto the gravel Botterberg road, passing Capia winery and ducking left along a dirt track for 1.8km to avoid the busy N7. After a small farm dam, turn right and cross the N7. You should start getting a kelpy whiff of sea air; the ocean is just 10km away.

The dirt road does a zig, a zag, then sharp right around Olifantskop with its distinctive concentric vineyards. Keep going left around the *kop*, through a farmstead, then turn right at a gravel pit opposite a copse of gum trees. At Die Anker cattle farm the road turns from north to west. Just before the R304, turn right (north) to keep off the tar, then swing over the road at the blue gums at the Sout River. Cross the railway line; keep heading west on the gravel till the houses of Duinefontein appear. You hit the R27 at the Melkbosstrand 4x4 track, where you have to turn left. Follow the main coastal road south for about 10km to Bloubergstrand. Turn right at Big Bay Boulevard and wend your way down to Big Bay – the Blue Peter Hotel has a prime spot in Popham Street looking over the bay.

Pedalling along Bloubergstrand – we've come so far, and are now so close to home, I wonder what's for dinner?

STAGE 3
BLOUBERGSTRAND TO CAPE TOWN   22km

GRADE: Short, moderate
OVERNIGHT: Various options, see Useful contacts (p. 202)

IN A NUTSHELL

There's really not much to the route-finding on this stage – just keep the sea on your right and follow the cycle path signs into town. If the wind's behind you, it's a pleasant maritime kind of ride, with sail and steam craft anchored in Table Bay. If the wind's in your face, I imagine the 22km would seem a lot more like 44.

Snapshot of the experience

Steve, Les Girls (our ever-supportive partners who cheered us in) and I lingered over a lavish breakfast in the Blue Peter's stylish dining room – without question the best address at the Tavern of the Seas – as we watched Table Mountain across the bay playing now-you-see-me, now-you-don't among tumbling clouds. Motivation to go out there and put the final flourish on our ride was low.

If I had to ride my mountain bike into the jaws of death, into the mouth of hell, I'd be happy to do it in Steve the Navigator's slipstream ... Oh, hold on a minute, I already did. It's a place called Die Hel.

But eventually we did. We lubed our chains for the second-last run, put on wet-weather gear, fiddled about, hoisted the Blue Peter (ship ready to sail) and cast off into a raging northwesterly. It was a down-wind run most of the way into town, chasing the rain ahead of us at around 30km per hour. Once in town, we tacked up Bree Street to talk gear ratios and other twaddle with the good people at Revolution Cycles, who had been among our most ardent supporters.

The route

You start off riding around the houses of Big Bay, through the beach parking areas of Bloubergstrand, and finally onto a paved cycle track as you swing around the Dolphin Beach development on your right. Next is Rietvlei to your left, while you watch the commuters building road rage inside their worker chariots (much more chilled are the workers riding the Bus Rapid Transit System buses).

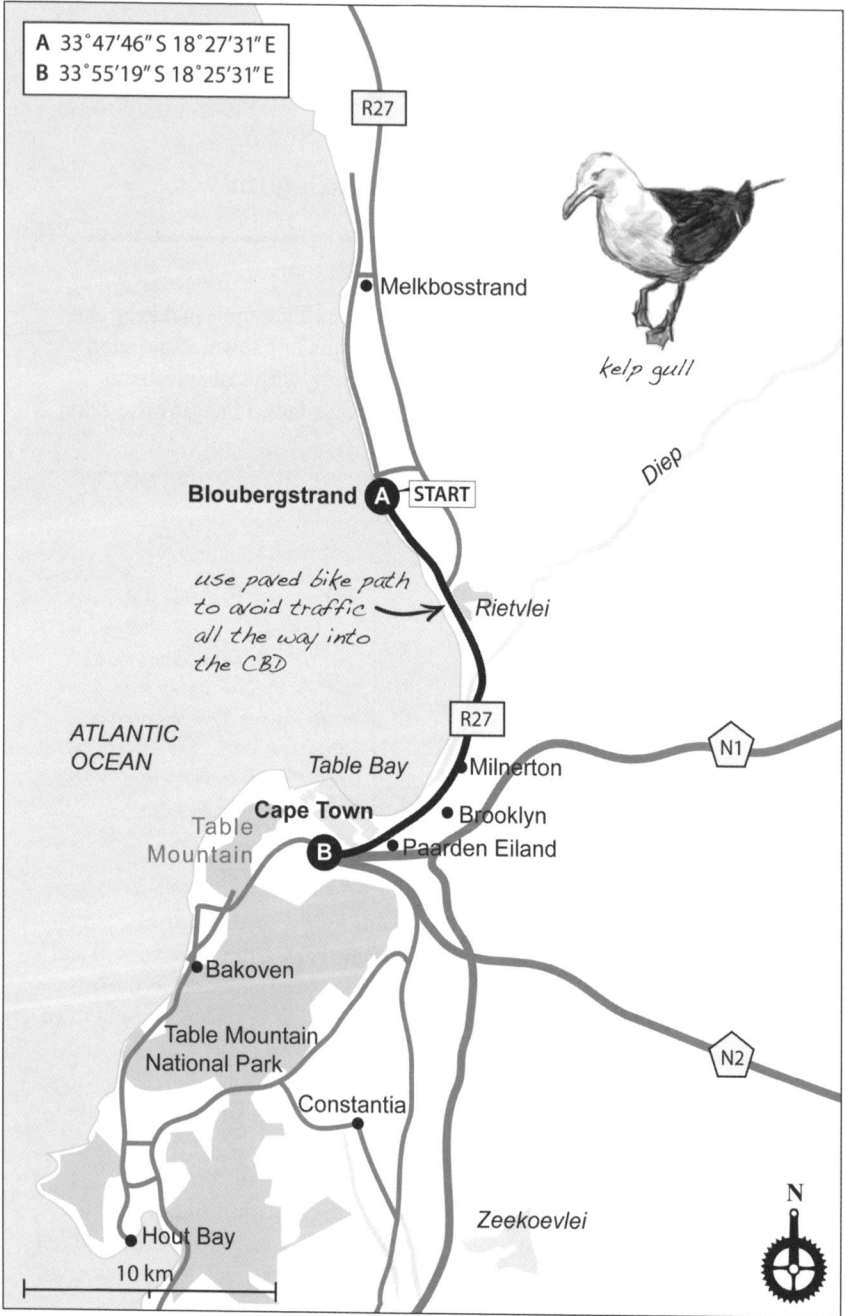

A 33°47'46"S 18°27'31"E
B 33°55'19"S 18°25'31"E

R27

● Melkbosstrand

kelp gull

Diep

Bloubergstrand Ⓐ START

*use paved bike path
to avoid traffic
all the way into
the CBD* → *Rietvlei*

R27

N1

*ATLANTIC
OCEAN*

Table Bay ● Milnerton

Cape Town ● Brooklyn

*Table
Mountain* Ⓑ ● Paarden Eiland

● Bakoven

*Table Mountain
National Park*

N2

Constantia

Zeekoevlei

N

● Hout Bay

10 km

Along the Rietvlei estuary and through Milnerton the track follows Marine Drive (R27). You pass Woodbridge Island with its lighthouse, duck through the back streets of Brooklyn (nothing like its Big Apple namesake), then through the maze of industrial Paarden Eiland. In times not too long ago this area was all salt marsh around the Sout River estuary. Now we have fewer fish and waterbirds, but lots of concrete sluices and factories.

As the curve of the bay swings from south to west, the cycle track ducks under the N1 freeway, along the railway lines, under the N2 and then around the back of the Civic Centre. The original configuration of Table Bay, before the Foreshore and Duncan Dock were built, was the same shape as the outward spiral of most sea shells. It's called a logarithmic spiral and it describes a precise geometric progression. Waves bending round a rocky headland will carve out this shape – it's the same one you see all the way up the Western Cape coast.

Eventually you come to lower Adderley Street (the name changes to the Heerengracht – 'gentleman's canal' – on the Foreshore) where statues of old luminaries (Jan and Maria van Riebeeck, Henry the Navigator, Forgotten Soldiers, Captain Robert Falcon Scott) mark the route. Should you venture into the station building, you can see a blue wavy line in the floor that marks the sea level back when Jan first set his beribboned shoe on the sand.

For some this will be the end point of the journey so, well done, you deserve to treat yourself to a double cheeseburger at the Royale Eatery on Long Street. It's not much use our suggesting places to stay in town. However, if our plan to create a mountain bike route to Cape Point comes off, the SANParks Washhouses in Vredehoek will be the place.

. . . .

STAGE 4
CAPE TOWN (CITY CENTRE) TO CAPE POINT   73km

GRADE: Long, moderate; riding highly variable
OVERNIGHT: Various options, see Useful contacts (p. 202)

IN A NUTSHELL
The distance of the False Bay route, versus our recommended 73km Atlantic coast route, is about 65km – really a very easy day's ride. So long as the weather behaves. If you fancy a picnic, Buffels Bay near Cape Point is the best place when the Southeaster isn't howling.

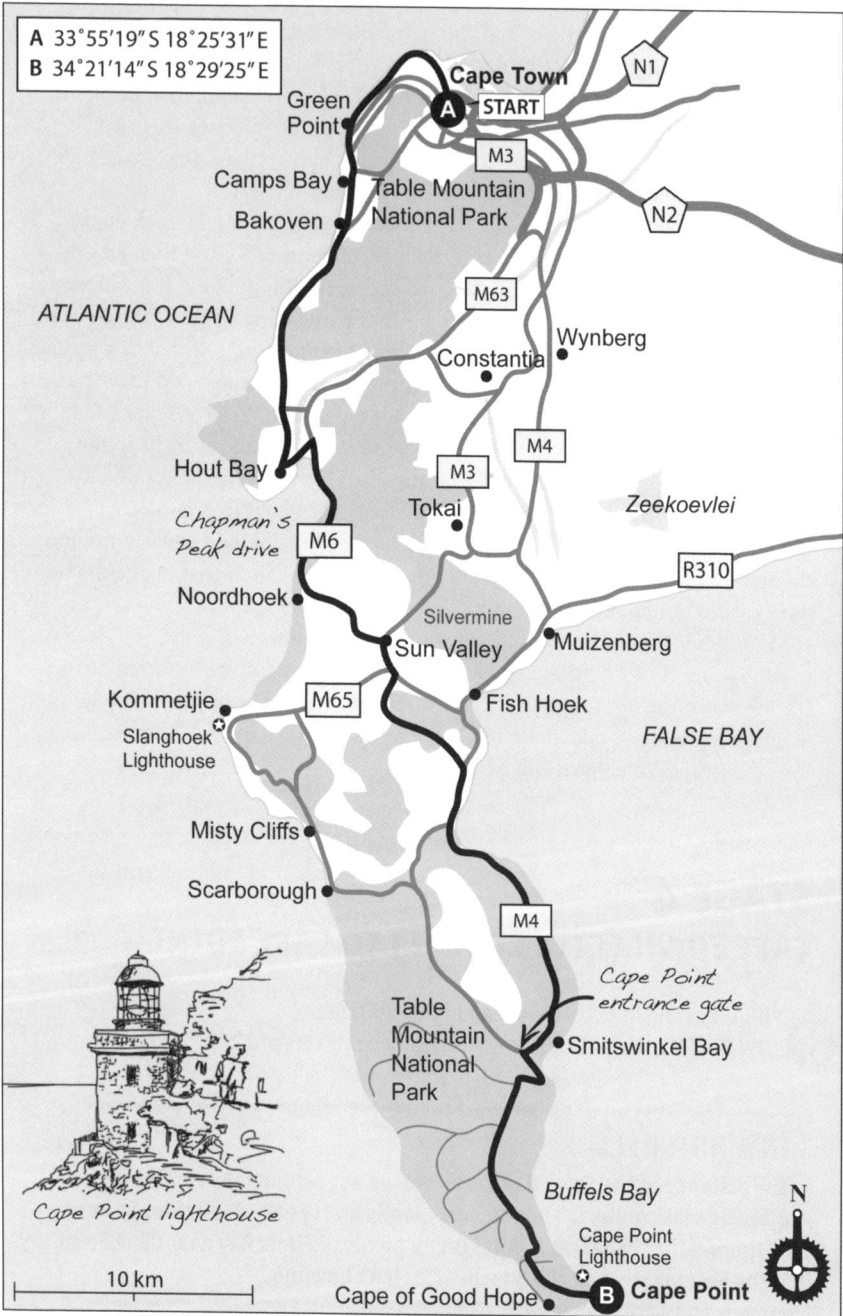

A 33°55'19"S 18°25'31"E
B 34°21'14"S 18°29'25"E

Green
Point

Cape Town
A START

Camps Bay

Bakoven

M3

Table Mountain
National Park

ATLANTIC OCEAN

N1

N2

M63

Wynberg

Constantia

M4

M3

Hout Bay

Chapman's
Peak drive   M6

Tokai

Zeekoevlei

R310

Noordhoek

Silvermine

Sun Valley

Muizenberg

Kommetjie

M65

Fish Hoek

FALSE BAY

Slanghoek
Lighthouse

Misty Cliffs

Scarborough

M4

Table
Mountain
National
Park

Cape Point
entrance gate

Smitswinkel Bay

Cape Point lighthouse

Buffels Bay

N

Cape Point
Lighthouse

10 km

Cape of Good Hope   **B** Cape Point

Snapshot of the experience

The tourist brochures won't tell you so best we do: this is a windy city, and when it blows it's seldom just a sea breeze. Riding a wild downwind into Hout Bay, we humoured amaDriver Ray by eating hake and chips at his boyhood haunt, Fish on the Rocks (and chips in the rain, we noted). Steve looked out at the blustery greyness, then at me, and said all Forrest Gump-like: 'I don't know about you, but I've had enough. I want to go home now.'

The route

There are various ways to ride from Cape Town to Cape Point. The two obvious routes are, firstly, along the False Bay coast of the Atlantic seaboard (two oceans do **not** meet anywhere near Cape Point, so both sides are washed by the Atlantic Ocean). Secondly, the more varied and spectacular way is the Atlantic coast side, including as it does Hout Bay, Chapman's Peak drive and Noordhoek. The False Bay option has its many charms, but the least of them is getting down the highways to the sea at Muizenberg (about 25km from the CBD).

Both routes meet at the Cape of Good Hope gate, the most southerly section of Table Mountain National Park. There are numerous tracks in the park, but, for first-timers, the direct route from the gate to Cape Point on the main surfaced road is best. Unless you have a Wild Card, the entrance fee is quite rude.

More adventurous riders might be able to put together a more circuitous route taking in all the best mountain biking places, including Deer Park/King's Blockhouse, Newlands, Tokai, Silvermine and Red Hill.

There is a dream among many local riders that one day they'll be able to ride a bike trail all the way from Signal Hill, above the city centre, to Cape Point. As soon as we've spliced the many frayed trail-ends that still exist in the Spine of the Dragon project, we aim to turn our attentions and our wheels to – hopefully – working with SANParks to make this dream a reality.

In the meanwhile, stay cool, ride easy and don't ever stop dreaming dangerous dreams and making plans.

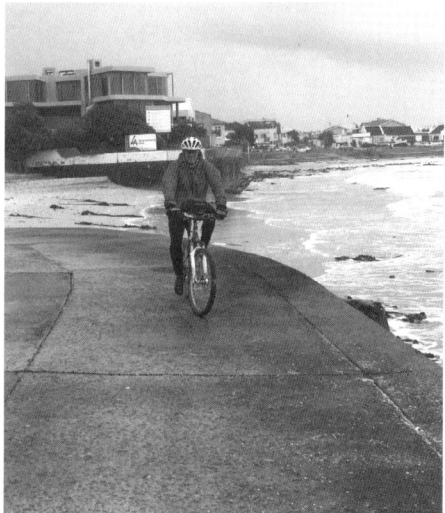

Finally heading for home – along Bloubergstrand's sea-lashed shoreline.

USEFUL CONTACTS

ACCOMMODATION

TRAIL SECTION & STAGE	LOCATION	ACCOMMODATION	CONTACT
BAOBAB TRAIL			
Stage 1	Musina	Forever Resorts Tshipise	Blikkies, Cynthia
	R525 T-junction	Popallin Ranch	
Stage 2	Gundani	Gundani Mutsiwa Campsite	Christopher Nethonzhe
Stage 3	Thohoyandou	Fig Tree Lodge	Rudi
Stage 4	Middle Letaba Dam	Middle Letaba Resort	Elvin Shondlani
		Some Werk Spaza	Colbert Mabunda
Stage 5	Modjadjiskloof	Sunland farm	Doug & Heather van Heerden
BUSHVELD AND BERG TRAIL			
Stage 1	near Magoebaskloof	Kurisa Moya Nature Lodge	Lisa Martus, David Letsoale
Stage 2	Haenertsburg	maGriet's Bed & Breakfast	Jessie, Magriet
	Wolkberg	Rheebokvlei	Dolf Harmse
Stage 3	Chuenespoort	Molapo-Matebele Resort	Masasa Frans Molopa
Stage 4	Burgersfort	Kusile Guest House	Pieter & Driekie Heyns
Stage 5	Ohrigstad	Iketla Lodge	Albert & Hennielene Botha
Stage 6	Pilgrim's Rest	Royal Hotel	Terence Ndlovu
TIMBERLANDS TRAIL			
Stage 1	Long Tom Pass	Misty Mountain	James & Lisa Sheard
	Graskop	Daan's Place	Ian Coetzee
Stage 2	Schoemanskloof	Die Rots Guesthouse	Elly & Kiewiet Pienaar
	Alkmaar	Eric's Chalets	
Stage 3	Kaapschehoop	Kaapsehoop Guesthouse	Neels & Ria Bothma
Stage 4	Badplaas	Forever Resorts Badplaas	Carolize Voges
Stage 5	Chrissiesmeer	Just Country (self-catering)	Heather, Cheryl Reum
Stage 6	Amsterdam	Glen Oak Lodge	Jean & Ray Walden
Stage 7	Piet Retief/Mkhondo	LA Guesthouse	Estee, Lynette & Arthur
Stage 8	Paulpietersburg	Natal Spa Hot Springs & Leisure Resort	Gail McCann
BATTLEFIELDS TRAIL			
Stage 1	Blood River	Blood River Heritage Site	Dons Grobler
Stage 2	Rorke's Drift	Rorke's Drift Lodge	Christy Gibson
Stage 3	Elandslaagte	Mawelawela Lodge	Herta Mitchell-Innes
Stage 4	Colling's Pass	Waterfall Farmstead B&B	Adele
	Swinburne	Mount Olive Stables Cottage	Karen & Christopher
	Harrismith	Various options	
Stage 5	Oliviershoek Pass	Windmill Lodge	Craig van Rensburg

HONE	CELL	E-MAIL	WEBSITE
	076-302-9383	tshipise@foreversa.co.za	www.forevertshipise.co.za
15-534-7904	082-903-0291	popallin@popallin.co.za	www.popallin.co.za
c/o BirdLife SA)	076-302-9383	chrisneth@vodamail.co.za	
15-964-1546	079-068-2644	figtreelodge@lantic.com	www.thefigtreelodge.com
	083-400-3085		
	072-432-3414		
15-309-9039	082-413-2228	baobabbars@mweb.co.za	www.bigbaobab.co.za
15-276-1131	083-568-4678	info@krm.co.za	www.krm.co.za
15-276-4762	083-683-1847	magrietsbnb@mweb.co.za	www.mountain-getaways.co.za
15-297-1248	082-639-5877	dolf@baobab.co.za	www.rheebokvlei.com
	082-720-2902 082-720-1530	phahos@limpopoleg.gov.za	
	087-752-0181	kusile01@vodamail.co.za	www.kusileguesthouse.co.za
13-238-8900		relax@iketla.com	www.iketla.com
13-768-1100		royalres@rhpilgrims.co.za	www.royal-hotel.co.za
13-764-3377	073-375-1817	mistymtn@iafrica.com	www.mistymountain.co.za
	082-343-7888	daansplace@vodamail.co.za	www.daansplace.com
	082-865-6505	kiewiet@iafrica.com	
13-733-3213	072-795-9175	e-mail via website	www.ericschalets.co.za
13-734-4161	082-450-3466	info@kaapsehoopguesthouse.co.za	www.kaapsehoopguesthouse.co.za
17-844-8000		badplaas@foreversa.co.za	www.foreverbadplaas.co.za
13-751-3245	082-449-3457	cherylreum@mweb.co.za	www.wheretostay.co.za/justcountry
17-846-9208		jeanwalden49@gmail.com	www.glenoak-lodge.co.za
17-826-2837	082-292-2163	laguesthouse@telkomsa.net	www.pietretief.co.za/3mark.htm
31-337-4222	073-213-7242	adminspa@goodersons.co.za	www.goodersonleisure.co.za
34-632-1695	082-925-8560	bloedrivier@voortrekkermon.org.za	
34-642-7001	079-291-1477	info@rorkesdriftlodge.com	www.rorkesdriftlodge.com
36-421-1860	083-259-6394	mitchelinnes@mweb.co.za	www.wheretostay.co.za/mawelawela
	073-155-5118	e-mail via website	http://waterfallfarmstead.jimdo.com
	083-701-0029		www.wheretostay.co.za/mountolive
			www.wheretostay.co.za/fs/ef/accommodation/harrismith
	083-636-1166		

Stage 5 (cont.)	Phuthaditjhaba	Hae@home Guest House	
	Kestell	Various options	
	Sterkfontein dam	Qwantani Berg & Bush Resort	

ROOF OF AFRICA TRAIL

Stage 1	Ha Napo/Ha Mphakha	Chief Napo's household cottage	Contact Tumi Taabe
Stage 2	Oxbow	Oxbow Lodge	Costas Coccusalis
Stage 3	Motete	Motete Primary School	Contact Tumi Taabe
Stage 4	Ha Lejone	Motebong Village Holiday Resort	
Stage 5	Katse	Orion Katse Lodge	
Stage 6	Thaba-Tseka	The Buffalo's Hotel	Jo
Stage 7	Mantsonyane	St James Mission Hospital	John Maho
		Marakabei Lodge	
Stage 8	Semonkong	Semonkong Lodge	
Stage 9	Ketane	Nohana Lodge	Contact Malealea Tours
Stage 10	Ha Qiqita/Bethel	Bethel Lodge	Ivan Yaholnitsky
Stage 11	Holy Cross Mission	Holy Cross Mission	Sister Virginia, Sister Elizabe

WAR TRAIL

Stage 1	Wartrail district	Reedsdell Country Guest Farm	Chris & Kath Isted
Stage 2	Barkly East	Siskin's B&B	Chris & Kath Isted, Jo-Anne Prichard
Stage 3	Dordrecht	Bradgate farm	
Stage 4	Molteno	Olive Cottage	Jenny
Stage 5	Hofmeyr	Karoobos Lodge	Louise, Hylet
Stage 6	Middelburg	Various options	

GREAT KAROO TRAIL

Stage 1	Nieu Bethesda	Owlhouse Backpackers	Ian, Katrin
Stage 2	Graaff-Reinet	Betty's	
Stage 3	Jansenville	Oak Villa Guest House	
Stage 4	Steytlerville	Karroo Theatrical Hotel	Mark, Jacques
Stage 5	Willowmore	Willow Historical Guest House	Deon & Sophia van der Merw
Stage 6	Klaarstroom	Klaarstroom Guest House	Jeremy & Sharon Witts-Hewi
Stage 7	Prince Albert	Dennehof Guest House	Ria & Lindsay Steyn

FOLDED MOUNTAINS TRAIL

Stage 1	Gamkaskloof	Fonteinplaas	Annetjie, Bennie, Pieter, Mari
		CapeNature cottages	
Stage 2	Seweweekspoort	Seweweekspoort Guest Farm	Liezel Hunlun
	Rouxpos	Rouxpos farm	Ronel & Gerhard Roux

58-713-2972			
			www.kestell.co.za/services
27-586-230882		reservations@qwantani-resort.co.za	www.qwantani.co.za
266-5945-8479	+266-6305-1359	ttaabe@yahoo.com	http://enkosi.org/cyclinglesotho
51-933-2247		oxbowski@kingsley.co.za	www.oxbow.co.za
266-5945-8479	+266-6305-1359	ttaabe@yahoo.com	http://enkosi.org/cyclinglesotho
266-2222-7600	+266-5974-4567	info@motebong.com	www.motebong.com
266-2291-0202	+266-6332-0831	gmkatse@orion-hotels.co.za	www.oriongroup.co.za/katse
266-5882-1029	+266-2700-7339	senatentabe@leo.co.ls	
266-5250-0700	+266-2700-1111	johnmaho@leo.co.ls	
266-5250-1111			
266-2700-6037	+266-6202-1021	(fax-2-email)+266-2226-4043	www.placeofsmoke.co.ls
266-5896-0278			
266-5874-2991		ivan.yaholnitsky@gmail.com	www.visitlesotho.travel
266-5896-6279	+266-5879-5379		
45-974-9900	082-457-0909	isted@telkomsa.net	www.snowvalley.co.za
45-971-0528	082-457-0909	isted@telkomsa.net	www.snowvalley.co.za
45-941-1014		bradgate@vodamail.co.za	
	079-715-4852		
48-885-0395	082-830-8313	karoobos.jotter@gmail.com	
			www.middelburgec.co.za/accommodation
49-841-1642		backpackers@owlhouse.info	http://www.nieu-bethesda.com/en/accommodation.html
49-845-0253	082-413-0579	info@kadash.co.za	www.graaffreinetselfcatering.co.za
49-836-0465		elna001@telkomsa.net	
49 835 0010	072-424-7185	info@karroohotel.co.za	www.thekarroohotel.co.za
44-923-1574	082-414-8483	thewillow@telkomsa.net	www.willowguesthouse.co.za
23-541-1474	082-488-8370	klaarstroom@telkomsa.net	www.klaarstroom.co.za
23-541-1227	082-456-8848	ria@dennehof.co.za	www.dennehof.co.za
23-541-1107		info@diehel.com	www.diehel.com
			www.capenature.co.za/reserves.htm?reserve=Swartberg+Nature+Reserve
23-581-5005	082-504-8775	jghunlun@polka.co.za	www.seweweekspoortguestfarm.co.za
23-581-5021	084-663-3200	ronelr1812@gmail.com	

Stage 3	Anysberg Nature Reserve	CapeNature cottages	
Stage 4	Touws River	Loganda Karoo Lodge	Clive
Stage 5	Karbonaatjieskraal	Karoo1 Hotel Village	Retha
	Ceres (Koue Bokkeveld)	Forgotten Highway Manor	Stephanie & Johan Geldenhuy
		Village Guest House & Restaurant	
Stage 6	Tulbagh	Various options	

FAIREST CAPE TRAIL

Stage 1	Riebeek Kasteel	Môreson Manor	Natalie Becker
		Royal Hotel	Chrizelle
Stage 2	Bloubergstrand	The Blue Peter Hotel	
Stage 3	Cape Town	Various options	
Stage 4	Cape Point	Various options	

BIKE SHOPS EN ROUTE OR NEAR ROUTE & ADDITIONAL CONTACTS

BIKE SHOPS EN ROUTE OR NEAR ROUTE	Saloojees Cycles	Polokwane	
	Bell Cycling	Mbombela (Nelspruit)	
	Boulevard Cycles	Tzaneen	
	Cycle Junkies	Sabie	
	Long Tom Cycles	Mashishing (Lydenburg)	
	Dirty Harry MTB	Harrismith (club)	
	Tumi's Bicycle Clinic	Khubetsoana, Maseru	Tumi Taabe
	Cycle Inn	Graaff-Reinet	Frikkie Rossouw, Oom Bossie
	Ton's Sport & Cycle	Oudtshoorn	
	Revolution Cycles	Cape Town	Stirling Kotze (Snr or Jnr)
ADDITIONAL CONTACTS	Daytrippers	Bicycle tours and accommodation	Steve & Di Thomas
	Freedom Trail	Annual race and trail	David Waddilove
	Trans Lesotho Trail	Annual race and trail	David Waddilove
	Detour Trails	KwaZulu-Natal and Lesotho mtb tours	Rohan Surridge
	Roger Tool-hands	Oudtshoorn	Philippe Samouilhan
	Thaba Tours	Sani Pass and Lesotho 4x4 tours	Ray Wat
	Long Tom Pass permits	York Timbers	Suzette
		Komati Land Forests	Snatjie Madden
	Kaapsehoop Horse Trails and Accommodation	Kaapschehoop	Christo
	AMA Rider	Boland	Meurant Botha
	Operation Smile		

			www.capenature.co.za/reserves.htm?reserve=Anysberg+Nature+Reserve
23-358-1130		info@logandalodge.com	www.logandalodge.com
23-358-2131	071-510-5605	e-mail via website	www.karoo1.com
23-316-1397	082-576-8578	fhwmanor@gmail.com	www.thewesterncape.co.za/establishment/?id=306
23-316-2035		villageguest@telkomsa.net	http://www.ceres.org.za/stay/b-b-guesthouses.html
			www.capedutchquarter.co.za
22-448-1379	072-805-3031		www.moresonmanor.co.za
22-448-1378		gm@royalinriebeek.com	www.royalinriebeek.com
21-554-1956		info@bluepeter.co.za	www.bluepeter.co.za
			www.capestay.co.za
			www.capestay.co.za
15-297-2766			
13-757-0920			
15-307-2512			
13-764-1149			
13-235-2355			
73-436-7879		chair@harrismithcycling.co.za	
266-5949-8479	+266-6305-1359	ttaabe@yahoo.com	www.enkosi.org/cyclinglesotho
49-892-4870	084-5040-762		
44-279-2423			
21 423 5191 / 21 424 5823		info@revolutioncycles.co.za	www.revolutioncycles.co.za
21-511-4766	082-807-9522	info@daytrippers.co.za	www.daytrippers.co.za
	084-567-4152	e-mail via website	www.freedomchallenge.org.za
	084-567-4152	e-mail via website	www.freedomchallenge.org.za
	082-896-0392	rohan@detourtrails.co.za	www.detourtrails.co.za
	082-538-3115		
	083-353-5958	thabatours@futurenet.co.za	www.thabatours.co.za
13-764-9200			
13-764-1215			
	086-537-0520 / 082-774-5826		www.horsebacktrails.co.za
		info@amarider.co.za	www.amarider.co.za
21-481-9103			www.southafrica.operationsmile.org

GLOSSARY

ama- (in amaMapper, amaWriter, amaDriver) – a prefix, like 'the'
bakkie – light truck, pick-up truck
bliksems – very, damn
bry – a burr (in speech)
Canis africanis – a strain of African dog
chakalaka – a spicy relish
Daytripper – Steve Thomas, the mapper
Difaqane wars – tribal wars that decimated much of Southern Africa between the 1750s and the 1830s
donga – drainage ditch, erosion gully
dorp – village, small town
Eardstapper – David Bristow, the writer
goggas – small bugs
klaar – finished
knyp – squeeze
kop/koppie – head, mountain peak
laager – wagon encampment, defensive formation
lekker – nice, great
lus – long, yearn for
meer – lake
mlungus – white people
moerse – very, 'hell of a'
Nagmaal – holy communion
nogal – would you believe, *really*!

ntsu – bearded vulture
oord – a folksy resort
O waar, be-waar, Bewaarkloof – Oh where, beware, the hidden canyon
padkos – food for the road
pap – stiff maize porridge
pap-en-vleis braai – stiff maize porridge and meat barbecue
plaaslike bevolking – rural inhabitants
platteland – rural area, countryside
poort – canyon
potbrood – pot bread
pundamatenga – pick up and carry
saamwerk – work together, cooperate
sho't left/sho't right – shoot (turn) left/right
slap chips – fried chips, as in 'fish and chips'
snor – moustache
spruit – stream
stimela – train, from steam train
Stoel monument – Chair monument (where Boer sympathisers were presumably tied to chairs and shot as traitors by the British)
stoep – veranda
'terrs' – terrorists or freedom fighters
tokoloshe – a sneaky or vindictive spirit
vergadering – meeting
vlaktes – plain, steppe
werf – farmstead